BISHOP PETER'S PILGI
HIS DIARY AND SKETC

ST. JAMES'S PALACE

How wonderful that a bishop should make a pilgrimage through his diocese! Bishop Peter's love for the churches and people of Norfolk shines out through the pages of his informative and entertaining diary. It is a remarkable story of a crowded year visiting every part of the Diocese of Norwich, and a remarkable achievement too. As Patron of the Norfolk Churches Trust, I share his enthusiasm for the magnificent churches of East Anglia, as well as his determination that we should do all in our power to keep this unique national treasure in good order for the benefit of future generations. I very much hope that the publication of this diary will inspire others with a sense of wonder and gratitude for the simple faith and intuitive craftsmanship of the people who built these unique monuments to the glory of God.

Bishop Peter's Pilgrimage

His Diary and Sketchbook 1995–96

A year's journey to celebrate 900 years of the Diocese of Norwich

by

THE RT REVD PETER NOTT

Bishop of Norwich

CANTERBURY PRESS

Norwich

First published 1996 by The Canterbury Press Norwich
(a publishing imprint of Hymns Ancient & Modern Limited,
a registered charity)
St Mary's Works, St Mary's Plain,
Norwich, Norfolk, NR3 3BH
Reprinted with amendments 1997

British Library Cataloguing in Publication Data

A catalogue record for this book is available
from the British Library

ISBN 1–85311–145–7

*Typeset by Watermark, Norfolk, and
printed and bound in Great Britain by
The Lavenham Press
Suffolk*

Commendation by His Grace The Archbishop of Canterbury

In the order of service for the Consecration of a Bishop, the Archbishop's Charge includes the words, 'He is to know his people and be known by them.' This diary provides a marvellous account of one bishop's response to that Charge, as in the space of a single year he met thousands of people throughout the Diocese of Norwich in a series of personal encounters.

Peter Nott has been a bishop for nineteen years, first in Somerset and now in the east of England. He has long experience of ministry in a variety of places, but especially in rural areas, and his diary vividly portrays what life is like in those parishes. The truth he reveals from first-hand experience is not at all the one which is so often portrayed by the media, of a Church demoralised and shrinking. On the contrary he produces solid evidence of a Church that is lively, growing, adventurous and hopeful – and where the level of churchgoing is proportionately far higher than in many urban and suburban areas.

The Diocese of Norwich does not consist only of rural parishes. There are country towns, ports and a large city, in all of which there are places of deprivation, poverty and suffering. The descriptions of his meetings with people in these areas are amongst the most moving passages of his diary.

To spend twenty whole weeks in a single year visiting parishes, in addition to his other duties, has been an extraordinary achievement, and I know of no other bishop in living memory who has attempted such an enterprise. It must have been exhausting, but the result will be that the love he so evidently has for the people of his diocese will have been warmly reciprocated. Bishop Peter's Pilgrimage Diary is a wonderful and very readable story – full of humour, compassion and faith. It is a book which I believe will be a great encouragement to all who read it.

+George Cantuar

The BISHOP of NORWICH "OPEN DOOR" PILGRIMAGE

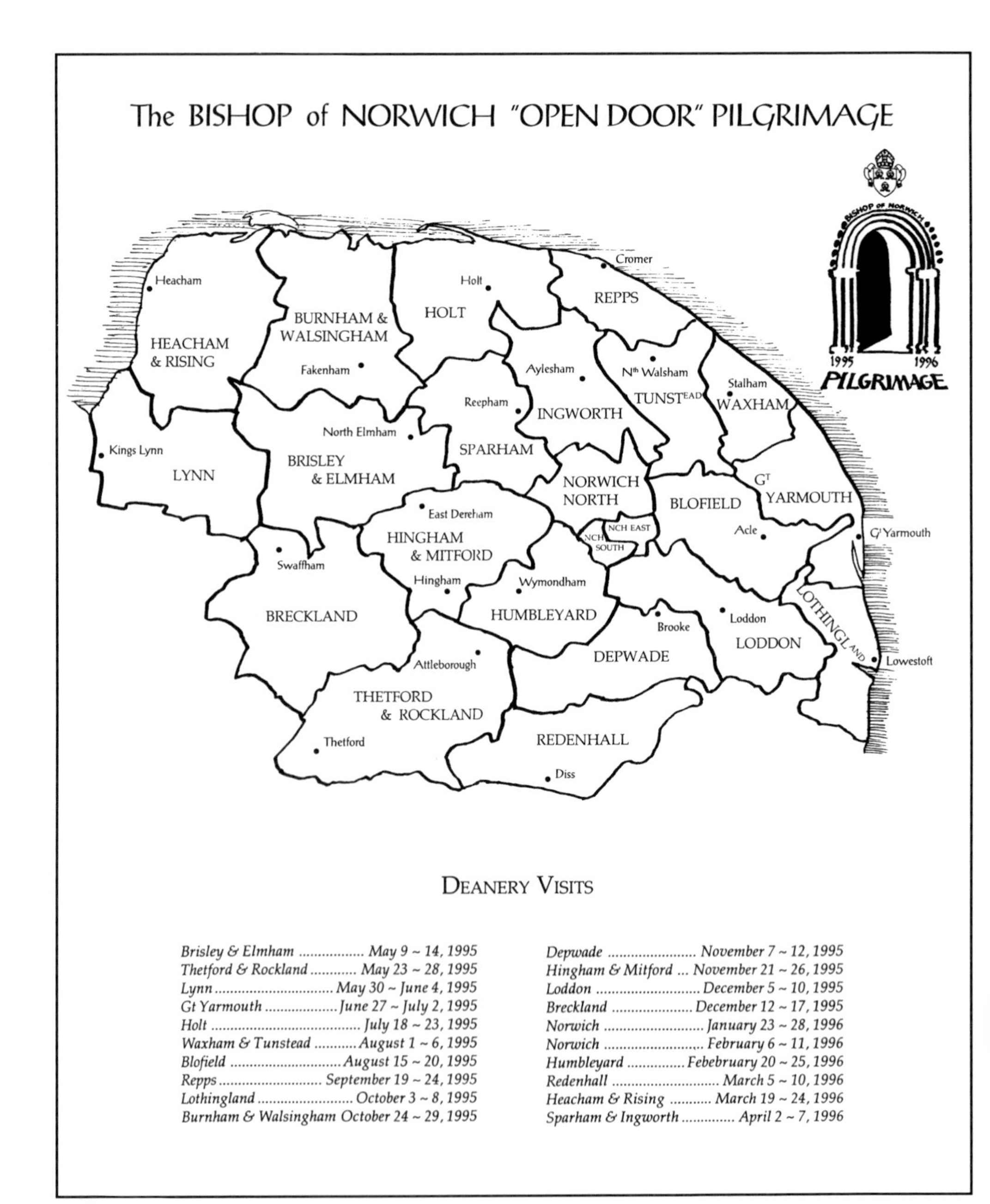

Deanery Visits

Brisley & Elmham	*May 9 ~ 14, 1995*
Thetford & Rockland	*May 23 ~ 28, 1995*
Lynn	*May 30 ~ June 4, 1995*
Gt Yarmouth	*June 27 ~ July 2, 1995*
Holt	*July 18 ~ 23, 1995*
Waxham & Tunstead	*August 1 ~ 6, 1995*
Blofield	*August 15 ~ 20, 1995*
Repps	*September 19 ~ 24, 1995*
Lothingland	*October 3 ~ 8, 1995*
Burnham & Walsingham	*October 24 ~ 29, 1995*
Depwade	*November 7 ~ 12, 1995*
Hingham & Mitford	*November 21 ~ 26, 1995*
Loddon	*December 5 ~ 10, 1995*
Breckland	*December 12 ~ 17, 1995*
Norwich	*January 23 ~ 28, 1996*
Norwich	*February 6 ~ 11, 1996*
Humbleyard	*Febebruary 20 ~ 25, 1996*
Redenhall	*March 5 ~ 10, 1996*
Heacham & Rising	*March 19 ~ 24, 1996*
Sparham & Ingworth	*April 2 ~ 7, 1996*

CONTENTS

Foreword by HRH The Prince of Wales		iii
Commendation by His Grace The Archbishop of Canterbury		vii
Map of diocese		viii
List of illustrations		xi
Introduction		xiii
Diary		
1	The French connection	1
2	Arrival	9
3	Brisley and Elmham	13
Interlude		23
4	Thetford and Rockland	27
5	Lynn	39
Interlude		47
6	Great Yarmouth	53
Interlude		62
7	Holt	65
8	Waxham and Tunstead	77
9	Blofield	89
Interlude		100
10	Repps	103
11	Lothingland	111
Interlude		120
12	Burnham and Walsingham	125
13	Depwade	137
14	Hingham and Mitford	145
15	Loddon	155
16	Breckland	165
Interlude		177
17	Norwich (first week)	179
Interlude		186
18	Norwich (second week)	189
Interlude		201

19 Humbleyard 203
20 Redenhall 215
Interlude 227
21 Heacham and Rising 231
22 Sparham and Ingworth 241
The Bishop's Pilgrimage Prayer 256
Some Comments 257

BLACK AND WHITE ILLUSTRATIONS

Rouen 5
Castle Acre Priory 22
Archdeacons 25
Thetford Priory 29
House of Bishops 48
House of Bishops 49
Martham 59
The Bishop of Sheffield 63
Worstead 79
Waxham Old Barn 81
St Benet's Abbey 87
Little Plumstead (pencil) 91
Fishley 94
Surgères 101
Cromer 107
Lambeth Palace 121
Wells Rectory 126
Café in Wells 127
Barns at Tasburgh 143
Farmyard near Mattishall 147
Chedgrave 157
Loddon 161
Caston 167
Watton 169
Near Holme Hale 171
Swaffham 175
House of Lords 178
Earlham Cemetery 191
Bishop's House Garden (pencil) 199
House of Lords 202
Bawburgh 204
Tacolneston 207
Barns at Swardeston 209
Swardeston (pencil) 210
Swardeston 211
Morley 212
Redenhall (pencil) 219
Brockdish (pencil) 221

Diss Rectory 225
Pulham Market 226
Brancaster 233
Shernborne 239
Itteringham 243
Cawston (pencil) 247
Erpingham Rectory 251
Near Weston Longville 254

WATERCOLOUR ILLUSTRATIONS

(Between pages 116 and 117)

PLATE
1 Reedham
2 River Yare
3 Breydon Water
4 East Bilney
5 Newton
6 Worthing
7 Larling
8 Longham
9 Rougham
10 Gaywood Rectory
11 Near Burnham Norton
12 Whissonsett
13 Horsey
14 Attleborough Rectory
15 Ranworth Vicarage
16 Horning

PLATE
17 Bacton
18 Honing Hall
19 Hassingham
20 Mundesley
21 Kessingland
22 Kessingland
23 Oulton Broad
24 North Creake
25 Great Ryburgh
26 Near Brooke
27 Caston
28 Rowley Farm Hilborough
29 Near Wheatacre
30 Bergh Apton
31 Near Docking
32 Ingoldisthorpe

INTRODUCTION

1996 marked the 900th anniversary of the building of Norwich Cathedral and the transfer of the Bishopric from Thetford to Norwich. Some years ago I decided to mark this anniversary by carrying out an episcopal visitation during the year leading up to the celebrations.

I wanted to do more than carry out a formal visitation, but rather to travel around the diocese visiting the parishes in person. So the idea of a Year of Pilgrimage was born. I met with a small group over a period of months, and together we planned an itinerary, consisting of twenty weeks spent in the parishes, from Tuesday morning to Sunday evening. I am very grateful to this group, which included the Reverend Phillip McFadyen, who wrote a commentary on St Luke especially for the pilgrimage, and which proved a great stimulus to the Bible studies in the parishes. Various common elements were decided: that my visits should be to the community at large as well as to the church; that we would systematically study Luke's Gospel throughout the year; and that I should spend as much time as possible informally with parishioners.

I am very grateful to so many people who have helped in the planning, particularly the rural deans, lay chairmen, my chaplain, Steven Betts, and to all those who have guided me on my pilgrimage. It has been the most rewarding year of my ministry, and the most exhausting. It could not have happened without the generous co-operation of my brother bishops and archdeacons who have dealt with the day to day running of the diocese while I have been away from Norwich. Above all, I am grateful to my wife, Betty, for her patience and loving understanding during a year in which she has seen little of me.

Before I set out in April 1995 I was asked to keep a diary because, as someone said, the account of a bishop spending a year visiting his diocese could prove in time to be a valuable historical record. The Canterbury Press, based in Norwich, suggested that a version of it would be of interest now, hence this publication. I am very grateful to the Reverend Robert Backhouse for his expert help and advice, and to my daughter, Lucy Stone, for her assistance in correcting her father's grammar.

This is the story of a year's journey which records only first impressions, rather like my sketches. I want now to reflect more carefully on the many lessons I learned, which I hope may give us guidance on the way ahead for the Church locally.

Above all, I am deeply grateful to the clergy and people of the diocese who have everywhere been generous, kind and welcoming, and who have given me a fresh and encouraging vision of the Body of Christ.

+Peter Norvic:

1

The French Connection

Taizé: Friday 28 April 1995

(Taizé is a monastic community founded in 1940. There are now about a hundred brothers of many nationalities and Christian denominations, catholic and reformed, some of whom live in the community at Taizé, and others in various places overseas. It is a place which has had a great influence on the young, and is visited by thousands of young people each year. It has been a formative influence on my own Christian life and ministry since I took a party of students there in 1966.)

Is this where the pilgrimage begins or is this a preparation for the pilgrimage? It is not clear and perhaps that is just as well because most pilgrimages do not seem to begin in a tidy way. One can set off from any place and indeed in any state of mind. The important thing about a pilgrimage is the journey and the direction; even the journey's end in many cases may not be clear. Frère Marc, here for a few weeks from Korea, gave me a card on which he wrote a quotation from St Gregory of Nyssa, the fourth-century theologian: *Et maintenant, je sais que je suis dans la voie droite, parce que je ne sais pas où je vais* – 'And now I know that I am on the right road, because I do not know where I am going!'

Arriving in the early evening I met the brothers in ones and twos, and they greeted me warmly as always. Some knew I was coming, others did not but just welcomed back their *frère-évêque* as if I had been away for a few weeks. I am living in a small room at the top of a house within the community, which consists of old farm buildings and converted barns. This house, which was once a small farmhouse, is now known to some as 'Lambeth Palace' because this is where Archbishop George Carey stayed when he came in 1992.

I have learned from past experience here not to try too hard to have profound thoughts, but simply to allow the place to take hold, and so it does in a kind of gentle embrace. The Prior of Taizé, Roger, wanted me to pray with the brothers, so for the evening prayer there I was in a simple white robe – just one of the older brothers. The simplicity and peace of the liturgy was very healing. The difficulties of the last few months will not just fade away but here they can, I hope, be put into perspective. The first two chants were especially apt. *Dans nos obscurités allume le feu qui ne s'éteint, jamais* – 'In our darknesses, O Lord, light the fire which never is extinguished.' And then later, *Jésus Christ, lumière intérieure, ne laisse pas mes ténèbres me parler* – 'Jesus Christ, inner light, do not let my darknesses speak to me.'

Saturday 29 April

After morning prayer I had breakfast with the Walters family who are here for a few days: Chris, a curate in Fakenham, Molly his wife and their two grown-up sons, Simon and John. Simon is terminally ill with an acute form of leukaemia, but is an immensely brave young man, who spoke movingly about his illness and how he has come to terms with it, the bad days as well as the good. He talked about the book he is writing which he hopes will help others in the same situation. For the rest of the morning and after lunch I worked at my address for the visitation next week. After tea with Frère Eric, the artist, I celebrated Communion in the beautiful little village church which has been restored by the brothers and was used by them in the early days of the community. It is still kept as a place of quiet and there are occasional small celebrations of Holy Communion.

Each Saturday evening there is an Anglican Eucharist, not specifically to provide a separate Communion, but aimed particularly at those who may have to leave early on Sunday morning before the main Eucharist in the church. It was a very beautiful and simple service to which Frères Stephen and Grégoire both came. I greeted everybody afterwards and gave them a Pilgrimage Prayer. The last person to emerge was a French lady who rather huffily said she had not understood a word. She brought me back down to earth, because she was like the difficult elderly parishioner who sits at the back of the church refusing to switch on a hearing aid and complaining afterwards.

Supper again with Roger and then the evening prayer. Saturday's prayer is always followed by a somewhat lengthy dissertation from Roger. Flowers were then given out by Samuel, one of the young boys who lives in the village, to all the representatives of the various nationality groups. I gave my fine sprig of lilac to the Walters family in the hope that it might last the journey back to England, which they begin tomorrow morning.

Sunday 30 April

The President at the Eucharist was Max Thurian, who some years ago became a Roman Catholic priest but still belongs to the community. He is a theologian of international repute who spends most of his time in Italy but returns regularly to Taizé. After the service he took me aside and said that throughout the Eucharist he had thought of me and felt strongly that as the only bishop present it was I who should have presided. He said, 'There is no difference whatever in our eucharistic doctrine and, indeed, in theology as a whole we are divided only on minor matters.' And I told him that it was because of that knowledge of closeness that these matters of protocol and custom which still separate our Churches did not matter to me. 'But they do to me,' he said.

Sunday lunch is always a big occasion when guests are invited and any families of the brothers who happen to be staying in Taizé are welcomed. Guillaume's family of ten, whom he had not seen for some years, were there, and the parents of Josef. The community is very understanding about families, so parents, brothers and sisters regularly come to stay, and from time to time the brothers visit their homes, however far away. Also at lunch was a young father and his three children from Rwanda. He had escaped the massacres because he was studying in Europe, and his children were smuggled out; but his wife was killed. Occasions such as these illustrate the broad perspective of Taizé and how open they are to all that is happening in the world: far more open, indeed, than we often are in the Church in England, not least because the brothers have such close personal contacts with these people.

At 4 o'clock Roger left for South Africa where he is to spend two or three weeks. He took three brothers with him and we all stood outside the house to see him go. The brothers sang *Laudate Omnes Gentes* and Roger went round kissing everyone goodbye on both cheeks. Stephen thinks this might be Roger's last great trip abroad. He will celebrate his eightieth birthday in South Africa and he is really getting a little too frail for long journeys and tough programmes abroad.

After the prayer at 5 pm I had a long talk with Grégoire, whom I knew first when we were both young and I was a chaplain leading one of my first groups of students from Cambridge in the 1960s. He has spent most of his time with a group of brothers in Africa, but is now here in Taizé and has a very weak heart indeed. He does not think he has long to live, but is not in the least worried by that and is, as he said, 'looking forward to heaven'. He is a delightful man, with a very good mind and deep interest in political issues, especially Northern Ireland about which he has thought and written a great deal. He also has a great devotion to Julian of Norwich and thinks we should have a campaign to get her canonised, which he believes would be a great ecumenical step forward. He gets very breathless, has to use an inhaler frequently and takes thirty pills daily. He drives the short distance from the house to the church, and this evening I drove him to the evening prayer because he was very short of breath. He is so weak that he has to have sixteen hours' sleep each day, but this does not affect his mind in his waking hours and he is always delightful company.

The times of prayer as usual are beautiful and it is a great privilege to pray with the community. After one of the prayers on my arrival Frère John, one of the Americans, told me that he was kneeling behind me, and not knowing I was arriving spent the whole prayer wondering who this older brother was whose back he did not recognise. He wondered if it was a brother who had lived abroad for many years, but also worried that his mind was going because he could not recognise someone he should know well. He said it was a great relief afterward to see my face, which he recognised, though the prayer had rather passed him by.

I had supper with Jean-Marie, another American, and Bishop Gérard Daucourt, who is the Bishop of Troyes. We had an animated discussion over supper in El Abiodh (one of the guest houses) about many aspects of the ministry of a bishop and the problems in rural parishes. He said his English was useless so we agreed to talk in French, which I suppose was good for me. The plight of the Church in rural France is far worse than it is in England and I think much can be gained by closer exchanges between our two Churches because, conversely, they have much to teach us about ministry to the young, baptism, confirmation and first Communion. Also they are making great strides in the development of lay ministry. Like us, the Church in France has to cope with a very secular society and hostile media. Because of the Church's position in France, and because of its history of independence, it really has much in common with the Church of England, rather more than with the Roman Catholic Church in England.

After the evening prayer I talked to Guillaume, one of the brothers from Bangladesh, a Dutchman who is home after three years for a short break. I sent messages to Frank, who has been in Bangladesh for twenty years, and was the very first brother I met when I came to Taizé. Then after hot chocolate with some brothers chatting in the kitchen, I returned to my room to pack and get ready for the next stage of the journey tomorrow morning.

Monday 1 May

After breakfast I drove to Paris where I met Hugo de Waal and David Conner (the Bishops of Thetford and Lynn) at Orly Airport. We drove on to Rouen where we stayed in the heart of the old city, which is full of half-timbered houses and the glorious abbey church of St Ouen – more beautiful, I thought, than the cathedral itself which is being heavily restored after bomb damage.

Rouen

The restoration, in fact, has been going on for forty years. We had a meal together in a tiny restaurant in a back street where for the first time we all had *briks*, which is a kind of pancake, followed by *couscous*, which is a Moroccan dish consisting of a kind of semolina-like rice with vegetables in a sauce and various kinds of meat – an enormous meal with very friendly French people at tables around us. Because both they and we are approaching the VE Day celebrations we toasted the *entente cordiale*.

Tuesday 2 May

We left Rouen before breakfast and drove through the gently rolling Normandy countryside so reminiscent of Norfolk, but with more grass and cows, in contrast to the arable crops of East Anglia. We stopped in a village for *le petit déjeuner*, which consisted of two long loaves put on the table, a dish of rich Normandy butter, jam and the most delicious coffee we have tasted so far. We arrived at Fécamp as the bright sun dispersed the mist and eventually found the little hotel next to one of the big churches. I think it must be better known as a restaurant because the accommodation was pretty simple but at 120 francs per night (about £14), I suppose one could not expect too much. The *patron* and his wife were away and we were welcomed by a shaven-headed young man dressed in jeans, vest and a scarf round his neck. He had several earrings in each ear, and looked rather frightening, but he was immensely friendly and polite.

When I first wrote to the priest at Fécamp, there was also a letter in return written in good colloquial English from a M. Leo Boucher, offering to make arrangements and to translate for us if necessary. I assumed he was French and telephoned his number saying, '*Je voudrais parler avec Monsieur Bouché.*'

'Oh yes,' he said, 'Leo Bowcher here, I'm Welsh actually.'

Leo is a former schoolteacher who has known Fécamp for some years and has a tiny house here. He is very friendly and talkative and has made arrangements for us to visit various places. Charles Roberts, a senior feature writer from the *EDP* (*Eastern Daily Press*), is here, too. He knows France well, speaks the language fluently and is always good company. From the start he has taken a great interest in the 900 anniversary celebrations and in the pilgrimage. He has friends not far away and he is spending the two days here to cover our visit.

Fécamp is a town of some 20,000 inhabitants, a working port and seaside resort but not in the least *chic* or geared to foreign tourists. The architecture in places is unattractive but interspersed with buildings which are very old and beautiful, some of them the half-timbered buildings that are everywhere in Rouen. There was considerable destruction during the war, particularly before the invasion and during the liberation of the town in September 1944, so there is a great deal of building which is post-war, concrete and ugly.

We walked to the abbey church, *La Trinité*, of the former Benedictine community. The exterior is not striking but immediately we walked inside we entered a building which is lofty, elegant and light. We walked in through the west end and down a series of steps into the central aisle. The resemblance to Norwich Cathedral is astonishing. The arches are Gothic, with a trace of Norman arches here and there, but the proportions and the whole impression are very similar indeed to Norwich. The transepts, too, are in a similar place. Charles Roberts and I even measured the floor area to compare it with Norwich. It is only now that we can understand a little note in a book somewhere which says that when Herbert de Losinga built the cathedral at Norwich he was influenced by the abbey church at Fécamp. He must have been more than influenced. We know he sent his cook from England back to Fécamp to learn how to do the Norman cooking he loved so much, and more importantly it is almost certain his masons would have been told to study the abbey very carefully. We met Père Jacques Soulé, a warm and friendly priest in his late fifties, and some of his parishioners, one of them an Englishwoman who married a Frenchman thirty years ago.

After prayer together we walked to a modern primary school run by nuns where we had lunch with the Sisters, some parishioners and the Bishop of Le Havre. It was a jolly occasion, stretching over three hours, the nuns serving a marvellous meal of five courses and many different kinds of drink from kir through beer or cider, to red and white wine. Like the Bishop of Troyes at Taizé, Bishop Michel Saudreau talked of the great difficulty over vocations for the priesthood, but also of the development of lay ministry, which is hopeful. Their catechesis or Christian instruction seems effective; certainly it is very thorough. The Bishop of Le Havre was friendly and talked openly about many issues. He has an extraordinarily loud voice, I suppose developed from years of talking in very large churches which could not afford amplification. One of the parishioners remarked, 'He never needs a microphone, as you can see.' Whenever he spoke all conversation ceased, rather in the same way that everything stops when a jet flies low overhead.

After lunch we walked to the *Palais Bénédictine*, which is part museum, and part factory where they make Benedictine. It was a most interesting tour, through rooms of treasures collected by the man who rediscovered the recipe for Benedictine one hundred years ago and marketed it very successfully. We then went through various rooms where we saw the herbs that go into the liqueur and finally to the place where it is made, in the basement. There are modern bottling plants on the edge of the town but Benedictine is made exclusively here. They knew the story about 'Benny and hot' and were proud to relate it again. In the First World War soldiers from Burnley discovered Benedictine and invented their own drink, Benedictine and hot water, which they took as a hot toddy. In the Second World War soldiers from the same area were also stationed near here and remembered the tradition of their fathers. So now Burnley is the place in England where most of the Benedictine coming to the UK is actually consumed.

After being presented by the Managing Director with bottles of Benedictine and commemorative books, we walked to the seafront and sat for a while looking at the white cliffs (whiter than the cliffs of Dover according to the locals). It was a long walk to the hotel, but Leo insisted on taking us further to show us *le source* which is a little well where, according to legend, a phial of the precious blood of Jesus was swept through currents from the Holy Land. It was not impressive, and covered with the kind of memorials one finds littering the sites of some holy places where no taste or discretion has been applied.

Footsore, we went back to the hotel to change into our purple cassocks and then returned to the abbey for mass, which we shared with Jacques Soulé. I read a lesson and we stood around the altar with him. He would have been quite willing for me to have presided and saw no tension, no difficulty whatever, about completely sharing in the Communion in every way. He had spoken to his Bishop about it and he too had raised no difficulty.

It is all so different from the nature of our relationships with Roman Catholics in England, understandably I suppose, because of our history, but the more we talked the more everyone, both French and English, agreed that there was an enormous amount in common between our Churches. Clergy here, if they wear dog collars at all, wear grey clerical shirts and seem very

Anglican in every way. Hugo, David and I took to Jacques Soulé very much and said on our way home how much we would like to have him in the diocese. It was such a natural thing to say – and only half a joke.

In the evening we went to dinner at a new restaurant run by two young women and a young chef. The meal was excellent and more conventional than last night. Charles Roberts, who writes regularly about restaurants and wine, gave the place his seal of approval. We had coffee sitting outside on a terrace: a balmy evening, which felt as if we were much further south than Normandy. Charles gave us an extract from his one-man performance of Martin Chuzzlewit – his rendition of Mrs Gamp – which was hilarious. And so to bed in very simple accommodation with old-fashioned bolsters instead of pillows.

Wednesday 3 May

Breakfast was served by the friendly skinhead, who sat in a corner and quietly sang a folk song, almost to himself. He had a beautiful and gentle voice. How wrong it is to judge by appearances.

After breakfast Leo took us up the hill above the dock area, along a winding road to the summit on the cliff overlooking the bay. At the top there is a church dedicated to *Notre Dame de Salut*, which is full of oil paintings of old ships and memorials to those who have lost their life on that coast. Jacques Soulé joined us, gave us a tour of the church and then we walked along the cliffs past massive fortifications left by the Germans. Fécamp had been the centre of very heavy fighting after the Normandy invasion and was not liberated until mid-September 1944. The town was shelled and bombed and the evidence in new buildings is everywhere. The deserted fortifications reminded one sharply of those further down the coast of Normandy, which feature in so many films.

Back at the house Charles and I had coffee alone together to discuss our feelings about the visit, which he will write in an article, and then we said goodbye to him because he was off to visit a friend in the Loire valley, and to Leo Boucher who had been kind and helpful, and very talkative.

The three of us drove back to Orly Airport, stopping for an hour en route to visit Monet's house and garden at Giverny; the latter was beautiful, and the day as hot as midsummer. The smells in this garden were as memorable as the flowers, shrubs and trees. I made a couple of quick sketches near the famous water lily pool which Monet painted often. It was good to be able to draw, however badly, in this place where he must have drawn and painted hundreds of times.

The flight was on time and because of the changes of hour we arrived back at Stansted at 5.55 pm, having left France at 6.15 pm. Hugo drove me home (David was met by Jayne) and I quickly unpacked and prepared for the next day.

2

Arrival

Thursday 4 May

A memorable day began when the bishops and archdeacons with their wives assembled outside Bishop's House and prayed the Pilgrimage Prayer together before setting off for Yarmouth. There we were greeted by clergy and parishioners, and a group of primary school children who presented me with their project on Herbert de Losinga. It was sunny and very warm as we embarked, at 9.30 am, on the old wherry *Norada* skippered by Peter Bower.

As we passed out of Yarmouth the huge bridge on the main road was raised so that we could pass through under sail. All the time we were being photographed by television and press photographers. We shortly passed out of camera range, changed into casual clothes, and spent a long, lazy day cruising with a warm southerly wind up the River Yare towards Norwich. Michael Handley, the Archdeacon of Norfolk, and I spent some time sketching and painting very fast watercolours with the boat moving past paintable scene after paintable scene. Small informal staff meetings were held from time to time between bishops and archdeacons but most of the time we talked, ate our picnic lunches and watched the scenery and birdlife.

With impeccable timing we arrived at Pulls Ferry at 6 pm to be greeted by about one hundred people, including the Vice Lord Lieutenant, the Mayor and Sheriff of Norwich, Chairman of the County Council and Chairman of the local Tourist Board. A group of schoolchildren, the Falconers Marching Band (from Falcon Middle School), was there, the band consisting of recorders and tambourines. Their leader had composed music for an 'Our Father' which they sang, and then they led me, in an informal procession, from Pulls Ferry to the cathedral. It was all very warm and welcoming with a general air of happiness and celebration.

At the cathedral door I was met by Michael Perham, the Precentor (and Vice Dean during the interregnum), the cathedral choir and honorary canons. We processed into the cathedral to the tomb of Herbert de Losinga which is in the presbytery just below the high altar. As we processed the choir sang psalms in plainsong, the kind of music Herbert himself would have heard. Kneeling at his tomb, I felt the link between us very strongly, particularly having just come from Fécamp. I prayed a prayer of St Benedict which Herbert certainly knew –

Gracious and Holy Father,
give us wisdom to perceive you,
diligence to seek you,
patience to wait for you,
eyes to behold you,
a heart to meditate on you,
and a life to proclaim you;
through the power of the Spirit
of Jesus Christ our Lord.

Then the choir sang the Pilgrimage Prayer which the choirmaster David Cooper had set to music. I knelt in front of the high altar where Michael Perham blessed me, together with all the chapter and honorary canons. After that we went to the cloisters for refreshments. It had been both a joyful and deeply moving ceremony.

A little later, at 7.30, the central visitation took place in the cathedral; 1,500 clergy and churchwardens were present and I addressed them on the subject of the proper place of law and of the fundamental necessity of unity in the Christian life. I had worried a great deal about this address, which I wrote while I was at Taizé the previous week, but everyone afterwards seemed to think it was right and helpful. Hugo, David and I spent more than half an hour saying farewell to the congregation as they left. It was a good occasion and I think must have been heartening, particularly for those rural churchwardens, so used to small numbers and tiny congregations, to be part of something so enormous, strong and hopeful. The singing of 'O Jesus, I have promised' as I moved up the steps to the ancient throne to give the blessing was memorable because it is truly a pilgrim hymn, and although I have sung it hundreds of times at confirmations, it took on fresh meaning this evening.

Friday 5 May

A day of catching up with correspondence, and putting some thoughts together for a sermon for VE Day. It was my granddaughter Alexandra's third birthday today. She came round in the morning and we gave her a doctor's set with plastic stethoscopes, syringes and thermometers, with which she proceeded to examine us. It is interesting the way children are not as conscious as grown-ups are, of time passing during absences. She had been told that I was away, but had little conception of what a time gap means. I suppose it is perhaps that little children live in the present moment quite intensely and time passing has a different meaning for them. The past does not seem to be so important, nor the future because it is not conceivable. The present, and each succeeding present moment, matter very much indeed. Of course history and memory are important, as well as the contemplation of the future, but a small child's witness to the priority of the present is very important. It is something of this, perhaps, that de Caussade means by the 'Sacrament of the Present Moment'.

The media are full of the local election results, which are disastrous for the Conservative Party, who have lost 2,000 seats and control of all but a minority of local councils. The other major news item, of course, is the VE Day celebrations, which feature in every newspaper, and on television and radio programmes, often reproducing fascinating original material. In spite of these major news items, the *EDP* today ran an excellent full page article by Charles Roberts about our visit to Fécamp, which brought back happy memories.

Late in the evening I finished a draft of my sermon for Sunday. I showed it to Betty, who lovingly but firmly rejected it. Back to the drawing board.

Sunday 7 May

The fiftieth anniversary of VE Day was celebrated with a great service in the cathedral attended by veterans' organisations and about 500 former American airmen and their families who were stationed in Norfolk. It was a moving service with a specially written fanfare for the Americans, which included a recording of Flying Fortresses taking off. I finally finished my sermon about five minutes before I had to go to the cathedral, but after such a long struggle it did seem to go down well. It is so difficult to get the balance right between thanksgiving for victory, recognition of the tragedy of war, the importance of reconciliation and of hope for the future. Afterwards I stood outside the west door and greeted the congregation. There were a number of American airmen wearing their original uniforms, which they had preserved and which amazingly still fitted them after fifty years.

After lunch I went to 'Living Waters' at the Norwich Showground. This is a renewal rally, taking place over the weekend. The meetings were in one of the main halls, which seats 1,000 people. It was stiflingly hot, but I enjoyed listening to the evangelist J. John. He could easily make a living as a stand-up comedian; he was quite brilliant and communicated exceptionally well – not quite my style, but I certainly learnt some things this afternoon. I rather enjoy these charismatic occasions, but never feel quite comfortable about joining wholeheartedly in all the movements. When we sang the songs people all around were jigging and waving their arms. I did however manage to keep up a rhythmic clap, and swayed a bit, to show solidarity.

Monday 8 May

The fiftieth anniversary of VE Day. Celebrations are going on all over the country with street parties, rallies, concerts and huge gatherings in London. The weather has been perfect throughout the weekend, enhancing what has been the most positive national occasion for many years.

Tomorrow the first deanery visit begins. I do not feel well prepared – not least because there has been insufficient time to do the Bible study and preparation that I had hoped, but in a pilgrimage it is the journeying not the preparation for the journey which matters; and if the Holy Spirit is truly to guide us, then perhaps a certain lack of preparation is not altogether a bad thing. When expressing these fears to Betty, she silenced me by saying, 'Look, at long last for a while you are going to do what you love best, being a priest. So just do that, and forget the rest.' She was right of course. 'The rest' does impinge so much in one's ministry as a bishop – the expectations of others and those one has of one's self, the consciousness of being in the public eye, all of which can seriously distract from the heart of ministry.

3

Brisley and Elmham

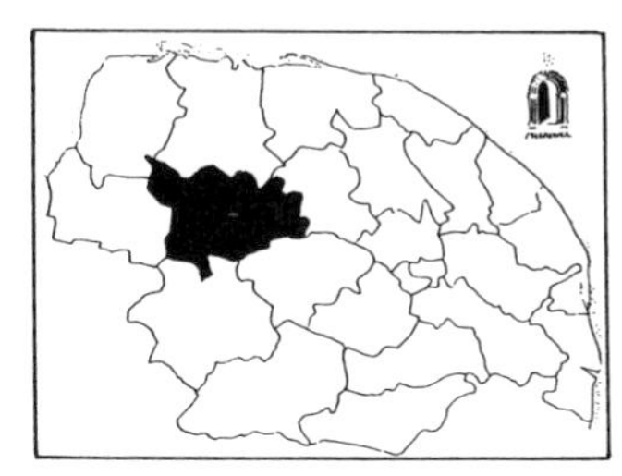

(A rural area in the heart of Norfolk, centred on the site of the Saxon cathedral at Elmham, now a ruin.)

Tuesday 9 May
Before Steven Betts, my chaplain, drove me to Castle Acre, the secretaries Mel and Vanessa said goodbye to me and gave me a handsome sketchbook with a set of drawing pencils. It was a touching beginning. We arrived at the house of Mr and Mrs Peter Smalls (he is a lay reader) and there we had a chapter meeting where we talked about the week ahead and I told them a little of my visit to France. At noon I celebrated Communion at Castle Acre Church, with a congregation of twenty-five parishioners.

After talking to the parishioners, Jim Gyton, the parish priest, drove me to Rougham where we had lunch at Ponders Farm with John and Irene Ringer. I met Mrs North, who lives at the Hall and whose family have lived here for 300 years. She is quite a character. Rougham Church is, like Castle Acre, a gem and very well kept, with many interesting features including some medieval brasses. After lunch, we drove back to Castle Acre where the school were having an open-air street party and I spent time with the children and their mothers. Afterwards I went to the school with the children, where they eagerly questioned me about my part in the war. They had obviously been well taught in preparation for VE Day, and were full of questions. It was interesting that when I talked to their mothers I realised that the history of the Second World War did not feature in their schooldays at all.

At 3.30 we drove to Newton Church on the Swaffham to Fakenham road. This is a church with Saxon features and is, I was told, the oldest church in the diocese: it is very small and was beautifully restored in the 1920s, having been mercifully untouched by the Victorians. The congregation is small and most of them were there. After a prayer together we drove to South Acre Church where Wendy, the churchwarden, met us and showed us round this interesting building with its Templar tomb and beautiful wood carvings made by a rector in the early part of the century. The lectern is a copy of the one in Norwich Cathedral, with two bishops at the base; the one with a beard I think must be Sheepshanks. After tea with Wendy and her daughter, Jim drove me back to his home at Ashill, and showed me round his tiny but interesting garden. Nan gave us supper and we chatted until it was time to return to Castle Acre Church for the Bible study.

The introduction by Huib van Hoeven was good but rather long. We split into small groups for quarter of an hour and then had a plenary session. As always, the discussion warmed up most towards the end. I concluded the evening by leading them into silence for fifteen minutes. When John Long (my part-time driver) arrived to take me back to Norwich, I felt very tired, but I expect it was partly the strangeness of a new kind of day and I shall doubtless get into some kind of rhythm soon.

Wednesday 10 May

Steven drove me to Great Dunham rectory, where I was met by Brian Cole, the Rural Dean. We first visited Sporle Church with its fabulous medieval wall painting of St Catherine, then Sporle First School for assembly with the children, where I did my usual thing with bishop's gear and herded them round with my shepherd's crook. At Little Fransham we met churchwardens and a few members of the congregations, and at Great Dunham the proud parishioners showed us this delightful small church, which is Saxon in origin and claims, like Newton yesterday, to be the oldest church in the diocese. Like Newton, it was clearly built with the villagers in mind and is small, accommodating no more than forty or fifty people. At Little Dunham we visited a converted pub, now called the Crown Rest Home, which is owned by a former social worker who cares for old people. There were just three elderly residents and we drank coffee and chatted together. It is a good home, where the rooms are filled with their own belongings, and Sheila, the owner, is keen to keep them there until they die so that they have a real sense of security.

After leaving, we went via Little Dunham Church to the Old Rectory nearby, the home of Andrew and Diana Don, for lunch with members of the PCCs of Little and Great Dunham – a friendly gathering, with delicious wine brought back from France by Andy.

After Beetley Church, which I visited with Leslie Wilman, the Rector, we went to Swanton Morley School, which is a huge first school, large because it has served the local RAF station for many years, which is about to close so they are uncertain about the future and hope that the army may take over the camp. The children showed me their new pond and we discovered a few tadpoles. I sat with a group in the senior class where one child asked me searching questions about the nature of suffering and how God can be good and allow tragedy.

Swanton Morley Church is beautiful, vast, though well maintained, and clearly loved not just by villagers but by the Royal Air Force too. We visited the new village hall which is nearly completed, an astonishing edifice, quite unlike the rectangular brick room I was expecting. It is a great octagon, built in a modern style with large meeting room, committee rooms, bars and changing rooms, overlooking several acres of playing fields. It is an unusual and exciting project for a village hall and I hope to return for the opening.

I went with Leslie Wilman to an extraordinarily lively ecumenical prayer and discussion group of old ladies in one of the parishes. It was formed by two ladies, one Methodist and one Anglican, who walked home after shopping together fourteen years ago and suggested that they meet for Christian fellowship. The oldest member is ninety, the youngest about seventy. They meet every month in one of their homes and someone leads them in Bible study or else they have a discussion together – a very good initiative, totally independent of the clergy. Incidentally, Leslie Wilman is clearly an excellent parish priest. The radical edginess that is sometimes seen in diocesan meetings is not at all evident in his parishes, where he is warm, friendly and sensitive, and much loved by the people.

I was glad then to be taken for a break to Patricia Jeffery's house at the Old Rectory, East Bilney, a vast Victorian house further extended in the early part of the century by a bachelor rector. He married late in life and thought the accommodation inadequate for the additional servants necessary when his wife came to live there. Patricia is a great worker in the Mothers' Union, and at the heart of the life of the local church and community. She sensitively suggested that I spend an hour alone, and I was glad to go for a walk to the little church nearby and spend some time sketching in the evening light.

After supper we went to Beetley Church for the Bible study which was attended by a much larger crowd than yesterday. The Bible study was led by a reader, Ann Bone, and again we ended the evening with a period of silence.

Thursday 11 May

At Wellingham Church I was met by the churchwardens, John Timpson, Robin Ellis and their wives, and looked round this delightful small church which has been well restored and maintained – thanks largely to the efforts of John Timpson since he came to retire here a few years ago. After coffee at the Ellis' farmhouse next door, Peter Brown, a retired RAF officer, drove me in his Dormobile to Weasenham School. Peter had plastered the windows and front with a notice saying 'Bishop Peter's Pilgrimage', creating a kind of Popemobile. Weasenham School is tiny, just about thirty pupils, but still apparently safe and I had an enjoyable time with the children, who sang a song in Zulu.

Peter and I then visited the two parish churches, Weasenham St Peter, which was restored and catholicised by a member of the Coke family who was very keen on Walsingham, and All Saints, another small and airy church, but which looked rather sad. Their last service had been at Easter and none of the flowers had been cleared away. It is the only church I have seen so far that was uncared for. There has been a long-standing conflict between All Saints and St Peter's. They are in small villages, joined together, and logic says that one church ought to be made redundant, but it would only take one caring family to transform All Saints Church into something beautiful.

We then drove to Harpley village hall where I blessed the new extension and met members of the playgroup and hall committee – a lively group of people and evidently a good village community. At Little Massingham Church there was an extensive memorial still left from VE Day celebrations. From an RAF station nearby Blenheims and Mosquitoes flew sorties over France and the low countries. Many squadrons occupied the airbase, including a Free French squadron. There had been a close link between the church and the airbase, and the officers' mess was the Old Rectory where one of the churchwardens, Mr Brereton, grew up, and where a number of his ancestors have been vicars of the parish. Another beautiful church of manageable size for the village.

At Great Massingham I visited the school and church, then went to Cedric Bradbury's house for coffee. Cedric is still not well after his operation in St Luke's. At 2 o'clock Peter Brown dropped me at Brisley School which is a church aided school, recently extended, with marvellous facilities. It is quite large for a village school, and lively. The children had a long assembly where they sang songs. They are doing a project on Nigeria and I was shown the artwork, which was excellent. They are clearly very well taught. In the assembly some children who had been doing an art project on the impressionists produced paintings in impressionist style which were most interesting, and I told them about my visit to Giverny.

Peter Greenwood, the Lay Chairman, took me to meet a farmer, Andrew Hill, a young man in his thirties, and his wife, who farm 250 acres near Horningtoft. Andrew showed me round his farm and arable crops, and explained the difficulties of modern farming, how he rotated the crops and was fairly secure with a guaranteed sale to agents. But nothing is certain for very long in farming, particularly on what is a relatively small scale for Norfolk.

Afterwards I visited another young man's enterprise called 'Town and Country Conservatories'. Kevin, a farmer's son, whose mother is a churchwarden, had trained as a carpenter and established a business with a London friend building expensive tailor-made conservatories. It failed in 1981 because the London partner was too ambitious and spent too much money, but Kevin managed to recover, found a new partner in London and the business is now thriving. He employs eighteen people in the farm buildings constructing the conservatories.

At Whissonsett Church there was a remarkable VE Day display, including camouflage netting, models of the Mohne dam (with the bursting dam made from flowers) and a blitzed city. This is another church which has been well restored. This village of 400 people raised £27,000 two years ago and the spirit of these people is amazing. Their achievement is extraordinary. I told them that they should write of their experiences because their example is important and could give confidence to others in similar situations.

I was then driven to Colkirk Church where I was met by a churchwarden and her son who looked rather unhappy. I chatted away amiably and she asked me if I thought Norfolk people were difficult.

'No more than most country people,' I replied, 'and having spent some years in Cornwall I was used to people who live at the end of the country and think themselves not really part of England.'

'Do you think Norfolk people are stubborn?' she persisted.

'Yes, I do. But once Norfolk people see the point of something they do seem to manage to change with great rapidity, which is one of the reasons why Norfolk has remained prosperous through the centuries.'

This was clearly a prelude to her pouring out her disappointment because her beloved priest had been appointed by me to a parish in Norwich after four years in the parish. It was all rather difficult and negative, and very little of what I said seemed to be of any comfort. But I prayed with them, gave them a blessing, and left to go to the home of Kevin Blogg, an NSM (non-stipendiary minister) and teacher, and his wife, who with their three young daughters gave me a warm welcome. I went for a walk and then came back for high tea. The weather had been icy, and despite gloves, Barbour and cloth cap I was frozen to the bones after half an hour of brisk walking.

After tea I went briefly to visit the church at Brisley where again they have done remarkable restoration work, and was shown a fine tapestry of the pilgrimage map which an old lady had made. After a brief meeting with the local Girl Guides I went to Horningtoft Church for the Bible study taken by Peter Greenwood – another very good evening, with about thirty people present, and again we ended the evening with a time of silence. During the conducted meditation I put my chair in front of one of the Calor gas heaters and felt warm for the first time for hours.

Friday 12 May

Steven drove me to the Beeston Industrial Estate for the beginning of what looked like an impossibly full day. We were given a tour of Norfolk Canners, a huge canning factory specialising in carrots and potatoes, which serves supermarket chains. Today they were on carrots – a fascinating process. I spoke to the workers who all seemed happy but were completely put off carrots by handling them for several hours each day. The head of the firm is a Norwich City fan who is often seen in the Directors' Box. Like me he is not at all depressed about the prospect of Norwich being relegated because we both think they will move straight back again. (They didn't.)

Beeston Church is a gem in a field on its own, a large and beautifully maintained fourteenth-century church. There I mounted a horse while photographers busily snapped away, doubtless hoping I would fall off. I rode Murphy, a large and gentle hunter, who is clearly tolerant of a bad rider. With Tom Scott, the owner (whose wife, Jill, is greatly involved in the St John Ambulance nationally), we rode across beautiful rolling countryside, past the ruined church of Kempstone which has been maintained by the County Council at a cost of £30,000. I wonder if it is right for the Council to spend so much money on a ruin? I haven't sat on a horse for more than thirty-five years, but I think it must be like riding a bicycle because it all came back to me, even rising to the trot. After a thoroughly enjoyable ride, we arrived at Litcham where we were met by a crowd of people and more photographers. After saying goodbye to Murphy, I went to the playgroup which meets in Litcham village hall and talked to the children.

At Mileham I was taken by the Rector to meet an old lady who has had two strokes and we talked for a while and then I prayed with her and laid hands on her. At the primary school I sat down to lunch with the pupils. Not very appetising.

'You should have come on Wednesday,' said the boy next to me.

'Why?' I asked.

'Because it's chips on Wednesday.'

After coffee with parishioners at Litcham Jubilee Hall, Neil Foster took me to East Lexham, a beautiful Saxon church in the grounds of his estate. At West Lexham, another delightful small country church, the readers of the deanery held a short service of prayer. We returned to Mileham to meet the couple who have taken over the post office and shop. The husband, having been made redundant, had decided to buy a village post office, but knowing that so many went broke he wisely looked at the map and chose a village a long way from a main town supermarket, and his business seems thriving. They are happy and very much at the hub of the community.

To the vicarage at North Elmham, where Noel and Gill Tewkesbury welcomed me. By then I was ready for a break and they kindly allowed me to go for a short brisk walk rather than socialise. Afterwards I visited the grand new surgery in North Elmham, which is a modern, well appointed building serving a large area roughly the size of the deanery. A number of the doctors and staff are committed Christians and after showing me round the surgery and its facilities, which overlook a beautiful garden with a pond, we had coffee together and prayed the Pilgrimage Prayer.

North Elmham Primary School is well run, with friendly outgoing children. I was bombarded with questions ranging from, 'What does a bishop do?' to, 'How can you become a bishop?' and, 'What's the difference between you and our vicar?' They were uninhibited and lovely children. After this we walked to the ruins of the cathedral at North Elmham where Grahame Humphries interviewed me for Radio Norfolk. Then Noel drove me to Billingford, which is the problem church in this Group because it needs a great deal of money spent and there are just a few very dedicated churchgoers, whom I met. Afterwards we visited the churchwarden in his ancient cottage next to the church. He is a delightful old farmer, aged eighty-eight, who has been in office for nearly sixty years.

In the same benefice, Worthing is a very small church with the remains of a Saxon tower, which serves a tiny hamlet. The church was full with parishioners and Noel Tewkesbury took evensong and afterwards we talked. A very good congregation indeed. In this Group they have some quite powerful lay leaders like George Eve, Robin Don and John Labouchere, who have strong minds of their own, but Noel admits he would rather have that than people who do not take the initiative. He told me that before he came he had been unused to sharing with lay people and had done everything himself, but in his time there he had learned the value of sharing and letting go. I guess he maybe has a bit more to let go, but it was encouraging to hear him talk in this way.

After evensong Noel drove me to the Don's estate which produces excellent wine. Judy and Robin welcomed me, with their daughter Hettie, recently returned from a year in South America but unfortunately having caught a severe bout of hepatitis. She is now looking for a job in publishing where she worked before. Before supper Robin and I walked through the garden, which is delightful, and the whole estate is in a lovely setting overlooking a valley. As a special treat, with our salmon we had asparagus from their own bed. I had mentioned when walking round the garden that we had an asparagus bed, but didn't also say that we were eating it like cabbage at the moment.

The last Bible study took place in North Elmham Institute with about forty-five people present. Each night the Bible study has grown and this was another good evening, the people warm in their thanks. I hope some of them will continue with the Bible study. I sense from what people said that they valued especially the small talk I gave at the end introducing silent prayer.

John collected me and we were home within half an hour. Perhaps I am pacing myself a bit better, or getting used to the round of visits, but I found today, although theoretically very full, more manageable than the others.

Saturday 13 May

At Gressenhall village common I climbed on to an ancient farm cart, pulled by an old cart horse, and, sitting on straw bales, was taken to the Rural Life Museum on the outskirts of the village. Another bitterly cold morning. Riding on iron wheels for a mile along a country road made me realise why our forefathers had good livers. I am sure the vibration is therapeutic. The Museum has the best collection of rural farm implements, furniture and utensils in the country and has reproductions of cottage rooms, workshops and shops. It is housed in the old workhouse, a vast building begun in the eighteenth century. There was an imaginative talk, giving us a vivid picture of life in the old workhouse which was grim.

Lunch was at Wendling Grange with Sir Ralph and Lady Howell, the local MP and his wife, and another couple, Frank and June, who live in a cottage on their estate. John Belham, the Rector, said that these two couples had revitalised the life of the local church, Margaret Howell taking responsibility for the restoration of the building, and Frank and June founding a Sunday school which has grown so large that it is now taking place in the loft of the Grange. It is a wonderful example of the 'rich man in his castle and the poor man at his gate' working together. After lunch I spent an hour with parishioners in Wendling Church talking about life in rural parishes. Like so many other congregations I have visited, they were in good heart, and quite belie the image that is presented of low morale and falling numbers.

I then went to meet another congregation in the church at Longham, which, like Wendling, is a small church obviously built for the community. Throughout this week I have been struck by the fact that you can divide the churches of Norfolk into two categories. The first were built with the needs of the community in mind, with seating of up to one hundred and often much less. These churches were probably founded by monastic communities in the early days. The others are the churches built to the glory of God and of the benefactor who provided the money, and almost invariably were too large for the community's needs. I found some congregations in those large churches the least confident because they feel themselves to be small and insignificant when twenty are gathered in a church which seats 300. But the fact is that there were never 300 people sitting in those pews. For most of their history the congregations were as small as they are today.

After Longham I went to one of the smallest villages in Norfolk, Bittering Parva. I briefly visited the tiny church, the smallest in Norfolk they say, and then ninety per cent of the population (fourteen) gathered together for tea in the sitting room of a cottage owned by a former Metropolitan policeman who is a churchwarden. They are an interesting group of people, who keep themselves to themselves most of the time, but are friendly and help each other out when they need to do so. The village was mentioned in the Domesday Book and is very old, with Bronze Age remains which indicate that it is the oldest settlement in the area. The reason is that a spring rises there and the source was always the place to make a settlement since the water supply was guaranteed when no outsiders could divert or block it.

After Bittering I paid a brief visit to the attractive parish church at Gressenhall and then a mile away to the village green where I went to the village hall and met a large group of parishioners for yet more tea. Everyone has been warm and welcoming and has expressed real happiness that I am making this visit, giving so many people the opportunity of meeting the person they see on television and read about in the press. Of course I see parishioners every week, but not with the same intensity as during this pilgrimage. There were no evening engagements, so by 6.15 pm I was home, and welcomed the chance to rest and catch up a bit on correspondence.

Sunday 14 May

After a short service in Harpley Church attended by sixty people (they had anticipated twenty), we began walking the Peddars Way towards Massingham and eventually Castle Acre. The day was bright and warmer than of late, and most of the forty or fifty people who made the walk were dressed appropriately. One or two had dogs, and a couple of minibuses were strategically placed en route to help stragglers. One man did the entire walk in a blue suit and shiny black shoes because he thought he had better dress for church.

We arrived at Great Massingham and had a service of Holy Communion – the congregation had increased to just over one hundred – and afterwards we ate sandwiches and had coffee in the church. After lunch a pony and trap arrived, driven by Sheila Stangroom, whose son, Aaron, had told me he wished for chips at Beetley Primary School the other day. She is a midwife working from the North Elmham surgery, and the partner of Kevin who owns the Town and Country Conservatories. The complex links in Norfolk between various families are not limited to the Buxtons, Gurneys, Barclays and Birkbecks! The sturdy little horse Blackie trotted happily along the country road; the trap was very old, but a Rolls Royce compared to the bone-shaking farm cart yesterday. Sheila set me down on the Peddars Way and I joined the others for a continuation of the walk. After a few miles, Sheila picked me up again and I had another ride with Blackie. He was very good but had an inferiority complex – he would only move if one constantly talked to him and told him how marvellous he was. We stopped again a mile short of Castle Acre, waited a little while for the first of the walkers to catch up, and then walked together into Castle Acre village accompanied by the pony and trap, another horse and a mountain bike. Kevin was there with a camera, and disappointed that I was walking, so I got in the trap for the last few hundred yards, providing photo opportunities for all the people sitting outside in the cafés on a Sunday afternoon outing. We assembled at the Castle Acre Priory ruins and for the next hour or so people wandered around and had tea in the excellent cafés nearby. I spent some time at the Old Vicarage, putting one or two thoughts together for a short address in the evening.

After some hymn practice, at 6 o'clock Jim Gyton led evening prayer, with a superb organist who had taught the congregation half an hour earlier how to sing responsorial psalms – they learnt it inside ten minutes, he told me later – so much more satisfying for a congregation which is not particularly musical than struggling with Anglican chants. The congregation had grown yet again to about 150 or so, and at the end I talked informally about my impressions of the week which had indeed been memorable, though that word is hardly adequate. I spent half an hour saying goodbye to members of the congregation, most of whom were now familiar faces.

It has been a marvellous week, extremely well organised by Huib van Hoeven, a retired officer in the Royal Netherlands Navy, a week full of friendliness, welcome, mutual encouragement, hope and genuine meetings. We could not have had a better beginning.

Castle Acre Priory

Interlude

Wednesday 17 May

The staff meeting was chaired in the morning by David and in the afternoon by Hugo. This was a restful experience. Always after staff meetings I feel worn out because although we are very much at ease with each other, chairing the meeting demands considerable effort in making sure we get through all the items on time and enabling reticent members to be properly heard and the noisier ones curbed.

In the afternoon Canon Pamela Fawcett came to review the position of women after just over a year in priests' orders. *All seems to be going well in the diocese. We have made a number of appointments of women as incumbents and morale among the women is generally high, not least because the entire senior staff has always been strongly in favour of the ordination of women to the priesthood. Yet problems inevitably remain. We are appointing women as incumbents but although they may have been in active ministry for some years, as yet they are very new to priesthood, and that is showing in certain stresses they are experiencing. But in their parishes they are being generally well received. There is also the question of clergy husbands to be considered, and we shall need to tackle this in a systematic way quite soon.*

Pam also came to talk about spiritual direction, about which she feels strongly. We agreed with her about the need for guidance in prayer and we had a long and good discussion on the subject. There was a general feeling that we should give this priority in the near future, perhaps when the 900 celebrations are over. It is an area where I think retired clergy could have an important ministry, which is as yet untapped. We tend to use retired clergy to plug gaps in the parochial ministry, which is not in my view the best way of using them, for a number of reasons.

Today the papers were full of the Bishop of Edinburgh (Richard Holloway) having given a lecture which allegedly suggested that the Church should be more tolerant and understanding of adultery. Of course they misquoted him in a passage where he was talking about the built-in sex drive which human beings have. But he is experienced enough to realise that his remarks would be seized on, as they have been, by the popular Press. Richard is someone I admire as a good and holy man with a fine theological brain, but like David Jenkins he is something of a gadfly who in the laudable desire to stimulate actually provokes and shocks. One wonders how much that actually helps. Like David, his remarks in the context of an address to students would be entirely right and in place, but given the general publicity such lectures are bound to receive these days, the Press is handed just one more stick with which to beat the Church.

Thursday 18 May

After a day of meetings, Betty and I briefly visited the new Lord Mayor's reception at the castle. One of the delights was meeting the Barbadian Mayor of Ipswich and his wife, and the black Chairman of the Council of Broadland who is from Belize. We have so few West Indians in East Anglia that it is always such a treat to meet them and of course Betty (herself a Trinidadian) had a great chat with them all. We left just as the procession of dignitaries was entering the castle keep, oddly led by pipers. We slipped away early to go to the institution of the new priest at Eaton.

Friday 19 May

Hugo preached at the retired clergy Eucharist extremely well on the subject of the ministry of the retired, and in particular about the ministry of teaching prayer, which tied up closely with our conversation at the staff meeting two days before. Lunch in the cloisters was chilly, and I hardly blamed them for not taking up our invitation to come and stroll in the garden when they had finished.

Stephen and Rosslie Platten were up for the day, taking measurements at the deanery, and they came round for supper and to talk. They are excited about the prospect of coming and it will be good to have a young and energetic dean. I have known Stephen for some years, since I was in Taunton and he was in Portsmouth, when we met through the establishment of the Southern Dioceses Ministerial Training Scheme at Salisbury. At Lambeth he has been involved in the high life, with much travelling abroad, and it will probably take some time before he comes down to earth and gives himself to the narrower focus of this cathedral and diocese. But he is keen and though he is bound to make mistakes I am very happy about his appointment and look forward to working with him.

Saturday 20 May

Before leaving for London to spend the night with our daughter Victoria and

Archdeacons

her husband Angus, I visited Oliver Prior, the former registrar, now an old man, who has become a good friend. I was returning some novels he lent me and a record of traditional jazz which he bought in New Orleans and is one of the interests we share. He told me about the VE weekend when he was the guest of the Danish Government in Copenhagen. He was among the first British troops to enter Denmark in 1945 and there were tears in his eyes as he described the parade when veterans walked through the streets, lined seven deep with Danish people just saying, 'Thank you, thank you,' over and over again. Oliver's first wife died some years ago, and he married a widow who is, by coincidence, Danish. Nina is a marvellous character, full of enthusiasm and energy, and a wonderful companion for Oliver, sharing his great love of good food and drink, and trips abroad. I walked through the drawing room into the conservatory to see Nina, who was puffing a large cigar and filling the small conservatory with a pungent cloud of smoke.

4

Thetford and Rockland

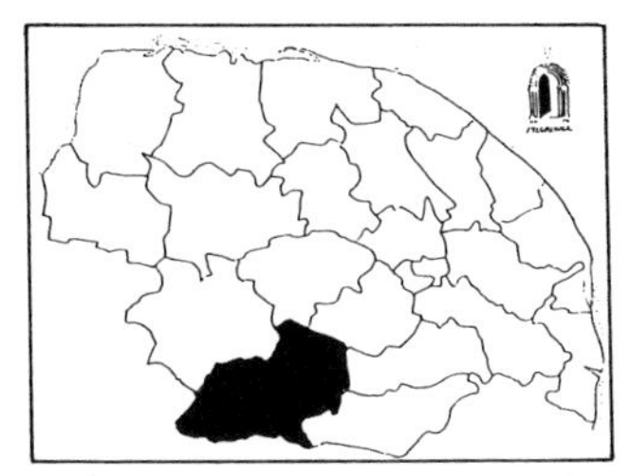

(This deanery is mostly rural, but at its centre is the old town of Thetford, formerly the seat of bishops of East Anglia, where Herbert de Losinga lived before moving to Norwich.)

Tuesday 23 May

At a chapter meeting at the home of Alistair McGregor, the Rural Dean and Team Rector of Thetford, I celebrated a very informal Communion service in the sitting room where the chapter normally meets for its Eucharist. I can understand how they wish to do this in the winter but I was unsure about not using a church in spring and summer. There does seem to be an entirely different attitude to church buildings, at least from the evidence of my first day, compared to that of the previous deanery where church buildings were a very important focus. Today I only entered one church, and that only because there was an exhibition of Thetford history. After breakfast the chapter held a Bible study on the first passage of St Luke for the week. Ten members were present and it was excellent, with good contributions coming from nearly everyone. I think ten is a good size for a chapter; any less and one would not have the stimulus and variety one experienced this morning. It is probably unusual for one hundred per cent attendance so perhaps the optimum size for a chapter would be about fifteen clergy. Many of our chapters are really far too small.

We walked from the pleasant suburb where Alistair lives through woodland and a park to the town centre. At the King's House we met the Deputy Mayor and Town Clerk who spoke about the history of the town, its present problems and hopes for the future. The town has had a chequered history for centuries and it has not been helped by local government reorganisation, which has taken away its decision-making powers while retaining its status as a town with a mayor and council. We had an interesting talk about centralisation and devolved decision making, which parallels many of the experiences we have in the Church. I think in the Church we are rather ahead of the thinking in local government in this respect.

We walked through the streets of Thetford and met a number of people en route, including the local undertaker, and he and Alistair talked about yesterday's funeral of a mother and three children. This was a tragic murder and suicide which has rocked the whole town. It was good to see such a close relationship between priest and undertaker which is potentially of such importance in a community.

We also met an unmarried mother whose boyfriend deserted her when she became pregnant. This sparked off a conversation between us about the problems of male confidence and a new lack of male responsibility which is puzzling, and not unrelated, of course, to the increasing emphasis on feminism or at least the place of women in society. Paradoxically, perhaps it is when men can come to terms more with the feminine side of their nature, that they will begin to exercise more responsibility.

We were joined for a ploughman's lunch at a local hotel by Tony Linge, the Lay Chairman, a retired engineer who lives in a tiny village but who worked in a large factory on one of the Thetford industrial estates. After lunch we walked through the ruins of the Old Priory. They are well kept and we were the only visitors. It is easy to underrate Thetford but there are some beautiful parts, a great deal of open space, riverside walks and some well-preserved old buildings.

After lunch we walked to the house of Keith Wilson, the industrial chaplain, and member of the Thetford team. He also has a great deal to do with schools and took me to a local sixth form centre. I spent some time in discussion with a group of sixth formers. The session was fine because the questions kept coming and I was able to give answers which I hoped were not too facile or complex, but I wished I could have spent more time with them because I felt that beneath the questions which had obviously been prepared in advance were some deeper issues which we could perhaps have explored together. Also the presence of three senior members of staff did not help. It inhibits the young and I think prevents them being as open with me as they might otherwise be. I think in future I must gently suggest that when I meet such groups of sixth formers I meet them entirely alone. Perhaps it is thought I need protecting and maybe I do, but I would rather take the risk.

After leaving the sixth form centre Keith returned me to Alistair McGregor's house where I spent an hour quietly in the shade.

Thetford Priory

At 5 o'clock I was taken to the home of Michael Hughes, who is a member of the team and also works part-time as a GP. He is looking after the brand new Cloverfield estate, a private development where the church meets in a local nursery school, the only public building on the estate. His wife and four delightful children, Xemian, Kerry, Javan and Naomi, showed me the new brood of rabbits (six of them) and then we had supper in the garden, which was very pleasant. The children were very chatty. One of them, Kerry, accompanied Michael and me in the early evening to the estate, where I spent the evening with the Crusader group. It had been set up in January and there were about twenty from the ages of eight to eleven.

They were a precocious group, well handled by the six young adults whom Michael had recruited as helpers. This is quite an achievement and bodes well for the future. It was actually quite unlike the Crusader classes I remember having attended for a brief period when I was aged eleven. I remember finding them too strict and religious, and unworthily only persevered until I qualified for the badge which attracted me. This lot were totally different. They played raucous games with enthusiasm, then bought tuck and finally I gave them a short talk and invited questions. I was bombarded for a full ten minutes and had to stop them because by then Steven had arrived to take me home.

It was a good and encouraging evening with lively young people whom I hope we can keep. If we have helpers of this quality then there is good hope.

Wednesday 24 May

At Banham rectory Michael Savage, Anne Hedges, Peter Knight and I said morning prayer together. They meet regularly to pray and talk, even though their groups of parishes are not officially united, which is good. I am finding that clergy are associating informally in many places in the diocese, and parishes are beginning to do the same without prompting and without making things official. This seems to be a very encouraging development.

After prayer we drove to a large arable and pig farm owned by Alan Wright, who is about to begin training as an LNSM (local non-stipendiary minister). He drove us around his farm in his Land Rover accompanied by Ron, a curiously named but very beautiful young female Springer, who was lively and affectionate and could obviously smell Carrie (my sixteen-year-old Springer). Alan took us to the middle of a huge thirty-acre field, from which little habitation could be seen, and he said, 'You can see why arable farmers get depressed if they are working on their own for up to ten hours a day without speaking to another soul.' He is very active in the Farmers' Helpline and counsels quite a few farmers, an increasing number of whom are suffering from depressive illnesses. We then visited his pig sheds, where 700 pigs are housed in good conditions, and we spent some time talking with his son Andrew who is to take over the farm when Alan retires next year. The smell was quite strong and Alan warned me that I would probably smell of pigs all day long, so if people backed away that would be the reason.

I was then dropped at Garboldisham rectory where Anne took me to a house Communion with an old lady whose husband was a chief instructor at Bovingdon in the 1930s and who was serving in the village shop when the news came through of the death of T. E. Lawrence in a motorcycle accident. (She called him 'Mr Shaw'.) Six friends had come to have coffee but arrived early and all joined in the informal Communion. Anne told me afterwards that previously she had always given Communion to this lady alone but they all so enjoyed the experience that they planned to meet together for Communion in future.

Peter Knight, the bearded curate of the Quidenham Group, took me to the old people's lunch club in the village hall, which was a jolly occasion but far too much food. These old people seem to have enormous appetites which I can't match. All the people there live on their own – single, widows or widowers. It was interesting that the men stuck together and refused absolutely to mix with the women. Having played cribbage all morning, they sat at a table by themselves for lunch.

Anne picked me up and took me back to her house for coffee and a short break, after which I went with her to Riddlesworth School where she is the part-time chaplain. After chatting to the Headmistress and almost being eaten alive by her large Labrador puppy, I spent three separate half hours with the three age groups at the school who asked me questions. The third group, seven- to nine-year-olds, gave me no time to do my usual explanation of the crook because they fired questions at me non-stop for half an hour, and afterwards half a dozen crowded round wanting to ask more questions. It was very stimulating but the questions were often unbelievably difficult, the first being, 'Who created God?' followed by, 'How do you know heaven exists?', 'What is your view of heaven?' and including such ambiguous questions as, 'How are human beings made?' I wasn't quite sure whether I should have given a biological or a theological answer. Afterwards I had tea with staff and visiting parents from another school which had come for rounders and swimming matches.

I felt quite exhausted by this experience, stimulating as it was, and I was ready for a rest, but first I visited the hospice for young children at Quidenham, which was very impressive and moving. It has been set up by voluntary donations, and is well equipped, but can cater for only four or five children. There were four there, three with serious congenital illnesses and one who had contracted encephalitis. One young boy was very distressed the whole time and obviously in pain. There seemed little they could do to comfort him and in the end they decided to give him a warm bath. I suppose he was aged about seven or eight but apparently gets wind very badly like a small baby and it was clearly very difficult to comfort him, poor child. After this I spent an hour at the Carmelite monastery. Because it is 'enclosed' I was not allowed inside, but was given a special guest room with a kitchen where I could make coffee.

Michael Savage picked me up at 7 o'clock and we drove to Kenninghall Church where we had refreshments and then a Bible study. It was an 'invitation only' evening to churchwardens, lay readers, lay chairmen and PCCs. There are no fewer than three potential LNSMs in this Group and predictably the Bible study was lively and well-informed. We ended with a period of silence as I have done before. It was a good evening but I rather regret that a more open invitation had not been issued to ordinary parishioners to take part. Steven picked me up just after 9 o'clock and told me that according to his calculations this had been my longest day; it was a good day but certainly felt long.

Thursday 25 May Ascension Day

A day in Attleborough began with a meeting at Besthorpe Hall, the home of John Alston, where I met local councillors from the Breckland District Council, town councils and one or two parish councillors. We had a long and interesting talk which followed up many of the subjects chewed over with the Deputy Mayor of Thetford on Tuesday.

The interesting thing about the meeting with the councillors was that they talked a lot about politics, and argued among themselves about the importance of national parties being involved with local party politics. But it was extremely difficult from their conversation to guess who was who. I was, for example, very surprised when a man who had been talking heatedly about common ownership was referred to in an argument as 'you Conservatives', and even more surprised when a lady who seemed obviously a great figure in the local Conservative Association afterwards told me proudly that she was a member of the Christian Socialist group.

Afterwards we went for a walk in the attractive gardens, which John is managing by means of a new use of manpower. He has a large farm and once a week brings in four or five farmworkers to spend a day in the garden. He reckons that will keep the garden going without the need for a full-time gardener. It is an interesting experiment, which might prove to be a cheaper option for other people with large gardens, like bishops, who could perhaps contract a few people for a day a week.

We returned to the new hall attached to the church at Attleborough, which is a splendid multipurpose building, for a bread and cheese lunch and a Bible study with a group of lay people. As with all such lay groups, the Bible study was very good. It wandered from the text but was nevertheless extremely valuable and was well organised by a young layman.

After an hour's break in the garden of Attleborough rectory, I went to the local old people's home, managed by Chris Mallett, an NSM. It was built in the 1960s, and extended in the 1980s when they took the opportunity to make considerable improvements to the layout of the accommodation. There are now no large rooms with chairs arranged round the edges, but rather a series of small dining rooms and sitting rooms which accommodate from three to ten people. I went round and talked to every person in the home, the large majority of whom expressed themselves happy to be there. People in their nineties abounded, and one lady of ninety-five talked to me about her family and about how much she admired her uncle, who had been born in the workhouse which I visited the other day and which is now the rural museum at Gressenhall. The odds were loaded against children born in the workhouse, but this young man made good, becoming a farmer and a Methodist local preacher. Another lady told me that when the rest of the family refused to look after her grandfather, she went to live with him in order to save him from the workhouse. It was extraordinary to hear living memories of a place I visited which seemed a part of history long ago. I wonder if young people are aware of some of the very important historical memories which are still around in places like this. If some of these conversations were recorded they could prove to be important sources for local history.

After supper with John and Anne Aves, and their sons Benjamin and Edmund, we made our way to the church for a deanery Eucharist. John organises such events with great flair and he had gathered together a choir of eighty-five. It was a great celebration and he preached a good sermon. I think the liturgy managed to meet most needs, combining *Ancient and Modern* and arm-waving charismatic choruses. Just before the final hymn children came through the congregation distributing helium-filled balloons, some of which escaped arthritic fingers and floated to the roof – for how long I can't imagine because the roof of Attleborough Church is very high indeed. I tied mine to my staff and we processed outside where the evening ended with a bang as John Aves had arranged for rockets to be let off. This memorable celebration of the Ascension ended another full and rewarding day.

Friday 26 May

From Great Ellingham rectory Mark Williams drove me to the nearby airfield at Deopham Green which was an airbase for the 452 Bomb Group in the Second World War. The fiftieth anniversary has seen many veterans returning and the old runways are still clearly visible. After the local farmer who cares for the memorial took photographs to send to the veterans' organisations in America, we returned to the rectory for coffee with about twenty parishioners. The group included some younger men who have been made redundant and are now engaged in new enterprises – one of them an aromatherapist.

We next visited Wayland Hospital where there are about seventy patients, many of them on courses of treatment following amputation and strokes. After an hour in the hospital we visited Great Ellingham Primary School where I met four separate age groups. The special pilgrimage badges for children have at last arrived and so I was able to give them out at the school, which delighted them. We seem to have hit on the right children's souvenir.

We returned to Rocklands village where an open day was being held at a parishioner's house. This is an annual event to raise funds for the church. The weather was lovely and I sat in the garden chatting to stallholders and visitors and ate a ploughman's lunch (again). Glancing at the programme, it did seem as if no break had been planned during the day and so I excused myself and walked for quarter of an hour down a nearby lane before returning for more chat until it was time to be taken to East Harling.

At East Harling John Handley whisked me straight to the local primary school which is large with 200 pupils, and there I talked to another four separate year groups. I ran out of pilgrimage badges but promised that they would be delivered after half term. I am quite looking forward to half term myself and a break from primary school children. After a time one does become a bit bored with one's own 'What's a shepherd?' routine, though occasionally one can be disconcerted by the sharpness of the questions, such as one from a ten-year-old at East Harling who asked, 'How can you possibly believe in God? I don't.' And from her friend at the same desk, 'Nor do I.' I really must prepare myself a little more for these fast balls but one hardly expects them from primary school children. It just shows how wrong I am. I learned afterwards that this particular child had raised this question more than once with John Handley during his assemblies and it seems as if she is being deliberately taught not to believe; because she worries at the questions perhaps there are already doubts in her young mind.

John then took me on a tour of the Group and for the first time this week I was taken to visit church buildings, which I enjoyed very much. We visited Rushford where a group of seven parishioners met me and we had a good time talking and then praying together. The delightful and dapper churchwarden walked me to the churchyard gate and told me a hair-raising story about his imprisonment by the Japanese. He was captured at Singapore, and after a spell in Changi, worked all the way up the Burma railroad to the end and still survived. Last year he felt a strange itch in his stomach and eventually went to hospital where they diagnosed some tropical parasite with which he had been infected in 1943 and which was only now working its way out through his skin. They managed to treat it and he is now perfectly well – a remarkable man.

After Bridgham, where again we met parishioners, we visited Brettenham which was built mainly as an estate church and is rather sad and deserted, the old Norman church having been heavily restored (vandalised, some would say) by a rich, enthusiastic Victorian lord of the manor. All that remains is a beautiful Norman porch. We then drove to Larling. To reach this we had to cross the A11 at 5 o'clock on a bank holiday Friday which was a nightmare. Eventually we made the northern side and drove a mile up a rough track to Larling Church where we were met by the farmer churchwardens and enjoyed looking round this lovely simple church with an outstanding Norman porch. A Victorian vicar had built a fine fireplace in the vestry, with a lavatory, fed by a tank from the rain gutter, with a pull up flush handle at the side of the seat, the like of which I've only seen before in Sandringham. It was evidently a rather plush little suite of rooms he had made for himself, perhaps to escape for some reason from the rectory.

We returned to East Harling, and the recrossing of the A11 was even worse than our journey out. We were stuck for a long time behind a young lady driver whose rear window was plastered with safety notices. She certainly took no risks, nor indeed opportunities, but at last we made it and arrived fifteen minutes late for the Bible study group at the rectory.

This group meets regularly, consists of a wide age range and was very good indeed, excellent contributions being made by some of the young mothers and teachers present. There was also a good rapport between young and old. They tackled the text with considerable seriousness and insight and did not use it simply as a stepping-stone for a general discussion which tends to happen in some groups. After supper with the Handleys, Joanna (my eldest daughter on her way from London for half term) arrived sweating from a tedious journey, and I drove home with her. The A11 was just as crowded but predictably (Joanna is an aggressive London driver) we managed to cross it very quickly to the accompaniment of flashing lights from a coach and mild swearing from Joanna.

Saturday 27 May

A day off from the pilgrimage today to attend the Consecration of the new Roman Catholic Bishop of East Anglia, Peter Smith. A glorious and very long service at St John's Roman Catholic Cathedral. The new Bishop Peter has been the Principal of St John's Seminary at Wonersh for some years and is fifty-one years old so will probably have a long stay in the diocese. I understand that his appointment was well received in the diocese, particularly by the number of priests who have been trained by him. By all accounts he will continue to foster the good ecumenical relationships we have enjoyed for many years.

As we entered the cathedral there was a demonstration with placards about the ordination of women to the priesthood. This was not the first such demonstration at St John's Cathedral and it is, I suppose, the shape of things to come for some years. We have of course become well used to this but the irritation of members of the congregation was very evident. I hope the campaign is conducted without some of the mistakes made by our own campaigners, which unnecessarily alienated some people. I was not pleased to notice some Anglicans among the demonstrators. This is hardly going to help the cause of women in the Roman Church.

The service of Consecration included Bishop Alan Clark, the retiring bishop, handing over the pastoral staff to the new bishop, so there was a nice sense of continuity which doesn't exist in our own Church, giving one food for thought. In both parishes and dioceses we have clean breaks and fresh beginnings, sometimes after quite a long interregnum. There are arguments in favour of this, but it does mean that we lack continuity and a strategy which does not depend on the personal gifts and inclinations of priest or bishop. As always, I felt the pain of not being able to receive Communion. At the very point where Christians should be most united one is most conscious of our unhappy divisions.

After the service we met Basil Hume, the new Bishop Peter, and John Drury, the Administrator of the cathedral, who embraced me warmly because he too is very sensitive about the division at the point of Communion. Like me he feels strongly that inter-Communion should be a means to unity and not the end of the process.

I spent the rest of the afternoon clearing the backlog of letters and then had a most enjoyable evening with the family who have all come for the weekend.

Sunday 28 May

The family Communion service at East Harling was attended by a marvellously mixed congregation of young, old and middle-aged. It was a fairly traditional Rite B with Merbecke, but they also have a monthly family service with a music group. John Handley, with a more evangelical background than his predecessors, has managed to draw people into the congregation who previously were involved in the Banham Free Church, founded by a former Anglican, which has always been a bit of a thorn in the side of local parishes here.

During coffee after the service we talked about the problems of keeping together both old and young, traditional and modern in the same congregation. I suggested that music was one way, if one could find a mean between traditional *Ancient and Modern* and choruses with drums and tambourines. I asked them if they had ever used responsorial psalms and it was a mystery to them, although they do use the *New English Hymnal* which has a selection of such psalms at the back. So when coffee was over I asked a group of a dozen or so if they would like to try; within five minutes they had learned to sing a responsorial psalm and enjoyed it immensely. Sometimes I long to be a parish priest again and be able to try out all these things I have learned during the last eighteen years.

Afterwards we crossed the road to the village hall where we had a sandwich and sausage roll lunch. John asked me to say grace, so we sang the response several times from the responsorial psalm a few had just learned. Of course the fifty or so present picked it up very quickly. A retired couple whom I met were confirmed last week in the cathedral and had found it a thrilling occasion. This is a good congregation and John is clearly leading them well.

Back home for a free afternoon with the children. We celebrated Carrie's sixteenth birthday and she much enjoyed the cake.

Songs of Praise in the evening at Banham was something of an anticlimax. I was given the second half of the evening to talk about prayer, so I talked once more about silence, and led them into two periods of quiet. But the context seemed rather discordant with a series of *Mission Praise* hymns preceding and following the half-hour I had with them. There were about forty people in church, not enough to justify the acoustic guitars, Yamaha keyboard and chancel floor festooned with wires, plugs and amplifiers. I suppose silence and noisy choruses can mix but probably only if the silence is really separated from the rest and not the filling in the sandwich.

So ended the second deanery visit. It was very different from the first, not least because the clergy were much more in evidence as leaders, although there are many active and very able laity in the deanery; I think there is probably potential for sharing leadership rather more. It was also noticeable that, excepting one benefice, I never went inside a church. I think this is possibly due to the fact that the clergy controlled the programme and gave low priority to visits to church buildings, either thinking I would not wish to go or, more likely, because they themselves did not value church buildings in the way that was apparent in the Brisley and Elmham deanery. Perhaps it was also true of the laity in their own deanery. We still need to reflect deeply about the place of the church building in the Christian community, the community at large and in the mission of the Church. I don't think this has been sufficiently clarified yet and it clearly marks an area of division between clergy and lay attitudes – but as always the division is not straightforward.

The pilgrimage badge

5

Lynn

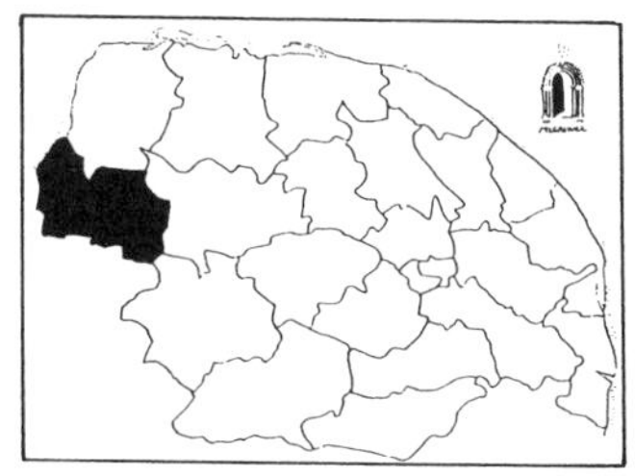

(The westernmost deanery of the diocese, bordering Ely and Lincoln, takes its name from King's Lynn, an historic town, once prosperous, which after a long period of decline is now reviving, but parts of the town remain very deprived. Like all the deaneries except Norwich, this also includes many country parishes.)

Tuesday 30 May

The week began with a celebration of Holy Communion at Narborough attended by the deanery chapter and half a dozen parishioners. After coffee in the garden at the rectory one of the chapter – Paul Bell – led a brief but well-introduced Bible study.

We walked together the two and a half miles to Pentney where we drank more coffee in the village hall and met a group of parishioners from this small village. Apart from the hall there is no public building left, the school, shop and pub having closed. Bob, the former publican, was there – an eighty-year-old who last year cycled round a record number of churches for the Norfolk Churches Trust. Stuart Nairn, the Rural Dean, took me to see the delightful church – a Norman foundation, clearly built by monks, which was unnecessarily extended at some period but is still a manageable size and very well kept and maintained. We returned to the village hall for a sandwich lunch (ham and cheese again), and then drove to Gaywood.

I spent the afternoon at Gaywood Church where parishioners had been invited to an 'episcopal drop in'. About twenty came and we had a good long discussion on a whole range of matters. These are lively parishioners who have been well taught and their long experience of close ecumenical relationships, combined with an outgoing church life, makes for a stimulating and stimulated congregation. Arthur Hawes, the Rector, extracted me from the meeting, although we could have gone on, but quite rightly took me back to his house to have a break and I sat in the garden sketching while he worked on papers for meetings.

After supper Arthur took me to a meeting of the Purfleet Trust of which he is Chairman. This is a project which is dedicated to the cause of single homeless people; they are obviously doing good work very successfully and are strongly supported by local authorities and the probation service. The meeting went on for two hours and was like a thousand other meetings I have attended and had hoped to avoid during the pilgrimage, but Arthur considered it exciting and thought I would enjoy attending. He will make a good archdeacon one day. (He was appointed Archdeacon of Lincoln two months later!)

Wednesday 31 May

The Wednesday morning Communion at Gaywood was celebrated by Kathleen Lees – the first celebration I have attended with a woman priest presiding. At least, I think it was – it seemed so normal that I find it difficult to believe I have not been present at such an occasion before. After talking with parishioners, I made five visits to the housebound who receive Communion at home. Imaginatively, the parish has formed them into the Order of St Faith and they are given work of intercession to do and simple forms of prayer to use. This is a good model for enabling housebound Christians to feel part of the community and continue to do important work within the life of the Church; some interesting characters including a former missionary with UMCA (Universities' Mission to Central Africa).

Lunch was at the Farrows' bungalow next to Gaywood Church where we met with the other ministers – Robert Dolman, the Methodist minister, Tony Shryane, the Roman Catholic priest, as well as Kathleen Lees and Peter and Olwen Farrow. Afterwards we had a Bible study led by Robert who until recently was a minister at the Central Methodist Church in Cambridge. We were all eager to know what Father Tony thought about the Pope's Encyclical on Unity which was announced yesterday.

'What encyclical?' he asked.

The afternoon was spent visiting old people in North and South Wootton. First, we visited a private nursing home where I spoke to all thirty-five residents; then on to an old people's home where one group was making model bird tables for sale at their fete, a second group was watching rugby on television and another small group was learning to swim in their splendid indoor swimming pool. I have an idea I have been shown the best of the homes in the area because they were certainly of a high standard and must be quite expensive although the people did not seem to be obviously wealthy.

I followed this with a visit to the Wootton Seniors' Club which was celebrating its seventh birthday. About twenty people were gathered there, including just two men, and we had a friendly chat while drinking tea and eating birthday cake together.

After talking solidly for more than two hours I was ready for a break, and was dropped at Gaywood rectory. Arthur and Melanie were away for the day but had left me the key of the house and I sat in the garden until a parishioner from the Woottons, Gerald Bell, collected me and took me to his home for supper, which was a relaxing occasion with his wife, mother and son, James.

The evening was spent at the home of Eric Hewer, a retired NSM living at Pott Row Grimston, where a large group was assembled for a Bible study. They meet regularly together as two groups and in many ways it was a good evening. In fact, it was rather difficult for me to get the chance of saying anything until ten minutes before the end when I asked if I might make a contribution. Eric is a very lively evangelical and many of the people there were like-minded, enthusiastically reading into the text rather more than was intended by Luke. I encouraged them, as I have the other groups, to continue the study of St Luke through the year. This systematic study is proving to be fascinating, not least in some of the themes which Luke brings out over and over again. For example, the themes of fear, hesitancy and of Jesus giving confidence; the desert and its inner significance for the life of prayer; the *via negativa* of the wilderness experience; the response to Jesus' call by the disciples and the demands made by Jesus for self-offering; and many more things besides.

Thursday 1 June

The day began at St Catherine's Court, a sheltered housing complex next to St John's Church, where I celebrated Communion in the large sitting room and chatted to residents over a cup of coffee. The churchwarden then drove me to West Winch where over a sandwich lunch I had a lively two hours with the PCCs of the parishes. We covered a number of issues and some strong opinions were expressed on both sides about church buildings. A group led by the Rector, Peter Brown, were resentful about the time and energy taken up in caring for church buildings while others felt equally strongly that this was a right use of time, energy and money. The latter group were mostly from the more rural parish of North Runcton, and were led by the local squire, Humphrey Gurney. West Winch is much more suburban in character. I have noticed so far that there does seem to be a real division, though there are exceptions, between urban and country parishes in that, in the country, care for the church building is given a high priority because it is much more the focus of Christian life than in the urban areas. There is more to this debate than merely a question of bricks and mortar. I sense it has something to do with attitudes to the place of worship in the life of the community, and it is something we need to continue to debate in depth.

After lunch I went with Bill Hurdman, the new Vicar of St Margaret's, King's Lynn, to the North Lynn estate, the most deprived area of the town and a place which is often highlighted in the local press because of its social problems. As always, the picture is not a simple one and I found this one of the most interesting visits I have made so far. We began at the community centre in the heart of the estate, a large, modern, ugly building surrounded by waste land with the Methodist Church not far away. I talked with a group who are working hard to revitalise the centre and I was especially impressed by four young mothers, all of them in their twenties or early thirties, who are determined to do something for their children. They have formed a play-group and one of them is keen to start a youth club. There are the usual problems with unemployment among the young adults, very few facilities and a small but significant percentage of the young involved in crime and extensive vandalism. It would have been a depressing picture but for the determination and hopes expressed by these people who live on the estate. They were tough and enthusiastic and left me both humbled and heartened.

Bill Hurdman, the new priest, is clearly at home in the environment of the North Lynn estate. He has come from Hackney, a large multi-racial parish in London, and has an instinctive understanding of the problems of the estate. Already, I sense, they feel his sympathy and they have great hopes that after years in the wilderness something good may begin to happen.

We next visited a lady who is the Chairman of the local Residents' Association in another part of the estate, not far away but in a road of neat, well-kept gardens, where she and her friends talked eloquently and forcefully about the poor image of the estate projected by the local press. They constantly try to correct this because they see, quite rightly, that the painting of a poor image is self-perpetuating. Again, this group of middle-aged people impressed me with their tough determination to work hard for the community.

The last visit was to the home of the former churchwarden of St Edmund's Church. He had gathered a group of mostly elderly people who had been worshippers at St Edmund's. This is a church built on the estate about forty years ago but closed in the 1970s because, in truth, it was never really viable from the beginning. It is now boarded up, badly vandalised, and is a danger to the children who play there, build fires inside and generally continue to wreck the building. From time to time there have been hopes that the church could be revived but these hopes are forlorn and, realistically, they now believe it is right that the building should be demolished and the site sold. They tried to sell it recently to a housing association who did not feel they could take it on. After talking it through we came to a common mind that whatever happens we should proceed with demolition and clearing the site to make it safe, and hopefully it can then be sold for building purposes. There is also the possibility that a congregation could be formed with the local Methodist Church near the community centre, particularly for the new generation. Again, I was immensely impressed with the faith and courage of these people to make such a hard decision. They included one woman whose husband's ashes are buried under a tree next to the church, and she too agreed with the decision to clear the site and was happy for her husband's ashes to be reburied at St Margaret's.

We spent far more time on these visits than scheduled and there was only time for a very short break at Gaywood before setting off for West Acre where the villagers were gathered on the picturesque green by the church, with stalls selling bric-a-brac, second-hand clothes and raffles. It was a delightful evening spent with lovely villagers in the company of Leonard Middleton, the parish priest. He has Parkinson's disease, though not too badly, and has the reputation of being irascible and no lover of bishops and archdeacons. Whatever the truth of that, he is clearly a good parish priest who has revitalised the life of the churches in his care and the villages also – especially the small ones – in which he takes a very full part. He is imaginative and has given people a real pride in their churches, establishing flower festivals and a number of village celebrations which have given encouragement and confidence to the locals.

Friday 2 June

Peter Farrow, the part-time industrial chaplain, took me to meet two officials of the King's Lynn Borough Council and we had an interesting discussion about the local economy. I spoke to them about my encounters in the North Lynn estate yesterday and I believe they are genuinely sympathetic to the estate's needs, wanting to be supportive particularly of the community trust. They complained, as have all local councillors whom I have met so far, about the restrictions imposed by central government spending or the lack of it, and the lack of freedom they have because of over-centralisation. They also talked of the frustrations they are encountering due to the resistance of some powerful people, by which they meant some of the local landowners and squires, to development and the necessity to promote better communications, particularly by road. I have found that the 'Norfolk Mafia' is divided over these issues. Most are farsighted and see the need for economic development which entails better roads, more light industry and job creation, particularly in rural areas, if the county is to remain viable and reasonably prosperous. A minority, however, are resistant in the name of conservation though in reality, self-interest is often the hidden motive.

This was followed by a visit to Dow Chemicals, a large eighty-acre site producing a variety of products from fertilisers to styrofoam materials for insulation. I spent some time in the huge insulation production plant, which is fully automated and controlled in a large room by a bank of computers. This major production area is controlled by only five men, all of whom are highly skilled. The company is successful, has close links with the continent of Europe, and is a vivid illustration of economic success through technology and the employment of very few people. Nevertheless, they are worried by the failure of the Government to be adventurous in communication links, particularly, they said, by rail. British Rail has just closed a rail link between the plant and the main line in preparation for privatisation, an extremely short-term economy given the prospect of rail links through the Tunnel with the continent. It is a sad irony that across the fence from this prosperous enterprise is the North Lynn estate with its very high levels of unemployment.

Lunch was at the Queen Elizabeth Hospital with senior members of staff – consultants, senior nurses and administrative staff. I had met the chief executive some weeks ago at a lunch given by the directors of Eastern Counties Newspapers and we had commiserated with each other about the difficulties of dealing with the Press. He has found it very difficult to counter the negative reporting about hospitals and health matters. The hospital seemed lively, modern, well-equipped and in good heart.

The Chairman of the Trust is Edward Dawnay, the squire of Hillington, who took me aside afterwards and said he did not wish me to leave without making his views known about the Hilborough situation. I winced until he said, 'I cannot tell you how appalled I am at the behaviour of these stupid people, their failure to listen to reason, and the way in which the Press has misrepresented you. I am entirely behind you and wanted you to know that, and how much I feel those people are living in an unreal world.'

With those comforting words I departed for a two hour visit to the wards. Andrew Haig, the hospital chaplain, who was spoken of warmly by people at lunch, very helpfully said that he had told two wards that I would be visiting and left me to my own devices. I visited every patient in these wards, about thirty or forty people, and much enjoyed the afternoon. I met two patients from the North Lynn estate who were pleased to hear my reactions to my visit yesterday. An old lady from Trinity Hospital, Castle Rising, remembered my visit to the church one Sunday nine years ago – the inhabitants of the hospital dress for church in quaint medieval uniform with tall, black witches' hats.

I had the longest conversation with a farmer's wife who was reticent at first but then talked at length about her son who was killed in a farming accident many years ago. She has never ceased to feel guilty because at breakfast, before he left for work that morning, she had ticked him off about the untidiness of his room. She has lived with guilt for sixteen years and although she has had some psychiatric help, still feels deep guilt about it, and anger at God who could allow such a thing to happen. We talked for quite a while and at the end she said, 'I would like some time to talk to a priest who could spend a long time with me.'

I told Andrew Haig about her and hope perhaps he may be able to help her. I much enjoy these pastoral visits, though of course there is the frustration of not being able to follow them through with some people as I should wish.

Andrew then drove me to Middleton vicarage where I had tea with Paul and Lucie Bell, after which a group of parishioners arrived. Paul led a Bible study with good contributions from the people there, most of whom, unusually, were in their forties and fifties.

Saturday 3 June

The morning was spent in St Margaret's Church, King's Lynn, where they have a cafeteria on Saturdays throughout the summer, so people can come in during the morning for coffee and snacks. It is an excellent facility which is much used by a wide variety of people. I met members of the congregation and of other churches in the area, German and Dutch tourists, local families who come to the Saturday market, and one or two people who had come in to find someone to talk to. Bill Hurdman is still new but a number of people have spoken warmly about him, not least Alan Glendining, a very old friend from Westcott days and one time Rector of Sandringham, who has retired to King's Lynn and who can be very critical of his fellow clergy, but thinks Bill will be very good. It is certainly a turning point for the town because the other churches in the city centre, St John's and All Saints, are now both vacant and we hope that new appointments will lead to much more collaboration.

Sunday 4 June

After an early start from Norwich I arrived at Ashwicken for the 8 o'clock Communion, celebrated by Leonard Middleton. The congregation of twenty-two, they told me afterwards, was smaller than usual because people were away on holiday. Since there are only about 200 people living in the village this again represents a far higher percentage of churchgoing than in urban and suburban areas, a perspective about which I keep reminding rural congregations. They often appear both surprised and encouraged by this simple fact, which needs more public emphasis.

We arrived a little late for the 9 o'clock Communion at Middleton where the congregation consisted almost entirely of the Bible study group that I met at Paul Bell's house on Friday evening. In contrast to the liveliness of the

Bible study, the worship in this large and heavily restored church was rather dull, the reason being that Paul is an excellent teacher of the Bible (and he preached a good Pentecost sermon) but lacks liturgical skills. Both the church and the liturgy could do with reordering, which would be a relatively simple matter – perhaps for Paul's successor.

Communion at St John's, King's Lynn, was well attended. I celebrated according to their tradition from the north end of the altar, which I find increasingly unsatisfactory. A great kneeler is placed at the north end, which makes it very difficult to read the book on the altar. It makes no sense at all liturgically or doctrinally, and only a minority of evangelical churches now insist on this historical curiosity; the remainder are perfectly happy with a westward celebration. The service was lively with a good cross section of people, but a twenty-minute sermon from a deputation preacher from a Bible Society did not make easy listening. I feel sorry for these men because they obviously preach the same sermon hundreds of times, with only small variations, and I think more would be gained by a simple exposition of the text of the day rather than the kind of advertising brochure address which is all too common.

We enjoyed a traditional Sunday lunch at the Nairns' home at Narborough and after a brief spell in the garden we had an open air service. The day had begun very wet, and was intermittently showery, so we were lucky that for two hours it remained fine, and Stuart Nairn had devised a good liturgy based on Iona and Taizé. About a hundred people were there, most benefices represented and nearly all the clergy present. After I gave the blessing the choir sang the Rutter anthem, 'The Lord bless you and keep you', which I always find very moving because it was sung at my enthronement as I mounted the steps of the ancient throne. I thanked them afterwards, thinking that perhaps this was the reason they had sung it, but it was sheer chance and of course they were delighted to know its special meaning for me. The service ended with the release of coloured balloons as we sang 'You shall go out with joy' – three yellow balloons for the bishops, twenty-three blue ones for the twenty-three deaneries of the diocese and twenty-two red ones for the twenty-two churches in the deanery – a nice final touch.

So ended another full week which was extremely well arranged. There had been less opportunity than before to talk about the prayer of silence, but it had been carefully paced and I was given the opportunity to meet hundreds of people, which I much enjoyed.

Interlude

Tuesday 6 June

Today Something to Celebrate *was published, an important Board for Social Responsibility report about the family. It is a thorough document, dealing with all aspects of family life, but predictably the Press seized on the sentence, 'The Church should abandon the phrase "living in sin" and respond with understanding and discernment to the widespread practice of cohabitation.' 'Living together is no longer a sin' was the headline on the BBC, though noticeably ITV gave a more balanced report. Equally predictably, the conservative right issued condemnations of a departure from biblical standards. The Church is still naïve about the way in which the media will react to its reports and pronouncements and that phrase was an obvious hostage to fortune. In articles written by intelligent journalists such as Janet Daley and Libby Purves, the tone has been not so much critical of the Church as sad – sad that the Church is not responding to the need they perceive to set an ideal in a secular world which has few ideals. On a first reading I cannot help thinking that this working party has missed the boat badly.*

Thursday 8 June

To London to take a General Synod Measure through the House of Lords. This is a duty which has to be performed from time to time when a Measure has to go through Parliament. This concerned amendments to the Pastoral Measure sections about Teams and Groups. The only controversial clause was that in future team rectors should no longer hold the freehold. In the Commons it had a rough ride because there were fears that this was an attempt to abolish the freehold by the back door. I prepared myself very carefully and at great length by studying all the documents in case some of the peers made the same points. In fact I had an easy ride and the only speech was made by Lord Beaumont who had for many years been campaigning for the abolition of the freehold! I might have saved myself a lot of trouble in preparation but it wasn't worth the risk.

Monday 12 June

We travelled by 'Sprinter' from Norwich to Liverpool (five and a half hours) for the Bishops' Meeting. It is being held at the Britannia Adelphi, an enormous hotel with many meeting rooms, well suited for our purposes. It was built in the golden days of the Cunard Line for rich passengers on the transatlantic routes. In its heyday it was obviously luxurious, with grand state rooms resembling those on board the great liners. It has an air of faded splendour now but is magnificent for all that.

It is always good to be with one's brother bishops because there is a very real sense of fellowship and mutual support. We always spend a day and a half doing some study together and this time the subject was 'feminist theology' – not everyone's favourite. But it is undoubtedly something which needs to be on the Church's agenda. The lectures and discussion groups were interesting, particularly the latter which were sometimes hilarious given the presence in our group of an elderly male chauvinist and two bright young suffragans, one of whom is married to a psychotherapist.

Tuesday 13 June

Another full day of meetings ending with a farewell dinner in the hotel in honour of John Habgood, the Archbishop of York, who is retiring this year. It was a wonderful evening, very convivial and with brilliant after-dinner speeches from David Sheppard, John Taylor and John Habgood himself. It is occasions like these which make one very proud to be a member of the Church of England, and privileged to be part of this fellowship of bishops –

House of Bishops

House of Bishops

so diverse and yet, particularly under George Carey's leadership, with a growing sense of unity and real friendship.

Wednesday 14 June

Another morning of lively discussion and then the suffragans left us at lunch-time and we continued in the afternoon with a very heavy agenda for the House of Bishops. I rather miss the suffragans and their lively presence because the business of the House of Bishops tends to be more formal, wading through masses of paper, and often I feel we make decisions with far too little time for discussion. The weather here is still dull and cool, though I hear even colder in East Anglia. We have not had fine weather since the wherry trip at the beginning of May – what a summer!

Monday 19 June

This morning in London I briefed a meeting of the Synod Working Party on Clergy Discipline with an account of the now notorious Chalcraft affair. We shall need to sharpen up our procedures, particularly in an age in which litigation is sadly becoming more common in the Church. Chalcraft and at least two other priests are going to industrial tribunals. The end result will, I fear, be bad for the clergy because bishops will naturally be much more cautious about divorced and remarried clergy, less willing to take risks and less generous. It will not be long before clergy will have to have contracts of employment, which would be a retrograde step, undermining traditional concepts of vocation, trust and pastoral relationships between bishops and clergy.

Tuesday 20 June

As part of Fitzwilliam College's 125th anniversary a cricket match was held between a team of former undergraduates and the college. The Old Boys were captained by Christopher Martin-Jenkins and apart from Derek Pringle (the former England player) who came to the college after my time, all the rest were 'my young men' – now aged fifty or thereabouts. I had not seen most of them for thirty years and it was marvellous to meet them again – balding, mostly prosperous, but quickly reverting to type in each other's company. As a purely pastoral chaplain I had the time to get to know every undergraduate in the college, regardless of religious affiliation or lack of it, and large numbers used me as a listening ear or a source of cheap sherry. Having always enjoyed sport, I spent some time playing hockey and cricket with them and supporting them on the touchline, river bank or from the boundary. Today I simply umpired, gave a couple of dubious decisions, and later enjoyed a dinner with them in hall. (They beat the undergraduates hollow – sporting standards have fallen, though the bulk of the Old Boys' team would not have made it academically to Cambridge nowadays!)

It was a very enjoyable and nostalgic evening, with fond remembrances of young Tony Cross (now a prosperous businessman and Vice Chairman of Warwickshire CC who agonised with me in his last year about whether to go all out for a cricket blue or a first and got neither), Chris Tod (a brilliant sportsman and one of the nicest men around, now a surveyor in Sussex), Nick Clarke (BBC World at One, who broke Ken Bulteel's nose in a football match and his snoring has been a plague to his wife ever since), Tom Moffatt (now a team rector in Liverpool, who met Emma from New Hall in our house, and whom I married, and who stayed with us on their honeymoon), Richard Frith (Archdeacon of Taunton, whom I still cannot think of as anything but an irresponsible twenty-year-old), Bob Hamilton (RC chaplain in London University, who told me today that my challenging his conservative theological views had made him a better priest), and all the rest.

Thursday 22 June

The news of John Major's resignation as party leader has filled the media, will doubtless continue to do so for days to come, and only time will tell whether he was courageous or foolhardy.

Sunday 25 June

To Horstead to celebrate the twenty-fifth anniversary of the founding of the youth centre. I had been doubtful about its viability, and established a working party to advise about its future. They were wholehearted in their support, and I gladly put aside my doubts, and am now trying to give them all the encouragement I can. The Warden, Val Khambatta, and her husband Neville, an NSM, are very professional, and I listened to warm, unsolicited testimonials from the large gathering of teachers and youth workers who came to lunch. In the afternoon there was a youth service in a marquee – all very well done with an excellent music group, but unremitting noisy praise choruses, with flag waving and arms aloft. I noticed some young people looking bemused. If something a bit more reflective had been interspersed, I wonder if it might have had more appeal to the unconverted.

6

Great Yarmouth

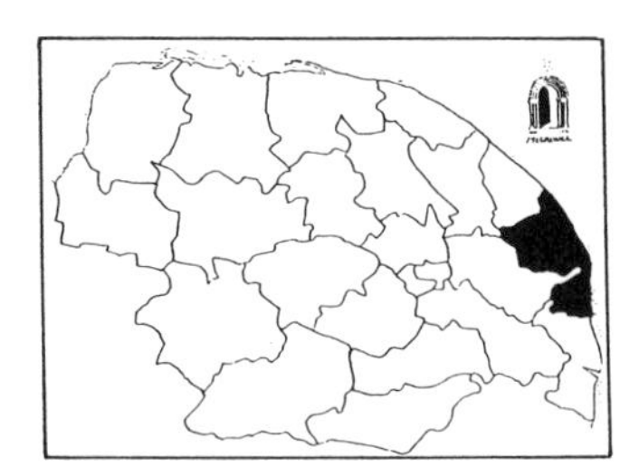

(The port and holiday centre of Great Yarmouth has been in decline for years, and the town has the highest unemployment rate in East Anglia. The deanery is extensive, and includes scores of rural parishes.)

Tuesday 27 June

It was good to be back on the pilgrimage road again, which began with Communion at St Andrew's, Gorleston, followed by a chapter meeting and Bible study. This was introduced by Chris Cousins, a relatively young rural dean, who has recently completed an MTh, quite an achievement for a busy parish priest. It was full of good theology and the quality of the discussion and fellowship was most encouraging. A few years ago this was reckoned by the senior staff to be one of the problem deaneries of the diocese but now, despite its many problems, it must be rated as one of the most hopeful, forward looking and adventurous, thanks to the appointment of a number of excellent new clergy. The chapter then adjourned for lunch at a local seaside hotel and afterwards I was taken by Chris Warner, who is the United Reformed Church industrial chaplain and a member of the Yarmouth Team, to visit Yarmouth F. E. College.

I spent time talking to a number of young people doing a variety of courses from theatre studies through computers to welding and bricklaying. One young man, who was doing the computer course, having graduated from the UEA (University of East Anglia), told me how important the cathedral was for him as a place where he loved to go and sit. I know the cathedral is special, but buildings do matter for their own sake because they sometimes speak a language which is deeper than human words. The saddest group were the young bricklayers, who were diligently learning their trade but for whom the prospect of work in Yarmouth is very bleak.

The next engagement on my schedule was Cobholm Tuesday Club, which I presumed to be an old people's club. It turned out to be an 'after school' club held in St Luke's Church under the guidance of Father Pat Kerley. Each Tuesday a group of thirty or so lively young primary school children gather for an hour for a kind of weekday Sunday school which is great fun. Today we did the good Samaritan and coloured pictures of the story afterwards. The twins Debbie and Diane gave me their pictures as a present, inscribed across the top 'with love from Debbie and Diane to Mr Fisher'. Rather a good mistake.

Pat Kerley drove me to Martham in his car, kept safe by a plastic Madonna glued to the dashboard. Martham is the only thatched vicarage left and a splendid house, not over-large, but doubtless there will be pressure to sell it at some time in the future which would be a pity. I went for a walk along a country lane, and sketched for a while. At long last the sun has come out but the north-east wind is still chilly.

After a light supper we went to Repps village hall for a Bible study with the Flegg Group ministry team. Most of them were fifty-plus but we had a good discussion led by Peter Paine which, however, was nothing to do with the Bible study set for the day. I must encourage rural deans to arrange for lay people to lead the Bible study as much as possible because I think they tend to be much more disciplined about sticking to the text and wrestling with it. Valuable as this general discussion was, during the last half hour I brought them back to the text a bit and then we had a period of conducted silence.

Wednesday 28 June

Because this was the first day of the Norfolk Show, I delayed my start until after lunch with the President of the Show. The weather has suddenly changed and it is now very hot, but with a light breeze, ideal conditions for the thousands of people who flock to the Showground.

The afternoon programme looked ordinary enough with a visit to two small country parishes and to the lifeboat station in Gorleston. The visits proved to be memorable in quite different ways. I was taken to Horsey, a tiny village of less than one hundred inhabitants, which is grouped with Winterton and Somerton. Parishioners from the two smallest parishes were gathered in the garden of a lady who had once been a nanny for a local family and then married and settled in the village, marrying again when her first husband died. Her attractive thatched house was the former coachhouse and stable block of Horsey Manor, with a beautiful garden full of trees and interesting plants. The dappled sun shining through the leaves made a perfect setting for an idyllic afternoon as I chatted to the villagers, most of whom had lived there all their lives.

The church next door is also thatched, a Saxon foundation and a much loved building with an immaculately kept churchyard. The church and old village houses are off the main road between Winterton and Sea Palling, completely hidden from view and mostly unvisited. There is therefore an air of peace and of days long past. The tea in the garden would have made a perfect scene for a Merchant Ivory film. The church itself has a genuine atmosphere and many people have written in the visitors' book about their sense of warmth and friendship when they entered the church although it was empty. There was certainly a strange and beautiful feeling of happiness throughout the two hours I spent there with people who are evidently content, warm-hearted and fond of each other across the wide age range that met together from toddlers to the very old. Horsey is very special; a rather magical place, I think.

Albert Cadmore, the NSM headmaster who is in charge of the three parishes, drove me to the Gorleston Lifeboat Station. He became involved accidentally through taking a lifeboat service one year and he and the lifeboat men adopted each other and established a close relationship which he still keeps going despite his many responsibilities. To my surprise and delight, I was told that we were going out in the lifeboat for an hour, and so I was kitted out with yellow boots, oilskins, pullovers and a life jacket. I was very hot but they said, 'Don't worry, you'll cool down when we get outside the harbour,' and the coxswain disconcertingly added, 'I hope you've got good sea legs, there's quite a chop out there today!'

So we boarded the lifeboat, and the crew, obviously extremely efficient and professional, made ready to set out through the harbour mouth into the North Sea. There was a fair wind blowing but it wasn't too bad and despite the heavy lunch I did not feel queasy. I was shown the various facilities below decks and then clung on as we drove at about twelve knots, with spray flying in our faces, towards the Scroby sandbank where we stopped and watched the seals until we got too close for their comfort and they took to the water. We then turned for home and after a simulated 'man overboard' exercise they let me steer, which was a great thrill, and so I took the boat right into the harbour, the coxswain only taking over for the final berthing.

We went upstairs to their rest room for a cup of tea and a chat with these very interesting and dedicated people. It is a sad reflection of our times that employers sometimes make it difficult for people to be lifeboatmen and resent the time taken off for this essential work of rescue. I thanked them warmly for a memorable experience and we departed for St Andrew's, Gorleston, where there was an ecumenical gathering in which I was able just to sit in the congregation – which was kind of them because I was too full of the other experiences to want to give out. After chatting over coffee, I returned home full of memories of an extraordinary and memorable day.

Thursday 29 June

St Mary's, Southtown, is due to close and this painful decision has been accepted by half of the small congregation. The other half buttonholed me after Communion and I tried to listen as sympathetically as I could as they expressed their feelings of hurt and disappointment. But the decision is right and has been taken after very long discussion between clergy and laity in all the churches. This, together with the closure of St James, is a bold, realistic and imaginative step in a move forward for the churches of Yarmouth where morale is rising rapidly thanks to the excellent team of clergy.

The rest of the day was spent in the company of Darren Thornton, the young Church Army officer who has proved to be an outstanding asset. We went first to the Northgate Hospital, a small hospital for geriatric and psychiatric patients, where Darren is part-time chaplain, and we visited two wards. Afterwards we walked to the Borough Council Offices, and had, as with other local government officers, a stimulating and worthwhile working lunch at which we discussed the problems of Yarmouth in some detail. The commitment of these local government officers is impressive and their hopes for the future are real but realistic hope depends on financial priority being given to what is a deprived area. Yarmouth will continue to suffer badly unless communications are improved, particularly the dualling of the A47 which has been a matter of contention for years but which I have always strongly supported. If communications were better and the outer harbour could be opened up, then there would be the possibility of a profitable direct link with Europe. They were very appreciative of the close working partnership with Michael Wood, Vicar of St Nicholas, and were glad to meet Darren Thornton and obviously interested in his experiences of working with young people in the poorer areas of the town.

After a sandwich lunch we went to Yarmouth High School and talked for a little while to the small Christian Union group which is led by Darren, again imaginatively, by the use of videos followed by discussion – not Christian videos but feature films such as *Ghost* which provoke interesting theological discussion about matters of life and death. We then took part in two assemblies led by Darren, with me saying a little about my pilgrimage. We had the pilgrimage badges available for all who wished to take them and thought that few would bother but curiously nearly every student took one, including the bolshie looking fifteen-year-olds. Many of them also took copies of the Pilgrimage Prayer which were left in the hall.

Darren and I then drove along the 'golden mile', parked beside a quiet stretch of beach and walked for a while, talking about his future. He is very keen to stay as long as possible, although his contract officially runs out in two years' time. He talked a lot about his vocation as a Church Army officer. He is a surprising candidate in a way because he has three 'A' levels from

Gresham's and chose not to go to university. He wanted to work full-time for the Church but not within the confines of the institution. I think one day he may be ordained, and probably should be, but his important gifts with the young must be used wisely. I hope very much we can keep him in the diocese and in the Yarmouth area where there are so many needs and where I sense we are on the verge of a breakthrough in the life of the Church.

We had high tea at St George's Hotel owned by Sylvia, a member of one of the congregations, and were joined by the Yarmouth Team staff, except Michael Woods who is on his way back from Germany where he has been serving as a chaplain to the Territorials. I had an hour's break in the garden of Malory Makower's house, which was welcome. Malory is very happy in Yarmouth where he has lived for ten years and hopes to remain when he becomes the full-time Director of the LNSM course, which I think would be right for him. He appears solemn but is a fulfilled man who is very excited by developments in the LNSM field and also in Yarmouth.

Darren collected me and took me to the parish youth club in St Paul's hall where fifty young people between the ages of twelve and sixteen were gathered with four adult helpers. It was noisy, lively and well controlled, providing more evidence of the new life that is to be seen in many places in Yarmouth.

Friday 30 June

The day began with a visit to Homefield First School at Bradwell. The senior year took assembly and I was glad simply to sit with the parents and teachers. They produced a marvellous assembly on the theme of weather, including poems, prayers, 'O what a beautiful morning' from *Oklahoma* and, dressed as Indians, they danced round a totem pole to the music of a steel band. The Headmistress told me that they were the most outstanding senior year she had ever had. It may perhaps have something to do with the presence of Lucy among them, a little girl with Harlequin's disease. This is a terrible and incurable skin complaint for which the life expectancy is not long and Lucy is now nearly blind, but she joined fully in the assembly and the children evidently care very much for her. Afterwards I met her parents who have another child with the same disease who also suffers from cerebral palsy. They are obviously a very special couple, who are deeply grateful for the support they have from the community and the church as well as from the school.

After a brief visit to a baby and toddler group in the hall of St Mary's, Southtown, where as a grandfather I was able to talk knowledgeably about the age when children walk and talk, we went to a young women's project run by the Girls' Friendly Society, which cares for single parents, many of them teenage mothers. They provide a number of services, including basic education, for most of these girls left school without any exams at all. The courses include parenting and pre- and post-natal classes; they also provide accommodation for some of the girls. There are three full-time workers, all of them high calibre people, who get very angry when it is suggested that girls become pregnant in order to obtain council accommodation. I talked to a number of the mothers and played with the children, including one little girl, Lindsay, who followed me everywhere and when I picked her up proceeded to stuff my pectoral cross into my mouth, much to everyone's amusement. This is a very worthwhile project which deserves strong support. They are looking for better accommodation and I promised to do all that I could to help and I certainly want to take an interest in its future.

Lunch was at Hemsby, in the small hotel next to the rectory, with William Williams, the colourful and sometimes controversial rector, and a mixed group of Roman Catholics and Anglicans. Roman Catholics have for a long time shared the church in Hemsby and there are close relationships between them which was evident in the good fellowship during the lunch. Afterwards I had coffee with William and two elderly lady friends from one of his former parishes, both staunch members of the Mothers' Union, who had come to stay for a few days and evidently adore him.

We drove in his Mercedes with the registration letters 'REV' to Martham, where I was decanted into Peter Paine's minibus, and thence to Thurne. Here I spent the afternoon with parishioners from this small parish, meeting in the house of a churchwarden which was once the village school. A thoroughly enjoyable time with a wide variety of parishioners – farmers, retired schoolteachers, a council worker and housewives. Peter Paine then took me to Ormesby rectory where I had a break in the garden of Chris and Jenny Cousins.

In contrast to last evening's end, filled with the ear-blasting noise of a disco, we had quiet Taizé-style worship and meditation at Ormesby St Margaret Church led by Chris, Peter Paine and the local Baptist minister with whom he works closely. So home through the sea mist which, like last night, had rolled in from the North Sea in the early evening.

Saturday 1 July

At the James Paget Hospital in Gorleston I visited a number of patients, and had to wash my hands between each ward visit because they have had an infection recently which has emptied half the hospital and they are taking rigorous precautions about passing infection. The chaplain said it was time for us to go to my next engagement but as I walked past a small ward I noticed a young woman in her twenties in a bed at the end and felt a sort of instinct that I should visit her, which I did and we had quite a long talk. She had been admitted with a severe chest infection and was a friendly girl in her early twenties, with a baby, living with her partner in a house in St Mary Magdalene parish. Without prompting she told me about her grandmother who used to take her to church.

Martham

She said she hasn't been much in recent years but has sometimes felt the urge to return. So I told her all about her new vicar, Trevor Riess. She told me that she and her boyfriend would like to get married some time and I think needs only a little encouragement to do so, and perhaps even to return to regular church-going. So I urged her to think about having the baby baptised, perhaps get married at the same time and make a new start. Her name is Elaine and I asked the chaplain to find out her address in order that Trevor can visit them. So perhaps the visit had a purpose – who knows?

At Caister vicarage we had a buffet lunch and talked with parishioners, who are delighted to have a young family living in the house again, and Tim Thompson seems to have made a good start. There was a good group of young people and in fact the parish is wide open for the development of ministry among children and young people. Jack Chase, the father of Robert Chase (Chairman of the Norwich City Football Club), was there, whom I know quite well from visits to Carrow Road. Himself a third generation builder, he talked about his sons, two of whom are, in contrast to Robert and his father, very clever academics, one a university professor. The afternoon was spent at Martham carnival on the green, which was less well attended than usual, so the Rector, Peter Paine, told me. Partly this was because of the weather which, although bright, was very chilly in the north-east wind.

After visiting an art exhibition in the church, I sat down to a strawberry tea in the rectory garden next to an old man who had served with the Special Forces during the war. He was parachuted into France, Belgium and Holland to work with the Resistance. He had obviously led an adventurous life during the war and became very attached to the Belgian and Dutch Resistance but said he did not like the French because of their lack of punctuality. He was an explosives expert and would arrange to meet the local Resistance to blow up a bridge at 9 o'clock in the morning, but they used not to turn up until five or ten minutes afterwards, which put everyone in great danger.

Peter then drove me to Billockby, a tiny hamlet of sixty people, where at the Hall we had tea on the terrace with Margaret Alston, the Lay Chairman, a widow who runs the huge farm herself, and a group of delightful parishioners including Nellie, a ninety-three-year-old who rules the roost and is a great pillar of the local church. Margaret told me later that when her husband died tragically twelve years ago (two years after the death of one of her sons), she completely lost her faith, but Nellie gradually weaned her back. The BBC are coming to the house to film an episode of a series starring Patricia Routledge. The villagers all say that if Patricia Routledge falls sick then Margaret Alston could easily deputise for her. There is a certain similarity. Margaret is a strong character, and a considerable leader with a marvellous sense of humour, a mixture of Patricia Routledge and Penelope Keith. She told us about her daily help who had finally retired after seventeen years. She had engaged, on recommendation, a new help whom she had not met, who telephoned her and said, 'Hello, Maggie, when shall I come and talk to you about the job?' Again, it was an encouraging afternoon, with a group of friendly parishioners right across the social spectrum. Nellie is very persuasive and only pretends to be a feeble old lady. She forced me to promise to go to the harvest festival at Billockby in 1996, which I had better note.

I returned to Norwich in time to walk to the cathedral and catch the last of the service for the ordination of priests. It was moving to sit on the steps at the west end and then to go and receive Communion from the new priests. Afterwards I greeted them all outside the west door and then had a welcome evening at home to celebrate our thirty-fourth wedding anniversary.

Sunday 2 July

At Caister Lifeboat Station we had a wonderful parish Eucharist attended by the whole congregation from both parish churches, lifeboatmen, their friends and relations. The place is full of history and heroism and before the service I met old Skipper Woodhouse, part of a famous family of skippers, some of whom lost their lives in the lifeboat. I blessed Scout colours, Guides and Brownies, and hidden behind them was a mini Brownie called, I gather, a 'Rainbow', a new organisation, who presented me not with a flag but with a teddy bear.

Standing behind the altar I looked through the open doors of the lifeboat station to the lifeboat on the slipway and the sea beyond, sparkling in cool morning sunshine. After the service we had coffee together and took many photographs as the tractor pushed the lifeboat down to the sea. We went for a trip to Yarmouth via Scroby Sands again, which this time at high tide were covered, but seals were playing in the surf which was breaking over the sands. They let me steer again, right into the harbour past the Gorleston lifeboat who were doing an exercise and waved to us, and then we tied up at the town quay beside the *Lydia Eve*, where we met local councillors and together with the lifeboatmen had a sandwich lunch. They showed me the old steam drifter which has been lovingly preserved, and I heard tales of herring fishermen and the hard life they lived.

After lunch Tim Thompson drove me to Belton where we had a long Eucharist lasting almost two hours. I had never before witnessed a choir raising their hands as they processed in at the beginning of the service. Before the Peace I blessed the newly finished church room attached to the parish church. The Peace itself was like a football half-time and lasted a full ten minutes. But it was a friendly, lively gathering with large numbers of children and young people present. Afterwards, I went back to the rectory, where John Quinn deposited me in the garden so I could start sketching, but soon the rain came on and I was driven indoors where I chatted to John and Sadie before driving to Clippesby, arriving just in time for the 6.30 pm evening service, a celebration of their Patronal Festival of St Peter.

Just before the blessing I thanked them all for the week, which had been truly memorable. I used the illustration of the little girl called a Rainbow and spoke of how it linked with the call of the Twelve (one of the readings from St Luke this week); of the kaleidoscope of people I had met, the variety of parishioners, old, young and middle-aged, town and country, rich and poor, with all shades of churchmanship but working together hopefully; of how the lifeboat crews know the dangers and difficulties but still love their work and thrive through good teamwork, which is becoming an encouraging mark of the churches in this deanery in particular. So home through driving rain, very tired but very happy, and once again greatly encouraged by the experiences of the week.

Interlude

Tuesday 4 July

John Major 218 votes, John Redwood 89. End of media hype about Tory leadership?

Saturday 8 July

I hoped that the test match commentary would keep me company on the long drive to York for the General Synod, but England were defeated before I reached Dereham. As a consolation, the women's tennis final was exciting: a large part of which I listened to in a solid traffic jam on the A1. York is very hot, and I am lucky to be in a cool room in an annexe of Langwith College overlooking the car park, so it should be quiet. Unless one finds liturgical business exciting the agenda is unbelievably mundane. I am sure there must be a better way for the Church of England to conduct its affairs than by these expensive sessions. But we are so locked into this democratic way of governing ourselves that I cannot see much hope of real reform, though perhaps the forthcoming Turnbull Commission will say something useful. To be fair, there are occasionally marvellous and informative debates but they are the exception rather than the rule. The one consolation of the York meeting is that it is residential and therefore one has time to meet people and catch up with some old friends.

Sunday 9 July

At the Eucharist in York Minster George Carey preached about the rich young man in Luke, a good parish Communion sermon rather than a great national address, but that was perfectly acceptable. In the course of it, he told us that when the young man went to see Jesus it is said in the text 'he ran' and the same word is used for the father running to meet the prodigal son. An interesting point I'm sure, but for the life of me I could not see its significance. Perhaps it will become clearer when we study these passages in the pilgrimage Bible

The Bishop of Sheffield

studies. The music is always wonderful in York, not least the ethereal singing of Psalm 150 at the end of the service as the procession moves out through the side aisle, which never fails to bring tears. Afterwards, mopping my eyes as surreptitiously as I could, my embarrassment was somewhat alleviated by the sight of others doing the same.

Lunch was in a hotel in York with a group of Old Alleynians (old boys of Dulwich College). The conversation was always more interesting when talking about general matters than when reminiscing about schooldays which for some of those present were the happiest days of their lives. For others they were definitely not. I sat next to Michael Walker who was a year senior to me at school but has now taken early retirement because he has Parkinson's disease; he keeps going but looks frail. Norman Warren, the Archdeacon of Rochester and a year my junior, was always insufferably good at everything at school: academically bright, a very good musician, and a brilliant cricketer. As a boy, and still now, he was full of confidence and is proud that his record of 8 for 34 against Bedford still stands. Brian McHenry, a government lawyer, and David Webster, until retirement a journalist with the Financial Times, drove back with me but were as hopeless about directions as I am – the five minute journey from the centre of York to the university took thirty minutes by the time we had traversed various ring roads.

The highlight of the Synod occurred after the evening session when we had a concert party organised by Sue Page. She didn't take part but produced a show of almost professional standards with very funny sketches, a stand-up *comedian, witty songs and a young female Synod member who sang beautifully. The evening ended with a memorable sketch performed by all the Synod staff: General Secretary, lawyers and secretaries, having a dig at the members, which they clearly much enjoyed, and so did we.*

Tuesday 11 July

A long liturgical debate – there will be many more of these in the years leading up to 2000 and the revision of the ASB. *It was followed by farewells to the leaving members of the Synod and in particular, of course, John Habgood. I sat next to David Bentley – a moving moment because he and I had been at Westcott together when John was Vice-principal. In the Peace during the little liturgy which followed we greeted him together and said farewell, as we had said hello thirty-seven years ago. He is a truly great man, as I am sure history will testify; certainly someone who was an important influence in my formative years, and although we have not been close in recent years I have always sought his advice when making crucial decisions. He is one of those people who knows one frighteningly well, whom one can never fool, and his advice is always ruthlessly honest. Many years ago I was asked to consider the post of principal of a theological college. I agonised about it for weeks and then went to see John Habgood. After listening as I spelled out in detail the pros and cons and all my agonisings, he said, 'Peter, you would be hopeless.' So that was that, and helpful, if deflating. Some months later I was appointed Bishop of Taunton and I simply had a postcard from him saying, 'That's more like it,' which few words meant more to me than effusive congratulations.*

Our bishops' cell group assembled in the afternoon at Riber Hall near Matlock for our annual meeting together with our wives. The group was only formed three years ago and consists of Nigel McCulloch (my successor at Taunton, now at Wakefield) and his wife Celia, David Smith (Bradford) and Mary, Steven Sykes (Ely) and Joy, and John Oliver (Hereford) and Meriel. David led the two days together which were very relaxing and informal.

The comfortable hotel, beautiful countryside, outing to Chatsworth, and long leisurely meals together proved therapeutic for us all. Everyone, of course, is very tired at this time of year and some had been through difficult periods for one reason or another, so we simply needed to relax together and talk. I am the oldest member of the group but proved the least tired, oddly enough. I think it must be the pilgrimage which is such a refreshment of the spirit.

7

Holt

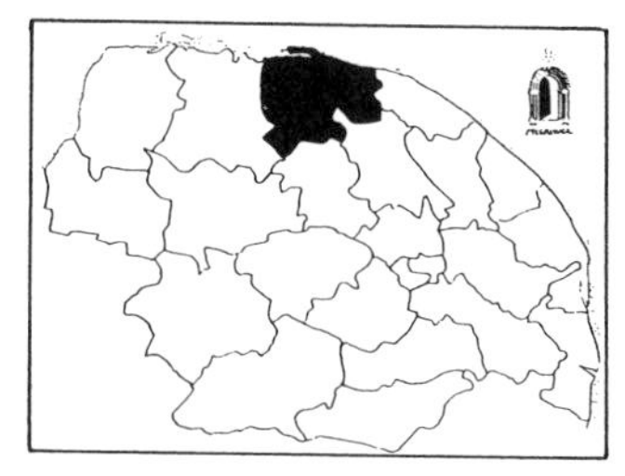

(A pretty area of North Norfolk, much favoured by the retired and holidaymakers, with a series of small, mostly prosperous, towns and large villages, though 'small' and 'large' tend to have different meanings in Norfolk from most other places. We regard a village of 500 inhabitants as large.)

Tuesday 18 July

An exhausting and exciting day began quietly enough with a Bible study in Briston Church with a dozen mostly elderly people. Before we had time to finish, the church was invaded by a hundred toddlers with about fifty parents and helpers from the local nursery school which is so well known and successful that it draws children from miles around. John Blacker led a simple service during which I spoke to them and gave out badges, having chosen helpers born in the same month and year as my two oldest grandchildren. After the service we went to the village hall for coffee and to talk with the parents.

This was followed by an interesting visit to a firm which makes caravans that fold in half and become compact trailers, a thriving small company which has been relatively unaffected by the recession. All their marketing and manufacture is centralised here in Melton Constable in an industrial estate built on the site of the old railway works, which were a major feature in the past. There are people in Melton who can still remember when 160 trains a day passed through the junction, until the Beeching axe. The town went through the doldrums but now is reviving through this estate, and the population is increasing again. Afterwards, at a large lunch party at the vicarage, I talked with parishioners and then John Blacker drove me to Weybourne via the ruined church of Burgh Parva which is being restored by the County Council.

After a ten minute break at Weybourne rectory, the home of Peter Barnes-Clay, the Rural Dean, I was driven to the Muckleburgh Collection nearby which is an amazing place full of vehicles, guns, tanks, models, diaries, uniforms and military memorabilia. It has been the work of Berry Savory who greeted me with his brother John whom I have met before. I met Berry's wife who is suffering terribly from Alzheimer's disease. She sat in the car while I chatted to her and she smiled sweetly as I blessed her and then was driven away with a friend.

Later came the highlight of the day when I drove a Sherman tank. The German engineer, called Gerry (appropriately), was a wonderful character who has married a local girl and maintains the large collection of World War II tanks in working order. The last time I drove a Sherman was in Germany in 1955 when serving with the 6th Field Regiment where we had self-propelled twenty-five pounders mounted on Sherman chassis. I had learnt to drive at the Royal Armoured Corps Centre at Bovington Camp in Dorset, and kept my licence for tracked vehicles up to date ever since in the hope that one day I would have cause to use it again – and today I did. The driver's compartment in the Sherman is cramped and I had some difficulty getting in with my cassock, but strangely it all came back to me: the enormously heavy clutch which takes a tremendous effort to depress, the two steering sticks and starter where you have to press two levers at once. With Gerry sitting in the co-driver's seat, we set off on a circuit and it was wonderful to feel the power of the old Sherman and manage the incredibly heavy steering levers to manoeuvre the tank three times round a circuit and twice over ditches. The Press were there in force and insisted on having me photographed on top, and inside with a helmet on, helmet off etc, etc. It all got rather tedious but nobody seemed to mind including the large crowd of holiday visitors who wanted to see this curious sight. My morale shot up when Gerry told me that he had never seen a tank driven better by a civilian.

We then continued the walk around the Exhibition which I must visit again at more leisure. We finally left for a brief visit to Kelling Church, a little gem with a wonderful atmosphere, and to an art gallery which was stuffed with treasures, not only artistic but literary, including children's annuals and magazines I had not seen since I was young.

On our way to evensong at Bodham I looked at myself in the mirror of the car and realised I was filthy. What the people in the art gallery with whom I chatted must have thought, I cannot think – some strange old tramp in a purple gown, I guess. Of course, I had forgotten how dirty one gets in a tank with dust flying in through the driver's hatch. My hands and face were streaked with dirt and so we made a hasty visit to Weybourne rectory for a quick wash before evensong.

We had what Peter Barnes-Clay called 'solemn evensong' which meant long evensong with lots of hymns and incense swung at us by a high church server keen to sanctify us three or four times during the liturgy. The music was wonderful with a huge choir run by Angela Dugdale, a trainee LNSM and a well-known musician in the county. But it did go on rather and so left no time at all for a rest and we drove straight back to Weybourne rectory for supper. But the Barnes-Clays are kind and gracious, and it was a delicious supper.

The day ended with a Bible study at the home of Keith and Angela Dugdale, a beautiful cluster of buildings with barn, house and centre where children come to stay for musical holidays. About thirty parishioners gathered and the Bible study was very good, leaving sufficient time for a good session of silent prayer at the end, followed by strawberries and ice cream.

Wednesday 19 July

A day in the Glaven Group of parishes began with assembly at Blakeney Primary School. The children were full of questions, including, as so often, extremely difficult ones. 'Who is God?' said one. While thinking with one part of my mind what I could say about God as creator and saviour, always present, and so on, I passed the question back. 'Who do you think he is?'

One little girl said, 'God is love,' and there was no need for any further answer. I wish I had thought of that first of all – 'Out of the mouth of babes and sucklings. . . .'

Next door in the church we had a *BCP* (*Book of Common Prayer*) Communion service, followed by another Communion at Letheringsett Hall which is now a home for the elderly. I spoke to all who came and afterwards visited two ladies who are bed-ridden. One of them had had a stroke the day before and lost her speech. She just held out her arms, so I bent down and she embraced me for a while. I think she just wanted someone to hug.

After leaving Letheringsett we drove, as we did often that day, in Nick Martin's ancient Citroën 2CV, which was only marginally more comfortable than the Sherman tank. He drives extremely fast around the lanes which he knows well and I just trusted that he was a good driver. Later that day, in the lavatory at his house, I noticed a book with a title something like *The Art of Driving Well and Very Fast,* so I suppose at least he took it seriously. We visited the Glaven Caring Centre where the elderly from several villages come for lunch and baths and nursing care. Afterwards we visited two old ladies in their homes nearby: rather sad people, one waiting to die and impatient for the end which will not come, and the other full of complaints about how difficult life is for her; and I suppose it is.

Lunch in the rectory garden was attended by a large gathering of parishioners from the Group. There was a plague of thunderflies, small irritating insects which got into one's hair and everywhere. At first when I scratched my head with the irritation I thought that somewhere I had picked up nits or lice or something ghastly but was relieved when I noticed everyone else scratching. After lunch we visited Glandford where Roger Combe, the son of the local landowner who helps his father run the estate, showed us round a large number of barns which have been converted for use by small industries. We met an upholsterer, walked through a small plastics factory which makes imitation antiques for hotels, and spoke to a boat builder and engineer – good enterprises and much cared for by young Roger who said, 'I love my work and realise that I am a very lucky young man.' It was good to find a rich young man so obviously sensitive and caring.

After visiting the remarkable shell museum and lovely church at Glandford, off we went driving like Jehu through the lanes to Cley via a short stop at Wiveton Church, where a thriving Sunday school has been started from scratch by Sarah, the wife of Jim Woodhouse, the recently retired Headmaster of Lancing.

At Cley and Wiveton we saw work of recent restoration – as at Letheringsett earlier in the day, parishioners had raised huge sums of money out of all proportion to the size of the population. We walked through Cley village, Nick hoping to encounter lots of parishioners and shopkeepers, but it was half day closing and only a handful of shops were open. Nick Martin, over anxious to show me as much as he could in a day, maddeningly persisted, and so we visited a few, but I was much relieved that there were not more people about because I was desperate for a rest. The heat and the plague of flies were very oppressive and kept most people indoors. (It is interesting that without exception old villagers called it 'Clay' while newcomers and the middle classes called it 'Cly' – a strange class distinction which may be the same in places like Hunstanton and Garboldisham.)

After a rest in the garden, although it was still oppressively hot, we drove to the house of Mary Norwak in Cley. She is a churchwarden, author of cookery books and a considerable power in the land. It was a small Bible study group but very good, sharply intelligent and wrestling with the text in an impressive way. The hour and a half sped quickly by and then we drove to Letheringsett to meet the ecumenical prayer group which has been meeting for nearly thirty years and includes people from the Roman Catholic, Methodist and Presbyterian Churches and the Salvation Army. We were running very late by this time and I was glad to take my leave after a day which had been full to excess.

Thursday 20 July

The magnificent Binham Priory was wonderfully cool and a good Bible study began the day with thirty or forty parishioners present. Afterwards we paid a visit to the Langham Glass factory where we watched the fascinating process of glass blowing, making candelabra, and paper weights, with one of which I was presented later. The heat in the glass-blowing area was intense. The craftsmen put the long poles with glass being shaped into little furnaces and as we watched from a gallery with a running commentary, the heat rose and was well in excess of 100°F. Despite this, people were riveted by the skill of the glass blowers. The factory contains extensive shops, restaurant, a play area for children and a beautifully restored walled garden, which makes it a very attractive place for visitors.

At Stiffkey I met parishioners in the village hall, a friendly gathering, mostly of retired people with a sprinkling of locals. In most of these North Norfolk parishes the running is made either by incomers, squires or big farmers. The old locals are rather shy and hold back so I always make for the corners where they are usually to be found.

We next visited Morston Church, a beautiful and much painted building (by artists) on a crossroads. Inside I had a surprisingly sharp exchange with the churchwardens. They wanted to talk about the parish share and its iniquities. I told them that I hoped not to have conversations about these things during the pilgrimage, but they insisted and so we had a not very satisfactory conversation, until at last I told them firmly that I really ought to speak to other people, and left them – not very satisfied, I'm afraid. I was taken off for lunch by Andrew and Mary Athill who live in a house on the edge of the marsh. We enjoyed a simple lunch in their large kitchen and afterwards I was able to spend an hour sitting in the shade until it was time to drive to the Matlaske Group.

At the village of Hempstead we sat outside the village hall, under a lovely spreading chestnut tree, with a group of old people, members of the 'Evergreens', a club founded by church members for the elderly, and also with some children who belong to the new Sunday school, started by a young mother on her own initiative. The school bus emptied a few more children until there were about twenty, aged three to fourteen. We all went inside the hall for tea, a lovely, friendly gathering of old and young. They are looked after for the time being by a retired priest, Michael Shearman, who in his gentle way is leading them very effectively. Later, he took me to another little cottage in the village to visit an old lady who is housebound.

The next stop was Barningham where I visited the post office and village shop and then we assembled at Hall Farm, met by the farmer, his wife, six daughters and numerous grandchildren. We watched cows being milked by computer, and then went back a few years to travel with the children by trailer behind a tractor up to Barningham Hall itself. The heat was still intense and I wished I had brought a hat. But at the Hall I went inside with Stella Mott-Radclyffe for a quick cup of tea in the cool, lofty drawing room of this beautiful old house.

I was due to walk from here to the church at Matlaske but because we were badly behind our schedule I was driven instead, for which I was grateful because it was far too hot to walk the mile or two necessary. The church at Matlaske is a little round tower church, much loved and interesting inside and out. Again I talked to parishioners over tea and biscuits before travelling to a parishioner's house for a Bible study. They call themselves a Bible reading group because they say they are not experts but simply read chunks of St Luke and then discuss it. In fact they were very effective and most interesting in their handling of the text, as all the Bible study groups have been this week. It was led by a woman who will probably be an LNSM candidate soon.

We next visited Baconsthorpe village hall where the Carpet Bowls Club, heart of the village social life, was practising and I was invited to take part. The captain of the team gave me instructions as if I was a novice, but having played bowls in the garden at home I reckoned I knew a thing or two about the game. When I tried, I was utterly hopeless and could not keep a single bowl on the carpet, let alone get it anywhere near the jack. I played a game after ten practice bowls and still could not keep the wretched bowl in the same county, much to everyone's amusement. But they were patient, saying that I needed to come out on Tuesdays and do a bit of practice with them.

The last visit of the day was to St Michael's, Plumstead, where a group of twenty parishioners had gathered, evidently expecting a full-blown evensong. A churchwarden gave out hymn books and prayer books and the organist proceeded to unlock the organ.

I was asked if I would lead the service and I said, 'OK, but we won't need books.'

'Not even a hymn?' asked the churchwarden sadly.

'No,' I said, 'we'll do something different.'

So I led them in silence for twenty minutes and I think they got more out of that than they would have done from evensong. Certainly I had need of very few words at the end of a day full of talk.

Friday 21 July

After meeting parishioners at St Andrew's, Holt, we walked over to the yard of the Railway Arms, and boarded the Holt Flyer which is a horse-drawn wagon. We were driven by Gary Thompson, the publican, through the town to Kelling Hospital. Joe, the old grey who pulled us, is one of seven heavy horses (and the slowest) owned by Gary and his wife, so we had a gentle ride at roughly two miles per hour, contrasting sharply with the furious progress in the 2CV on Wednesday. At Kelling Hospital I celebrated in the chapel, took Communion to patients in the wards, and visited throughout the hospital for a couple of hours.

Lunch was at the home of Jean Smith, a churchwarden, and her friend Pat, both single, Jean a retired headmistress, Pat a mathematician. They have converted an old barn, appropriately named 'Bachelors', by a lake in an idyllic setting. The house is wonderful – full of light and coolness, with modern paintings, sculptures and furniture – quite unlike the kind of home one might expect of such a pair. The whole setting is somehow un-English, reminiscent more of the Dordogne, perhaps, or even Spain with its cool tile floors and rush mats. After lunch I walked around the lake and sketched for a while until I saw a small crowd arriving at the house and it was time for me to return.

The 'crowd' were mentally handicapped people from the training centre in Holt, waiting with their minibus to take me to the centre for the afternoon. About a hundred people with various kinds of handicap were there and I spent a happy time with them in their workshops as they cut firewood into bundles, made seed trays, bunches of lavender and engaged in other simple crafts. I also spent some time in the 'experience room' which I had seen only once before, in Quidenham, where the most severely handicapped lay on water beds or mattresses with coloured lights and music and all sorts of electronic devices producing peaceful sensations all around. I lay with them and chatted for a while before going out into the gardens to see them planting wallflowers by the thousand, ordered by a local nursery which they supply. There was much laughter, affection and beautiful courtesy, which is always the joyful experience of spending time with the mentally handicapped.

I was next taken to a private nursing home, arriving fifteen minutes late, and visited all the residents, some sitting in a day room, others in their rooms. All of them were glad to see me except one deaf lady in the day room. The Matron introduced me. 'Here's Bishop Peter come to see you, Nellie,' she yelled in her ear.

'I'm not at all pleased to see you,' she shouted back. 'It's long past time for tea.'

The little church of All Saints High Kelling, built in 1924, used to belong to the old TB Sanatorium and was converted to a church – not a tin tabernacle, as one might expect of that period, but a well found brick and flint building, set in a lush garden and quite charming. From there we walked to the village hall and had tea with parishioners, all of them retired, as seems to be the case for most of the population of this rather exclusive and pretty area.

After sandwiches and cake, which more than filled me, I was off to a barbecue with young people on the edge of Holt: servers as it turned out, from Holt Parish Church, a friendly young crowd with good adult helpers, and we spent a happy hour together, relaxing in the garden, though the weather was now cool enough, in contrast to yesterday, for some of them to be wearing anoraks. I was collected soon after 7 pm to drive back to the parish church for a Bible study, attended by a dozen or so lay people and led by Jean Smith. It was high-powered, due to the presence of a few people here with a theological background, and the lessons learned were valuable. Some of them had also been following the Bible studies from the beginning and I think this group will also continue through the Gospel until next Easter. Again, we ended the evening with silence which, as always, I think was welcomed after all the talk in the Bible study and throughout the day.

Saturday 22 July

A day of church-crawling began at Gunthorpe and ended in Swanton Novers with nine more churches in between. At every one I met parishioners and had a different and interesting conversation with each group. Nearly all the churches have recently completed considerable restoration work or are actively engaged in it. Over and over again it bears out the fact that this is indeed the greatest age of church restoration since the Middle Ages. When I told them, they seemed surprised, but it is a fact that church history in fifty years' time will certainly acknowledge. They have done wonders in raising money and the standard of the work, thanks to English Heritage and DACs (Diocesan Advisory Committees) who are often complained about, is always of the highest order and will last for generations to come. I tried to encourage them to see that this preoccupation with the building was not to be despised, but was perhaps our vocation in this age so that those who come after may be set free from this particular task. Indeed, in many places they acknowledged that the commitment to the church building, if undertaken wholeheartedly, drew people from the village at large and in some cases became the focal point for social activities.

The villages are nearly all very small indeed, with a hundred or so inhabitants, and again I tried to encourage them by pointing out that their level of churchgoing is much higher than any urban or suburban area. It is common for ten per cent of the population to be regular worshippers and in one case more than twenty per cent. They seemed surprised at this fact but need to be reminded for they are too modest, and are doing far better than they realise.

I was conducted in the morning around the five parishes of the Bale Group by the incumbent, Michael Ward, an enthusiast about church buildings and a great talker, who is married to Catherine ('Batwoman'), the controversial founder of MABIC (Movement against Bats in Churches).

In the Briningham Association in the afternoon, a retired priest, Frank Ward, took me round with meticulous timing. He is a former employee of British Rail and a stickler for timetables, as one might expect. After a large and convivial lunch in Sharrington village hall, we went to the church where children sang and played to us and then we had a Bible study, rather more desultory than the others this week, probably because it was the aftermath of a good lunch. I was then taken off by Ian and Meg Anderson to their house at Brinton for a rest. They had reserved a bedroom and bathroom for me and put up a hammock in the garden if I wanted it. They gave me strict orders to be on my own and refused to talk to me until they gave me tea, an hour or so later. They are a delightful couple, both in their second marriages after being widowed; the two families having been very close throughout their first married lives, it was a very suitable and happy match.

Most of the churches in their way are gems and all of them are clearly much loved and well cared for. It is difficult to single out the best, but Bale and Stody are outstanding. The list of churches visited today reads rather like a song by Donald Swann or poem by Betjeman – from Gunthorpe to Bale, Field Dalling and Saxlingham, through Sharrington, Brinton, Hunworth and Thornage, next Stody, Briningham and Swanton Novers. At Swanton Novers we had some good talk in rather general terms but when a man asked me to say something about the Taizé community and its possible relevance to rural churches, I introduced them to Taizé chanting and demonstrated how simple the chants are to learn. So we sang 'Jesus, remember me when you come into your kingdom', followed by silence and the Pilgrimage Prayer, after which I blessed them and we had refreshments in the church before driving home. Another memorable and very different day.

Sunday 23 July

The Sung Eucharist at Holt Parish Church was almost devoid of children because they were preparing the float for the Holt Carnival which was due to set off at midday. After greeting parishioners I was taken to a recreation ground where the floats were assembled. The parish church float was a model of the cathedral with children dressed as medieval labourers. Five ladies, who help with the young people, were dressed unflatteringly as Franciscan friars and walked beside the float when we got going. A bishop's chair was mounted on the truck and I sat with the children waiting for the judges to come round, sharing their crisps and cherryade. We didn't win a prize (but no-one seemed to mind – it was the fun that mattered), and set off with the twenty other floats through the streets of Holt, waving at the crowds, the children singing songs they'd learned at Sunday school. The smallest labourer got tired of the hard floor and sat on my lap most of the way, pointing out school friends and teachers as we passed. The sweating Franciscan friars handed out badges to children in the streets, and encouraged the labourers on the float to sing. After an hour or so we arrived at Kelling Sports Ground where the Carnival was in full swing with sideshows. There I left them and travelled with Jean Smith, the churchwarden, to the home of her fellow warden, Anne, where we had a light and delicious lunch. I spent some time in the garden afterwards trying to put together a few thoughts for the evening.

Thornage Hall is a Camphill Community for the Mentally Handicapped of which I am a patron, and there we spent a delightful time being shown around by members of the community. Dickon – tall and very handsome – led us through the model farm with a stick quite like my crook and a broad straw hat. Some of the residents I knew, one or two I had confirmed. In contrast to the training centre, these young people are rather privileged and many come from wealthy backgrounds. They are wonderfully cared for by a German couple, the Hoffmans, with helpers (some permanent, some temporary), many from the continent of Europe. They run a farm with cows, goats and arable fields and an extensive four acre garden, mostly growing vegetables. They are completely self-sufficient but occasionally produce a surplus which is sold in a nearby village. Thornage Hall was donated by Lord Hastings (whose son Justin is here), but before that, centuries ago, it was the property of the bishops of Norwich – one of the summer palaces, with farm buildings which have now been extensively and imaginatively converted. The residents live in the house with house parents, in flats housing four or five people, each with its own kitchen, dining room, sitting room and bedrooms. Like all the mentally handicapped they are immensely friendly and affectionate and eager to tell me of all they are doing, and were thrilled to bits to be given badges. David, the oldest resident, made a speech at the end and presented me with a box of vegetables grown by them, then James Stratton also made a speech and Justin Hastings insisted on producing a third, involuntary speech. It was all great fun.

We arrived at Blakeney just in time for the closing service with the church reasonably full, including many people whom I had met during the week, and all the clergy were there. The service was a little long but beautiful and simple in its Taizé style. I spoke informally for ten or fifteen minutes about my impressions of the week, which of course were just first impressions. I ended by reading George Herbert's poem *Love Bade me Welcome* which Phillip McFadyen had recommended in one of the commentaries on the Bible readings for the week. Its note of modesty, hesitancy and growing confidence seemed in many ways to sum up some of the experiences of this overcrowded but heartwarming week.

Love bade me welcome; yet my soul drew back
    Guilty of dust and sin.
But quick-eyed Love, observing me grow slack
    From my first entrance in,
Drew nearer to me, sweetly questioning
    If I lacked anything.

'A guest,' I answered, 'worthy to be here.'
    Love said, 'You shall be he.'
'I, the unkind, the ungrateful? Ah, my dear,
    I cannot look on Thee.'
Love took my hand, and smiling, did reply,

'Who made the eyes but I?'

'Truth, Lord, but I have marred them: let my shame
Go where it doth deserve.'
'And know you not,' says Love, 'who bore the blame?'
'My dear, then I will serve.'
'You must sit down,' says Love, 'and taste my meat.'
So I did sit and eat.

8

Waxham and Tunstead

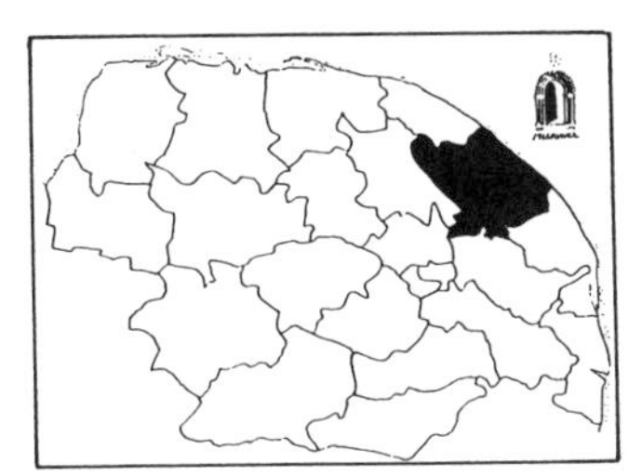

(These two small deaneries, recently amalgamated, run from the east coast north of Great Yarmouth inland to the Broads. Its focus is the lively old town of North Walsham.)

Tuesday 1 August

The first day of a pilgrimage week is always the most tiring because the adrenalin levels have dropped during the days since the last visit, so it was good that today's pace was reasonable. After a Eucharist at North Walsham Parish Church there was a Bible study in the church hall with clergy, readers and deanery synod officers from both deaneries. It was well led by Jim Cameron, the Rural Dean of Waxham, who has experience in modern training methods (he used to work for the General Synod Board of Education). He and Martin Smith, the Rural Dean of Tunstead, have been working well towards amalgamating their two deaneries and the occasion was used imaginatively to further that joining by mixing small groups for the Bible study. The subject of the text from the first three verses of Luke 8 was largely concerned with the place of women, and the resulting discussion was remarkably friendly considering the presence of two or three priests strongly opposed to the ordination of women.

We had a sandwich lunch at North Walsham vicarage with a group of people from the town including the Mayor, two undertakers, shopkeepers, an architect and builder. Interestingly, most of the people there had been born in North Walsham, in contrast to my experience in the villages where a high proportion of people I meet are incomers. The reason is probably that local people can find work in towns like North Walsham, whereas in the villages they nearly all emigrate since farming employs so few people.

After lunch the curates, Valerie Watts and Richard Stainer, took me on a round of visits to the sick and housebound, which, as always, I much enjoyed. It included a visit to Cherrie Moland's mother (Cherrie's husband, Bob, used to be diocesan secretary). The old lady is a great bird lover and wild birds regularly come into the house at teatime and are quite tame. She is still mourning the loss of her granddaughter, Sarah, a brilliant young graduate who was killed in a car accident when coming home from Cranwell where she was a star student. She had hoped, she said, that she would not recover from her last operation because she so wanted to go and be with Sarah again.

After visiting various houses we went to a small unit for the mentally ill attached to the local cottage hospital. It is modern, extremely well run, and I spent a short time with most of the twenty patients. Some of them were pointed out to me as churchgoers, and I gave them all a blessing, and in many cases there was a distinct response, in one case the woman repeating with me word for word the blessing from the Communion service.

Tim Lawes, the Rector of Felmingham, picked me up from the hospital and drove me to his home for an hour's break, which I took in the garden because a breeze had sprung up and the temperature was reasonable. Afterwards we drove to Banningham for Prayer Book evensong and then I was whisked off to Skeyton Church to see their flower festival. This is a lovely single aisle church on a high point which can be seen for miles around. We then drove back to a farm at Felmingham where the whole congregation gathered, about thirty in all, for supper in the garden – a very pleasant occasion. In contrast to this morning, a large proportion were incomers.

So ended a rather easier day than I have had for some time. Apart from the usual round of talking to lots of people and visiting the sick, not a great deal had been demanded of me, for Martin Smith celebrated Communion this morning, Jim Cameron led the Bible study and Tim Lawes conducted and preached at evensong. Martin tends to be bossy but is a first-class parish priest and his staff are very happy and loyal, as are his parishioners with whom he clearly has a good relationship. Tim is still suffering from his depressive illness which is not unconnected to his lack of confidence in himself and in other people. He is a far better priest than he gives himself credit for and I just wish he would believe it and relax.

Wednesday 2 August

Another day of cloudless skies with no wind to alleviate the heat. First stop was Worstead Church, a magnificent building much loved by its priest, Anthony Long, a local Norfolk man and expert local historian. After coffee and chatting to parishioners, we climbed the church tower. I had not told them in advance about my fear of heights so set off with some trepidation, but since I was escorted by one or two aged parishioners and two young girls,

Worstead

I put a brave face on it and climbed the hundred odd steps to the tower. I stood firmly in the middle and enjoyed the magnificent views. One could see all the parishes of the benefice and in the far distance the spire of Norwich Cathedral was just discernible. We drove past Westwick and Sloley to the home of a parishioner at Tunstead for a Bible study with their regular Bible study group, a good session, well led by Anthony Long who is clearly adored, particularly by the old ladies. Instead of coffee which I expected, white wine was served during the Bible study and then afterwards in the garden.

At Scottow, our next stop, there is a beautifully proportioned church with many interesting features including a bench with bishop's mitres carved into the arms. Since this church was in the patronage of the Abbot of St Benet's in the fourteenth century, and then passed to the bishop, I have an idea this might once have been an item of furniture in the Bishop's Palace. It is a handsome piece which I would dearly love to pinch. We walked over to Scottow Hall, the home of James Shaw and his wife. James is a shy and gracious squire who plied us yet again with wine, and I enjoyed looking at some of their paintings, including several by Edward Seago.

We returned for lunch at Anthony Long's chalet vicarage which suits him as a bachelor very well but I doubt would be large enough for a family. Lunch had been cooked by Janet, his housekeeper, who calls herself a household executive since she does everything from cooking and cleaning to answering the telephone and generally managing Anthony – a cheerful soul who comes in two or three times a week. Anthony is an interesting priest, deeply committed to the care of church buildings which he fervently believes can be an important means of evangelism. There was a picture of a woman priest in a room at the vicarage, which shocked me because Anthony is a convinced opponent. On looking closer I realised it was actually of Anthony himself, taken in the days when long hair was the fashion, and he has particularly beautiful curly hair, which made the mistake understandable.

At lunch we had champagne, and after this somewhat alcoholic morning we were joined by twenty or so others for a walk through Dilham Common. It was a longish walk, six miles or so, in the heat of the day and I was glad I had brought a floppy hat. Martin Smith, organising everyone as usual (but everyone seemed very content to be organised), was dressed in straw hat, shirt and shorts, and looked a little like a German tourist. He instructed everybody to walk with me for a period and give way from time to time and it worked well.

By the time we eventually returned I was pretty desperate for a rest and was taken off by Rachel Cubitt to Honing Hall. Here I met her husband Tom, a delightful man who is now completely blind, and unlike those born blind has great difficulty with co-ordinating and guessing where things are. He only inherited the house when he was seventy years old – it is a beautiful place, mostly Georgian, with soft coloured brick and set in a Repton garden. I cooled off for an hour or so in the garden, sketching the house, and then had supper with them. Tom Cubitt was captured at Singapore and worked on the Burma railroad, amazingly surviving, though I think the glaucoma which caused the blindness is partly a result of those awful experiences. He said that he could now talk about his years in prison camp, but still gets nightmares, and is longing for the fiftieth anniversary year to be over so that he can put the memories to rest. They both spoke warmly of Bishop Hugo's care for them and for their parishes and are very pleased with their new priest, which is good to hear.

After supper we went to the little church at Dilham, a curiosity entirely built in 1931, a cosy single aisle church rather like the one at Skeyton yesterday. Gordon Cordy, the previous vicar, just on the verge of retirement went over to Rome, much to everyone's surprise because he had been a good country parson, if a touch charismatic for most of them. He had instituted this weekly evening Eucharist beginning with the singing of choruses and informal prayer. It was a small gathering of fifteen or twenty parishioners which had a good feel.

Thursday 3 August

Another day near the sea began at Waxham Church near the famous old tithe barn. A group of delightful parishioners face an enormous bill for repairs and restoration on their church, but far from being downhearted,

Waxham Old Barn

they are actually quite excited by the prospect of all the work that needs to be done to raise the money. As with so many of these country parishioners, they really love their church and although they do not articulate it in precise words, see the work they do as an expression of their love for God.

We then went for a short walk along Eccles beach where the old church and village were swallowed by the sea many years ago. In a half a century or more our successors might be walking in other parts of this coast, looking at drowned villages, as this could be the fate of many parts of Norfolk.

'We're not going to the parish church at Sea Palling,' said the churchwardens. 'We're going to the Methodists. They make better coffee.' They work closely together, almost taking for granted a unity that far surpasses much that happens in well advertised Local Ecumenical Projects in other places. Here, the Methodists, for example, do all the training of children, Anglican and Methodist, because that is their particular skill, and they join happily together in worship. The warmth of the relationship between the churches was very evident in the half hour or so I spent with them.

Each church is different, and in its own way memorable, but I seem to be visiting so many churches this week that it is difficult at the end of a day to remember which ones I have seen; among them Happisburgh, Walcott, Hempstead (for a Bible study), and the village hall at Lessingham where we had lunch with a large group of parishioners. John Lines, the Vicar, is still grieving the death of his elderly mother who lived with him. He is a former Roman Catholic, and an honest man who wanted to talk to me about life after death because at times he felt shaky when reading some of the works of radical theologians. Such honest vulnerability, I think, is very close to the deepest kind of faith, and it is a faith which communicates with ordinary people, if we will only take the risk of sharing it.

Michael Pickering drove me in a beautifully restored Morris Minor van to the small village of Edingthorpe. We met in a farmyard and were taken in a trailer by tractor through the village, stopping on the way to meet old Bob, a retired farm labourer who now runs an allotment, and thence up the hill to the remarkable church of All Saints, Edingthorpe, a medieval gem which sits on a rise overlooking the sea. On his return from the trenches, Siegfried Sassoon wrote a memorable poem about Edingthorpe.

All Saints' is a monks' church, quite small, with a single aisle, kept open twenty-four hours a day for all the days of the year. The congregation of mixed age groups from this tiny village of no more than fifty houses regularly numbers twenty, that is, about twenty per cent of the population. They have recently restored their tower, which will now stand for centuries, and are tackling other work without anxiety.

Michael drove me down the hill again to Bacton village hall for tea, after which we went to his house for a rest. The vicarage is an elegant seventeenth-century house, not over-large, next to the fine church which in one direction looks out over lovely countryside and the open sea and in the other to the ugly gas terminal which mars the landscape but provides much needed employment.

Michael's parishes have grown in strength and numbers since he went there. He is not an obviously dynamic leader and I asked what his secret was.

'I let the lay people have their head, within reason, and advise them when they ask or I think they need it,' he replied. 'They were raring to go.'

An interesting comment about what may be increasingly needed of the leadership of clergy. 'Hands on' styles of leadership will become less appropriate as stipendiary clergy increasingly work as leaders of ministerial teams in larger areas.

After an hour in the shade we drove to Ludham where we had more food with parishioners and once again I circulated table by table to talk. Then we went into the fine but over-large church for a Bible study attended by thirty or so parishioners from the Group. Only recently amalgamated, they do seem to be working well and, unprompted, one or two parishioners said how much they appreciated the encouragement of working with other parishes. The Bible study was led by Diane Nicholson, widow of the former priest and a lay reader, and Julia, another newly licensed lay reader. Their competent introduction was followed by study in small groups and a good hour together ended with the usual pattern of my own exposition, comments on their discussion and a conducted period of silence.

Friday 4 August

A much more relaxing day began with a tour of Sutton, Catfield and Ingham. Each church interestingly had a two storey 'Parvis' porch, which contained a little room where the monks used to come from the local abbey or priory to stay for a night when they said mass and conducted occasional offices. The parish priest, Stephen Weston, was on holiday and the churchwardens took me round visiting small industrial estates, which included a potter and Sutton Mill – the largest mill in Norfolk with a tourist centre including an old-fashioned chemist's shop. The church at Sutton (a small monks' church) is in a very good state of repair, being cared for by a local builder, though I am not sure if they have always obeyed the faculty rules. Here I encountered a typical Norfolk attitude – that half a glass of beer is always 'half empty', never 'half full'. As we walked around this beautiful church I said, 'Your church seems in good nick.'

'No that isn't, Bishop – look at the roof.'

'What's wrong with the roof?' I asked.

'Look at the tiles – we have to spend £2,000 on them this year.'

'Well, your tower looks very good.'

'Oh, yes, we spent £15,000 on that last year – but look at the roof.'

The church at Catfield is enormous and they have worked hard to restore it, but still much needs to be done. Ingham Church, which I visited for the first time, is quite beautiful, tall and graceful, light and narrow. It has a French feel about it. The parishes are going to be split in the future, Catfield going to Ludham and Potter Heigham, about which they are quite content, and Sutton and Ingham with Stalham. Ingham are rather frightened about it because they think they will be swallowed up, but I doubt it because that church is so special and has the potential for being used for many things. I guess the acoustics are fine and it would make a marvellous place for concerts.

They took me to the ancient pub next door whose cellar had been the cellar of the priory attached to Ingham Church, very ancient, and the publican was glad to show us round.

I gave him some Pilgrimage Prayers and said, 'They're prayer cards not beer mats.'

'I'm the one who's supposed to make the jokes around here,' he said.

Andrew Parsons then collected me and took me to lunch at the Norfolk Broads Yacht Club at Wroxham. A regatta was in progress on a fine, windy day and I much enjoyed the two hours spent with them in the company of the Commodore, his wife, his fellow Commodore from Horning Yacht Club and John Aitken and his wife. (John, one of the sons of Bishop Aubrey Aitken, former Bishop of Lynn, is Headmaster of a primary school in North Walsham.) Afterwards we went in the Commodore's restored Edwardian wooden launch to Hoveton, just past Wroxham bridge, where we had a short outdoor service accompanied by the Salvation Army Band. A good crowd gathered and a huge sign had been posted up with the Pilgrimage Prayer painted on it. At the service I was presented with an appliqué design of the bishop's coat of arms for the back of my cope, which had been beautifully made by Bee Dashfield, a parishioner from Wroxham.

We then left for a journey down the river by canoe, another new experience for me. I used a canoe made by Andrew Parsons' father, which I was assured was stable but didn't feel it when I first got in. After a wobbly 200 yards, however, I got the hang of it and spent a happy hour paddling with three or four other canoes down the river. A photographer from the *EDP* had turned up with a reporter, in the hope of seeing me fall in, but I managed to keep upright though by the time we arrived at the meadow near Wroxham vicarage I had become pretty wet with the splashes I made with the paddles.

After a rest in the garden and supper with Andrew and Diane and their very lively girls, Clare, Joanna and Sarah, we went to Wroxham Church for a Bible study which again was good. At supper we discussed the service at St Benet's next day, and the girls debated whether they would come.

'It doesn't last long,' I assured them, 'and I don't preach long sermons.'

'That's good,' said Joanna, 'because Daddy preaches very long sermons.'

'How long?' I asked.

'Seven minutes,' she replied in disgust.

Saturday 5 August

Another pleasant day began early with a men's breakfast at Neatishead for the three parishes of Barton Turf, Neatishead and Irstead. About eighty men turned up at the village hall which surprised us all, but there was enough food for a great breakfast full of cholesterol. Only an hour had been allowed, which was really too short because I would have liked to have stayed and talked for longer, but the meal included a good, brief ten-minute address from Michael Reeder of the Church Army about his ministry in the hospital.

Richard Millard, a retired headmaster and NSM in charge of the parishes, drove me to Barton Church where ringers rang and we had a family service led by the reader, who preached a short address on the Bible study for the day. After talking to parishioners, we walked down to the Staithe for coffee and then set sail on a White Boat, the famous 'Yare and Bure One Design', a twenty-foot-long, elegant day boat, and we sailed across Barton Broad escorted by little girls in mini motor boats. We made a stop at a punt, afloat in the middle of the Broads, where there was a gathering of the Disabled Sailing Club, and I talked to some of the instructors and disabled people who have specially designed small dinghies to enable them to sail solo if they wish. We then proceeded to Irstead where we landed and walked up to the beautiful little Irstead Church where we had another short service and Bible study.

Again, all very friendly and welcoming.

We next drove to Neatishead for another service – a short hymn sandwich but made exceptional by the choir, led by Jeannie Peel, which was of a very high standard. After I gave the blessing they sang a sevenfold 'Amen', an old-fashioned musical custom which I have not encountered since Beaconsfield days. A thoroughly enjoyable and long morning ended when Richard Millard drove me to Horning vicarage for lunch with Hugh and Joy Edgell.

Hugh is due to retire in November. He has a bad heart and is retiring a year early, particularly since Joy has also not been well. Sensitive to my need sometimes to eat quietly rather than in a continuous round of conversation, the three of us had lunch alone, which I much appreciated. Afterwards we drove to Beeston, a much vandalised church on the main road, and met the churchwarden and his wife who faithfully care for the building. Even here there is a regular congregation of fifteen in a village with only forty-one inhabitants.

Ashmanhaugh was next, a pretty little church, tucked away in this tiny village off the beaten track but boasting a cricket field. They evidently love Hugh Edgell and will desperately miss him. They urged me to make a good appointment – not too high and not too low and let him be someone who will love the churches – 'or her,' they said – at least, some did.

Next stop was Horning Sailing Club where I met David Levy, the Commodore who had been at lunch yesterday at Wroxham. Horning Yacht Club is not as luxurious as Wroxham, nor so expensive, but very friendly. Here they don't have full-time people working at the Club but do it all themselves, so there is a strong feeling of fellowship. Again, I had a short sail in a White Boat to Horning village green not far away. They presented me with a burgee, with the arms of their Club, which are exactly the same as the arms of the Abbot of St Benet's. I shall fly it from the wherry tomorrow.

'It has been an honour to have you on board,' said the owner as I stepped off the boat on to the green. I hope he realised what pleasure he and others have given me with their generosity, kindness and warm welcome.

Parishioners sat around having tea and I chatted table by table and then there loomed over me a pretty lady in a floral dress, holding a guitar. 'Here's something for you, Bishop Peter,' said her companion and she proceeded to sing very sweetly the Pilgrimage Prayer which she had set to music. People gathered round and applauded warmly at the end, and Hugh Edgell invited her to come to St Benet's and sing it there tomorrow. The Pilgrimage Prayer was distributed and, as so often happens, one person asking me to sign a copy started a flood of requests for autographed prayers. It reminded me of the days when, as Bishop of Taunton, I used to sign Confirmation cards for little boys and told them if they collected fifty of my signatures they might be able to swap them for one of Ian Botham's.

After an hour or so we drove back to Horning vicarage, one of the most beautiful parsonages in England, let alone the diocese, with its matchless setting near the river. The Diocesan Board of Finance are bound to want to sell it when Hugh goes but I shall dig my heels in because the Church mustn't let this wonderful house go. In the church, another building much loved and well restored, and closely associated with St Benet's Abbey, the lay brothers joined their Prior (Hugh Edgell) to sing compline and I joined in the old-fashioned plainchant which a young man from Mattishall recorded for a special tape they are making. Traditionally the Vicar of Horning is the Prior of St Benet's, and according to very ancient custom he must maintain not less than twelve nor more than twenty-four lay brothers. So Hugh has chosen men from the congregation who have made a notable contribution to the church, and they meet once a month for compline and dinner.

(Hugh has an attractive husky speaking voice and sings well. Thank goodness the phenomenon of 'the parsonic voice' is almost a thing of the past. But still one does encounter it in strange forms. In Somerset I remember one or two native clergy with rich and attractive west country accents who changed in church and talked posh, which sounded very strange. Even odder is the phenomenon of 'the theological college principal's voice'. A former Cuddesdon man I know has a perfectly good voice, but it flattens out in church, which always puzzled me until I recognised it as an imitation of the flat tones of Robert Runcie, his Principal at Cuddesdon. Similarly, I knew a Cockney priest who in church adopted the fruity tones of Donald Coggan, his Principal at the London College of Divinity. And I remember someone else, trained at Westcott House, who talked about the 'fet cet set on the met' as Ken Carey used to do – a 1930s BBC English kind of accent, which sounded natural with Ken, but very odd from the mouth of his former pupil.)

We finished at about 6 o'clock and I was grateful for an evening free, and also for the sensitivity of people during the last few days who kept the pace of this week's pilgrimage more humane than some. So I was fresh enough to enjoy a family barbecue at Bishop's House to celebrate Andrew's thirty-first birthday, Peter's thirtieth, and the fifth wedding anniversary of Joanna and Simon.

Sunday 6 August

The last day in this deanery began with a Eucharist at Stalham, also attended by parishioners from Sutton, Ingham and Catfield with whom I had been the other day. After coffee in the church, we walked through Stalham to a large car park where carnival floats were assembling which I was asked to judge. It was not a task I relished but eventually I made a reasonably fair and diplomatic choice, giving first prize to the Cubs and their pirate ship, second to the playgroup with a display called 'Peace', which curiously featured a

St Benet's Abbey

tank, a warship and a jet fighter (they won last year), and third prize to the Brownies with a float illustrating their badges, the most spectacular of which was the 'Housekeeping' badge which featured a Brownie dressed in apron with mop and bucket, slippers and hair done up in curlers tied with a silk scarf.

After lunch in a parishioner's house with a group of a dozen or so, we drove to Horning vicarage to begin the wherry trip to St Benet's Abbey. Peter Bower as always was there as skipper with two young helpers and we set sail soon after we arrived, this time on *Hathor*. After years of sailing on the wherries once or twice a year, Peter now allows me to steer, which is great fun. But when I think I'm doing rather well he never fails to remind me of a disastrous occasion on Wroxham Broad when I was steering and we accidentally jibed and headed straight for the pristine landing stage of the Yacht Club. It took three of us straining on the heavy tiller to avoid a major catastrophe. Peter's elderly parents were there as usual with a few friends on a day's outing, together with Steven Betts and my son-in-law, Simon Pullen. The wind and tide were favourable and so we took the sail down and drifted into the rushy bank for quarter of an hour before making the final stretch down to the landing stage below the ruins of the Abbey.

A score of boats were tied up and many cars had made the journey across the causeway on the land side. With the lay brothers, we processed up to the ruins for the service which was attended by about 400 people and the Salvation Army Band. The singer was here from yesterday's little incident at Horning and sang to us again and later went back with some parishioners from

Hingham to Horning rectory for a sing-song. The old stagers all bring folding chairs while others stand or sit on the grass, though it is rather mucky from cows and several hundred geese. It was the last service for Hugh Edgell, though I will ask him back next year if we have not made a new appointment by then.

After the service I chatted to various visitors and signed autographs on the prayer cards. A lady took my photograph and said it would be placed in her house next to the picture of the Pope. ('Ecumenical breakthrough,' I thought. But the new Roman Catholic Bishop of East Anglia is also called Peter, so maybe it was a case of mistaken identity.) Another old lady, now aged ninety, who has been coming here since 1939 and never missed a year, said she looked forward to seeing me during the next deanery pilgrimage in Blofield when she will be attending a dinner in South Walsham at which I shall be present.

'I look forward to being with you, Bishop,' she said, 'and I promise not to drink too much.'

We joined two other wherries, *Olive* and *Norada* tied up nearby, for tea, and then sailed back in a stiff breeze, Peter again allowing me the helm despite some fairly tricky tacking in the reach past Ranworth.

'You did that quite well,' Peter said, 'but don't go round telling people you can now tack a wherry. Remember Wroxham Broad.'

We walked up from the quayside to the vicarage and found Deborah, the dusky folk singer, sitting next to an old man, singing together. He had obviously fallen badly for her.

So home, after another different, encouraging and enjoyable week, with clergy and laity in this deanery everywhere solicitous of my need for rest so that I felt very well cared for.

9

Blofield

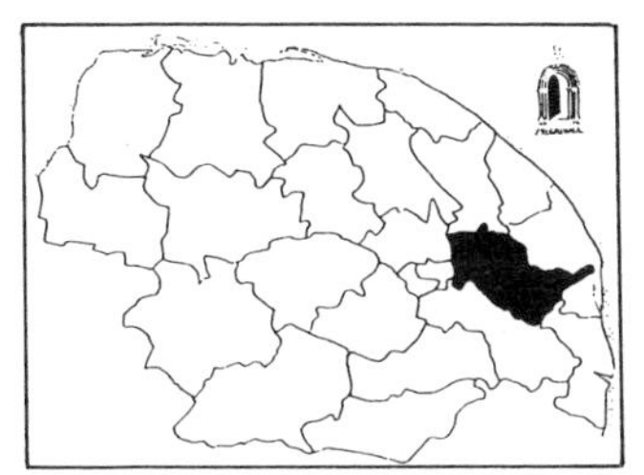

(A series of attractive villages stretching from the outskirts of Norwich along the rivers Yare and Bure to the heart of Broadland. A high proportion of the working population are Norwich commuters.)

Tuesday 15 August

After a few days of cooler weather, the temperatures are now soaring again and it was very hot with no wind as I began the next stage of the pilgrimage. At the home of the Lay Chairman, Sheila Ashford, at Strumpshaw, a group of parishioners met over coffee, followed by a walk to Strumpshaw Fen. This is an RSPB reserve and the young deputy warden took us to a hide and then for a walk through the reserve – only two or three miles long but very hot. The interesting group of parishioners included a couple new to the village, Peter and Marilyn. He is German and told me a fascinating story about his forebears who had been involved in left-wing politics in Germany, including a grandfather who was imprisoned as a trades unionist in Dachau concentration camp. Peter's one desire as a young man in 1945 was to leave Germany as soon as possible. He trained as a brewer, worked overseas for most of his life and is now happily settled with his wife in Strumpshaw.

After a light lunch, Sheila drove me to an industrial estate at Rackheath where I was to meet the inventor of the winning Olympic bicycle. In fact he was on holiday and I met his assistant who offered me a tricycle to ride. When I heard about this in advance I imagined one of those invalid tricycles, like a large version of an old-fashioned children's trike with a shopping basket in front. But this turned out to be an extraordinary machine with two wheels in front and one at the back. You lie prone (as in those one man sledges in the Olympic Games – a 'luge' I think they're called), with the pedals out in front. It is, in fact, used by professional cyclists for training and proved quite tricky to handle. I led a small group of cyclists away from the factory and down the main road for a couple of miles – rather a frightening experience being so close to the ground with cars and trucks overtaking. I had not been given a crash helmet and I just hoped the photographs from the *EDP* would not provoke a torrent of correspondence about bishops setting bad examples. We stopped at the little church in Rackheath, a modern building, not very beautiful but much cared for and loved by its parishioners. A feature is a fine mural of the feeding of the five thousand, painted recently by a young artist. After a welcome glass of lemonade, we continued the bicycle ride. It was even hotter by this time and the only way to create a breeze was to cycle fast but that made one sweat even more profusely. Catch 22.

We eventually arrived at our destination, the village hall at Salhouse, where parishioners had gathered for tea. Some who had been following us in a car said that we were doing between fifteen and twenty miles an hour at one stage. All the cyclists had been behind me, looking rather serious with their helmets and luminous sashes. I had been afraid that I was dawdling and they would become bored, but they told me afterwards that they had been straining to keep up. The machine goes rather faster than I thought. My shirt was wringing wet, and there was no chance to change, so I just dried out gradually, taking a dim view of Jesus' instructions to the Twelve in today's Bible study to go out without taking an extra shirt.

We had a jolly supper at the home of David and Mary Benham in Salhouse with the table surrounded by friendly teenagers, including their two children, Josh and Jess; Jess' boyfriend, Charles, who used to be in the choir at the cathedral and is now a server; Josh's girlfriend, Zoë; Nicola, a girl from Crewkerne, and another girl from Germany.

After supper we went to the home of local Methodists, Graham and Marion Bunn, for Bible study. The group meets fortnightly and is a lively gathering of Methodists and Anglicans – another example of informal co-operation without benefit of ecumenical instruments. We sang some choruses together and then got down to the study led by Val, a churchwarden and candidate for readership. They were people who clearly knew each other well and trusted one another with confidences. They included an elderly lady who at a service attended by Bishop Hugo a few weeks ago had collapsed and felt she was on the edge of death. Apparently Hugo – according to them – rather dramatically stopped the ambulance men from coming down the aisle until he gave her a blessing at which, she said, she felt completely peaceful and that it did not matter whether she lived or died. She talked about the experience of being prayed for in an interesting and matter of fact way. I left them as they began a supper party; having eaten twice that day, with no more room for food, I was looking forward to the prospect of a cool shower and clean clothes.

Wednesday 16 August
I revisited the modern St David's Church at Thorpe End which I had dedicated two years ago and after talking to children at the holiday club we had a Bible study group in the well-equipped church. Our prayer at the end was blasted out by noise from the children singing in the room next door, who were accompanied by a recording of what sounded like the massed bands of the Royal Marines played at full volume. We then paid a visit to Richard Hale, an old retired bachelor priest, and a scholar who has produced a great amount of material for the history of the cathedral. He is cheerful, still working at various projects, but actually dying of cancer.

After visiting the churches at Great and Little Plumstead, we went to Little Plumstead Hall for a pre-lunch drinks party at the home of Mr and Mrs Wiley, who gave me some of their home-produced honey. We then called at the tiny church at Witton, serving a population of only fifteen people, but I am glad that everyone is determined to keep the church open because this parish is so near Norwich that one can envisage it being populated sometime in the next century.

Barry Tomlinson then drove me to Little Plumstead Hospital where I met senior members of the Norwich Community Health Partnership which is a huge organisation, headed by three women, dealing with mental illness, mental handicap (the politically correct term is now 'people with learning difficulties', but I find it a difficult and unnecessary mouthful), home care and the aged. After an interesting discussion we went to the chaplaincy centre in

Little Plumstead (pencil)

the hospital and had tea with patients, all of them quite severely mentally ill but friendly and full of smiles. One old lady told me she was a gypsy and offered to tell my fortune which I did not take up. I went round handing out biscuits which they all ate ravenously and a second tin had to be opened. I hope they are properly fed – perhaps they are just biscuit addicts.

Next stop was a memorable visit to St Edmund's, South Burlingham, where the roof was off, covered with plastic, being re-thatched. We met the builder from Ditchingham and Mrs Dixon, the churchwarden and prime mover in everything that happens at South Burlingham. They have done a marvellous job in raising money. The church is in the process of complete restoration. It is beautiful, untouched by the Victorians, with a magnificent wall painting of the murder of Thomas à Becket and an exquisite fifteenth-century pulpit alleged to be the best of its kind in the country, and one can believe it. Mrs Dixon is a marvellous lady and after complimenting her on all the work she and her fellow parishioners had done, I said, 'And of course you are also distinguished because you have one of the first women vicars in the diocese.' Later Vivien told me that she could hardly suppress her giggles because Mrs Dixon and the PCC of South Burlingham were the ones who at first did not wish to have her because she was a woman. In my innocence I hope I said the right thing.

I was driven away from the church and given a tour of Lingwood in a tractor driven by Mary, Mrs Dixon's daughter and a farmer's wife. We sat together in the cab of a brand new Massey Ferguson tractor, surrounded by glass, and in the heat I rather dreaded it. But she said, 'Don't worry. As soon as we get moving you'll get cool.' Trusting her advice, as soon as we started I opened my window to let the breeze flow in. Mary said, 'Shut that window or else you won't get the benefit of the air conditioning.' Things have come a long way since the days when I sold old Fordson tractors in 1957. The modern monster was also equipped with a computer which told you the depth and width of the furrow. We bounced a bit along the rough road but it was a comfortable ride, our conversation on the way suddenly deepening as Mary told me an interesting and touching story of her loss of faith when her daughter was diagnosed with multiple sclerosis, and its (her faith's) slow recovery. At the home of parishioners in Lingwood we sat in the garden for tea and another Bible study which was led by John, a candidate for LNSM.

I was very ready by now for a rest because there had been no spare moments at all thus far. After an hour's welcome break at a house in the beautiful hamlet of Hassingham, we drove to the Old Rectory at Buckenham for a barbecue and yet another Bible study. This is an amazing Victorian house, owned now by Tony and Sue Hedge. It used to be the home of an eccentric parson called William Haslem who built a pulpit in the rectory wall from which he addressed vast crowds who came from miles around to hear him. He was a great thorn in the bishop's side for preaching everywhere without permission, but was a huge popular attraction. Sue Hedge showed me an etching of a Sunday afternoon with thousands gathered in the field and Parson Haslem addressing them. About thirty or more parishioners gathered for the barbecue which was delicious. Tony led the Bible study imaginatively and there was a really good discussion first in groups and then all together, as the darkness gathered.

Thursday 17 August

Market day in Acle began at the parish church with a brief period of prayer with Colin Way, the Rector and Rural Dean, and his churchwardens, followed by a stroll through the market, chatting to the stallholders, villagers and holidaymakers. Regularly on these visits, as yesterday, one is suddenly plunged from light-hearted banter into a deep conversation. This happened when I met a stallholder whose husband, sitting behind the stall in a corner, suffers from motor neurone disease. He talked bravely and movingly about his condition, and of his gratitude for sixty-two years of life if it should end soon. Soon afterwards I met Joan in a wheelchair, who is very clever with her hands and makes delightful floral hats which a number of people were wearing around Acle. She promised to make one for me – white with a purple band if we could get the purple band. At another stall we found some purple material which the stallholder kindly gave us and which we passed to Joan.

We walked on through the little town, talking to people as we went, to the modern, well-equipped surgery which, like many of its kind in Norfolk, is self-contained with its own dispensary, play area for children and restroom for the staff. Then on the same site we visited the new sports complex where they have a huge indoor bowling green, and I saw there a picture of Timothy Stone who lives with his parents in Granary Cottage (part of Bishop's House) and is a member of the Norfolk Junior Team. I gained considerable 'street cred' because I know the Stone family. The site also includes a Methodist church, built thanks to the southern bypass which took the land of the old Methodist church and demolished the building. So they have a fine new church which also contains a centre like the one in Blakeney where people can come for treatment and the disabled for baths. It is run by Val, a member of the parish church congregation, who won the MBE for her work in establishing this service for all the surrounding villages.

We continued walking along an ancient pathway through a cornfield to Fishley Church, a tiny building set on a rise with no houses around – a Black Death church, they say, but possibly a Clearance church, when ruthless landowners, like their Highland counterparts, cleared the villages to make room for the sheep which made them prosperous in the Middle Ages. We had a picnic lunch in the churchyard. Often on these journeys a sense of timelessness

Fishley

comes over me for one reason or another. As I sat in the wide circle listening to the chatter I noticed three women, an elderly mother and her two unmarried daughters, all dressed elegantly in straw hats trimmed with ribbons and flowers. The daughters must have been in their late fifties, and were both very beautiful. I wondered why they had never married, and thought myself back in the early twenties when there would have been many such groups of mothers and daughters, with lost husbands and boyfriends, victims of the slaughter in the trenches.

I awoke from my reverie in time to comment on the Bible study, after which we continued along the old path through more fields to the village of Upton and walked on to Upton Dyke, a little staithe where there were boats and a couple restoring an old working wherry called *Maude*. There I met Miss Wilmott, a ninety-year-old former nanny, who looked very glamorous and well preserved although she can hardly walk now. She used to live near Hickling Broad in the thirties and went to the first service at St Benet's Abbey in 1938. When the service stopped during the war she wondered if a bishop would ever return to St Benet's and wrote a poem about it in 1940 which she gave me. I met another family, holidaymaking, which included an old lady in a wheelchair who told me she was ninety-one and born again and looking forward to the Second Coming.

I spotted a young boy, aged about ten, sitting on a bench and swinging his legs, dressed in a yellow and green football shirt.

'Good to see a Norwich City fan,' I greeted him.

'Nurridge?' he said. 'Ahm a Newcassle suppourtah,' and pointed to a Newcastle Football Club badge on his shirt (it must have been their 'away strip').

I told him he'd better be careful in that shirt if he met any Canary fans, and gave him a pilgrimage badge to pin on his shirt. 'That might keep you safe,' I said as I left him, bemused, still swinging his legs.

At St Margaret's Institute, a wooden village hall, we had tea and another Bible study, led expertly by Graham Hendy, the Rector. Another ride in the trailer of a tractor followed, to Dick Dewing's farm for a rest. He is a lay reader who with his wife Veronica recently volunteered to spend two years in northern Uganda, the poorest and most difficult part of that benighted country, training lay readers before returning to their farm; a dedicated and delightful couple who wore their real holiness without any sense of piety. I went with them to the Ship Inn opposite St Margaret's Church where the parish regularly hold functions, and we had a delicious supper with about twenty parishioners, including little William, aged eight, baptised last Sunday and in the Junior Squad of Norwich City Football Club. The group also included Edna, the ninety-year-old from St Benet's Abbey who promised not to drink too much. I told this story to someone who said that she is not supposed to drink at all, let alone 'not too much'.

Afterwards we went over to the church and had a simple and imaginative pilgrimage service devised by Graham and attended by forty or fifty parishioners, which made very effective use of the church building. Then on to the old St Lawrence building next door, which has been recently restored as a conference centre, for the third Bible study of the day, again led by Graham. Like all the Bible studies today, it was very worthwhile and ended with a time of conducted silence.

Friday 18 August

After coffee at Brundall rectory with Bob Baker, his curate and the readers, we walked through the attractive churchyard to the church room for a Bible study on the Transfiguration. While they were studying the passage in groups, I had a long conversation with Claire, a four-year-old, who told me all about her favourite television programmes, books, best friend and almost being able to swim without arm bands. A good session together was followed by a visit to the Brundall Medical Centre which is a carbon copy of the centre at Acle which I visited yesterday, indeed they are all partners in the same practice. The churchwardens joined staff at the centre for a sandwich lunch and talk and then I walked a short way to a parishioner's house for a brief rest in the garden.

A small group of us then walked through the suburban streets of Brundall and across fields to Braydeston Church, set on a hill, where we had a short act of Prayer Book worship attended by a large group of parishioners.

We left in a car with Bob Baker, Richard and Libby Espin-Bradley, the curate, his wife, and their three-year-old daughter Harriet, for Broom's Boatyard by the river at Brundall. Here we boarded a rich man's motor launch, a seagoing monster with luxuriously equipped cabin with double bed and single beds elsewhere, sitting room, kitchen, shower and two bathrooms. On deck there was every navigational aid possible. According to the skipper, who is one of the boatbuilders at the yard, these immensely expensive boats are hardly ever used, perhaps only once or twice a year, by their owners. This one was second-hand and for sale – a snip at £180,000. Bob Baker had completely miscalculated the time it would take to go from Brundall to Reedham Staithe where we were due to meet parishioners. He calculated one hour and it took us two. When we eventually got there the parishioners were somewhat restive, but did not make too much of a fuss. I had to work hard, however, to break a certain ice I sensed.

After chatting busily for half an hour, I boarded a pony and trap and was driven by a farmer's wife and her two sons, fanatical football supporters, through the village of Reedham, past old houses and interesting scenery, but the most important site was a large modern house – 'Ashley Ward lives there,' they said in awe. (He is a Norwich City striker.) Extraordinary how football has recurred so often; it must have something to do with the start of the football season.

I alighted at the village hall, which is a new building and very splendid, produced by the efforts of the villagers. By now everybody was warm and friendly. I then went back to the house of Alan and Babs Parrott for drinks and supper with friends, which was a jolly occasion. Alan is a kind of local squire who talked a lot but very knowledgeably about the church. I duly admired the interesting design for a stained glass window for Reedham Church which has been rejected by the Diocesan Advisory Committee.

The Bible study at Reedham Church was excellent. The church burnt down in 1981 and was completely rebuilt. It is a white-walled early English building, spacious, with wonderful acoustics but furnished with hideous pews which came from Keswick College. I commented upon the pews later over coffee and realised it was a hornet's nest. Some sensibly wanted to throw them out and have fewer chairs, and others wanted pews again. The lively Bible study was enhanced by the presence of one or two very articulate and thoughtful parishioners; one old lady who made a shy and valuable contribution and a young girl who yesterday heard that she had got three As at 'A' level and was going to Lincoln College, Oxford, to read Greats. I hope she retains her thoughtful agnosticism which was very positive and thought provoking, particularly given the presence of another quite powerful lady with strong evangelical views.

Saturday 19 August

This was one of the most enjoyable days of the pilgrimage. We drove through the beautiful village of Woodbastwick to the parish church on the green, surrounded by thatched cottages, for a short service of prayer led by Phillip McFadyen. On the green I met Valentine, a huge white bull, who snuffled my shirt with his wet nose – whether a friendly gesture or a sniff to see if I was good to eat, I don't know, but I was glad his keeper kept a firm hold on him.

Afterwards twenty of us mounted a farm trailer, a much more luxurious affair than on previous such expeditions. It was double the size of most trailers, with seating round the sides and a public address system. We were taken on a tour of the Woodbastwick estate, which is remarkable in many ways. It is owned by John Cator, and run by his sons, Henry and Alby. Before arriving on the estate proper, we drove through the village past a beautiful white house, which was once the village pub. When it became very rowdy the landowner of the time ejected the publican and installed the Rector, so for years it was a rectory. We had a running commentary by Henry Cator and Graham Bunn, the farm manager, who had been our host the other evening at the Bible study in Salhouse. It is a huge estate and run according to 'LEAF' principles (linking environment and farming) which combine conservation of the environment, modern farming methods, encouragement of local industry and care for the community. They are very much looking to the future and it is a model of what farming on a large scale can be. The tour, which lasted an hour and was fascinating, ended at the village hall for coffee with parishioners.

After coffee I boarded 'the bus', which was a large 1954 Ford van converted into a shooting brake with seats in the front for the 'guns' and a separate compartment in the back for loaders, with racks for the game above. We were driven by the Cators' housekeeper and her husband to a Scout camp site. This is a fine open space with a private Broad, where Scouts can learn to sail, canoe, study birds and learn about plants. This large Broad was blocked from the main river by John Cator so no cruisers can intrude. The whole thing is a model of the best kind of feudal landowning, which still survives in parts of Norfolk.

At a nearby staithe we boarded a beautifully restored Edwardian day boat, the *Princess Margaret*, a gracious launch, full of polished wood, brass and with a gently puttering engine which once belonged to a Morris 1100. Escorted by a Broads Authority boat, we motored to Hoveton Little Broad, which is quiet and picturesque, and not much visited by big launches since the entry is very narrow. We dropped a mud anchor and, with Derek, Joyce and Elaine, had a tranquil lunch until it was time to move off to Ranworth along the busy highway, always dangerous on a Saturday because of new holidaymakers hiring boats for the first time. We dropped anchor in Ranworth

Broad and I rowed the launch's dinghy for the last few yards to the quay where Phillip McFadyen was waiting for me.

I walked to the visitors' centre and chatted to people there, mostly day visitors from Norfolk rather than holidaymakers, and then to the church which is much visited and where the ministry of welcome is justly famous. In the background a tape recorder was playing, which lent a wonderful atmosphere to this beautiful church. I chatted to several visitors, including one family where the husband is head of music at King's College, Taunton, and his wife churchwarden at St John's. Small world. I returned to the vicarage for a break and sat in the garden sketching the house, which is one of the few surviving old vicarages of Norfolk and must never be lost to the Church. Afterwards we went on the 'Saturday Run' in an electric boat owned by the Broads Authority, visiting holidaymakers, distributing leaflets about the church and tomorrow's services and I gave badges to the children. Many of the holidaymakers were spending their first night on the Broads. One large and lovely Cockney family were delighted to see us.

'Is this your first time on the Broads?' asked Phillip.

'First time on the Broads, mate?' he replied. 'This is the first time we've ever been on a boat.'

There are a lot of minor accidents on Saturday night when people try to park their launches, but everyone is good-humoured.

On our way back we called briefly at the shop on the staithe and the village pub, before returning to the vicarage where a marquee had been set up in the garden. Here a large number of parishioners gathered for a Passover meal led by Phillip and Sheilagh Philips; Sheilagh is a theologian who has been teaching in Israel and has now retired to live in Brundall. She could be a great asset to the diocese. She and Phillip interpreted the meal throughout and taught us about Hebrew greetings and food, relating it all to the Last Supper. We ate traditional Jewish food – soup, a lamb stew, various nuts, raw vegetables and fruit – with real Israeli wine. The whole thing was imaginatively arranged and it was a memorable evening for everyone who shared it. Sheilagh and Phillip were dressed in skull cap and prayer shawl, while Brenda and her fellow helpers wore Arab headdress. After feeling very weary on Friday night, it was wonderful to have this day which was full but refreshing.

Sunday 20 August

There was welcome cloud cover as I went to Hemblington Church for the Eucharist and so for the first time this week wore a cassock. Parishioners from Blofield and Hemblington had gathered together and the lovely medieval church was almost full for a Eucharist at which I preached informally, or rather rambled, which I suppose is appropriate for a pilgrimage. I must have gone on for about twenty minutes but people afterwards said they found it interesting and wished I had continued, but that would have made us late for the next engagement which was coffee at Blofield Church across the southern bypass, followed by a Bible study led by Rosemary Hammond. Afterwards I went for lunch with Janet and Roger Shreeve, together with Brian Short and his wife, who retired through ill health a few years ago.

After a quick cup of coffee, we returned to Blofield Church for a deanery service, and another good liturgy devised by Graham Hendy. The large church was full and it was lovely to see people who had accompanied me on the pilgrimage through the week – no longer strangers, but friends and fellow pilgrims. At the end of the service, after giving a short address, we processed out singing, 'One more step along the way' and then had tea. We prayed especially today for Bishop Hugo, who is to preach at the VJ Day service this evening in the cathedral. It will be a difficult task, but he is the obvious person to preach, having been interned in Sumatra during the war; his father was taken away to a prison camp by the Japanese and for five years they did not know whether he was alive or dead.

The VJ Day service in the evening was truly memorable, the cathedral full of veterans, civic dignitaries and representatives of other Churches. There were scores of British Legion banners, rousing music and a good liturgy, but the highlight was Bishop Hugo's sermon, which was one of the most moving I have ever heard. With little reference to notes he spoke eloquently, painting pictures like icons which drew people in and beyond them. It was a long sermon but everyone was totally gripped from beginning to end. It had been an emotional week or two for Hugo as memories of those awful experiences revived for him, and the sermon was obviously forged at considerable cost. But it was a great gift to the people there which they will remember and treasure all their lives, as I shall.

Interlude

30 August to 15 September

Our holiday this year was itself a kind of pilgrimage. We travelled 3,000 miles through France into north-east Spain beginning, after crossing through Le Tunnel, with a tour of the Normandy beaches. There were memorials everywhere – the vast acres of sad and beautifully kept cemeteries – the impressive 'Memoriale' museum at Caen where the whole war is commemorated through film, displays and memorabilia – Sword, June and Omaha beaches – the Pont du Hoc where so many American Rangers lost their lives in a heroic scaling of the cliffs under fire, and which is little changed, including the barbed wire along the cliff edge. Not least moving were the signs everywhere expressing the gratitude of the people of Normandy to British, Canadian and American soldiers. Nowhere was there a note of bitterness at the suffering of French people as a consequence of the invasion and Normandy Campaign – more civilian lives were lost then than during all the years of occupation. The message seemed curiously akin to the feelings of Israel in Egypt and at various periods of Jewish history, that liberation at a heavy cost was better than slavery to a foreign power.

After leaving Normandy, we travelled to the town of Surgères, not far from La Rochelle, in the middle of rich dairy country, where Betty's family originated. It was her first visit and proved very exciting. An eighteenth-century ancestor, Joseph-Etienne Maingot, second son of the Marquis de Surgères and a major in the French army, left France to escape the guillotine and travelled to Trinidad where he was appointed Surveyor General to the Spanish Governor. When the British took Trinidad from Spain, he continued the same work for the Crown, and settled permanently on the island. From him the large West Indian branch of the family grew. We had always known that the Maingots came from Surgères, but were surprised to find them still very much remembered and venerated – the family coat of arms having been adopted as the town's. Little remains of the old château, except a few

Surgères

buildings, the walls and moat. But the magnificent Romanesque church is complete, built by Guillaume Maingot in 1100 – that is, at the same time as the building of Norwich Cathedral was proceeding. The mention of her maiden name produced enthusiastic reactions from the staff of the town library, and from the man in charge of the Syndicat d'Initiative, who is a local historian. Partly because Betty's parents had been killed in the war, and she had subsequently been brought up by her mother's (Scottish) side of the family, she had rather lost touch with her paternal roots, so the journey to Surgères was an exciting and emotional pilgrimage.

Our final night in France was spent at the Auberge de L'Evéché, the former Bishop's Palace next to a ruined eleventh-century abbey in a little village on the Aude, in an idyllic setting beside the river. It sounds romantic, but the hotel was truly awful and we were glad to leave early the next morning for the final stage of our journey south into Spain.

A leisurely week was spent in the sun at Aigua Blava, where the hotel was very comfortable and the staff immensely friendly and helpful. They spoke little English, though one waiter tried – a young version of Manuel in Fawlty Towers. *One evening I asked for 'una platta de patatas fritas' with my omelette.*

'Ah yes,' he said, 'you wanna a plat a shits.'

'No,' I hastily corrected him, 'a plate of chips.'

'Ah yes – a playit *a shits.'*

'Si – por favor.'

On Sunday we attended mass at the local church – totally incomprehensible because the whole thing was in Catalan, but the shape of the liturgy was exactly as we knew it, so were able to follow, more or less. The priest was served by a beautiful teenage girl with long golden hair, dressed in a white alb. Throughout the liturgy she stood beside the priest with her arms rebelliously folded and her eyes half shut – a bored Botticelli angel.

On the return journey, after visiting Monet's garden at Giverny, where Bishops Hugo, David and I had spent a happy hour in April, we made our final stop at Bayeux to see the tapestry. It is not only a remarkable work of art, but brought home once again the strong links between the English and the Normans. Like so many exhibitions we have seen, the whole place was very well organised and informative, with films, models and displays demonstrating the links between England and the Normans, paying particular attention to the ecclesiastical links and the building of cathedrals and abbeys by Norman bishops and monks. So there we were, linked once again to Herbert de Losinga and our Norman roots.

10

Repps

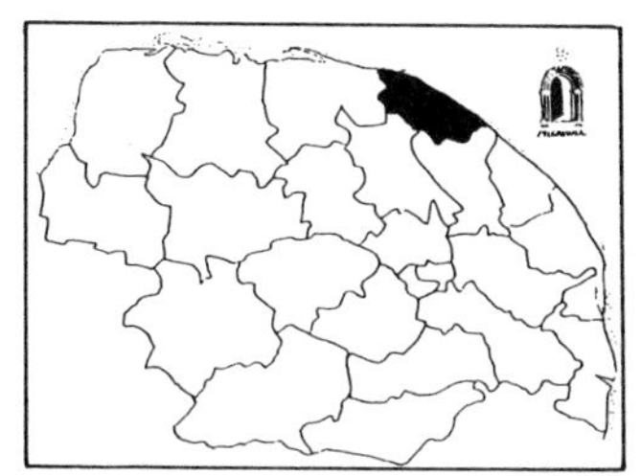

(A popular holiday and retirement area in the north east. The two towns in the deanery, Cromer and Sheringham, became fashionable in Edwardian days and still retain a genteel charm despite the crowds that flock to these popular resorts.)

Tuesday 19 September
Back on the road again to Mundesley Church, perched on the edge of the cliff top, for Communion and Bible study. The church is undistinguished, mostly rebuilt in 1910, the medieval church having been swallowed up by the sea many years before. This could be the fate of the present church in a few years' time because the cliffs are eroding steadily in this area of North Norfolk. Peter Allan, the long-haired leader of the Trunch Group, conducted me on a walkabout around the town visiting various shops. They all seemed to be run by hearty, jokey, incomers which I found a bit difficult at first though perhaps this was due to the problem of re-entry after the summer holiday. We went for lunch at the church hall with a group of old people who were, as always, interesting, friendly and grateful for all that the community was doing for them.

After a short stroll along Mundesley beach in a gale force wind but with patches of blue sky beginning to appear, Peter drove me to Sheringham where Anthony Lathe introduced me to the manager of Blyth & Wright's shop. This is quite an institution in Sheringham, an ironmongers which grew and grew and is one of the most comprehensive shops, outside a hypermarket, one could ever see: everything from lawnmowers to fine china, stacked higgledy-piggledy through this fascinating emporium run by two brothers with various sons, daughters and sons-in-law. Despite the end of the season, the shop was full of people who had wandered in and would be bound to buy something they had not anticipated because of the fascinating variety on the shelves.

After emerging, we walked towards the seafront, pausing at the clock tower, a local meeting place for old people and alcoholics, and I had a jovial conversation with two of the latter. A group of parishioners gathered on the pavement with whom we chatted and then we walked together to the seafront to see the fine new sea defences completed early this summer. By now the wind had whipped up to gale force but the sun was shining brightly as we walked along the front and back through ornamental gardens and suburban streets to the rectory, where I had a short break. We said evensong in the parish church with a group of about fifteen lay people, the service led by them, not Anthony. He faithfully says the offices of morning and evening prayer each day and is never alone in the church. In fact the lay people kept up the daily office throughout the long interregnum. I was much impressed. After evensong we returned to the vicarage for a light supper with Anthony and Carla Lathe, reliving the delights of Normandy where Carla had recently spent a week.

The first part of the evening was spent with the Crusaders at Felbrigg. Like the Crusaders I met in Thetford, this was certainly not a holy huddle but a lively group of youngsters from a local estate, many of the children from deprived homes with a high unemployment rate. It is always a surprise to encounter this deprivation in such idyllic rural surroundings but the hardship and the problems are very real, the children disorderly and often hard to control. I much admired the three women who ran the group, two of them in their late sixties and one younger woman in her thirties. After I had given out Crusader badges to those who had qualified by ten weeks' attendance, Keith James, the Rector, took me off to the Parsons Pleasure at Northrepps, a delightful pub where the clergy and their wives gathered for a pleasant social evening. I wonder if the publican realises that his hostelry shares the same name as the famous place on the river at Oxford where people used to bathe in the nude.

The two sons of a local vicar arrived early with their parents, and as the deanery clergy entered one by one I heard one boy say to his brother (they have recently arrived from a conservative parish in Wales) – 'Look, Harry, there's a woman priest! – and another!! – and another!!!' Many were asking me how I was enjoying my pilgrimage and among other things I boasted that, in the seven or eight weeks so far, I had not encountered a single day of rain, which was a pretty stupid thing to say in view of the weather forecast.

Wednesday 20 September

Half the morning was spent at the Belfry School in Overstrand, a church primary school which is very popular and has become overcrowded. Three-quarters of the school is accommodated in temporary classrooms, in some of which the present generation of children's parents were educated. The school was delightful, well disciplined and happy. All the children without exception were in school uniform and I enjoyed myself visiting the classes in turn and having a short assembly with them all.

I was collected mid-morning by Anthony Gurney who took me back through narrow country lanes which he explained to me were the old smugglers' routes from the coast. Smuggling apparently was the popular industry in this area in the eighteenth and nineteenth centuries. Many of the local villages had gangs which went in for smuggling, often on quite a large scale. Anthony told me that about 150 years ago the gang from Southrepps turned king's evidence against the gang from Northrepps and ever since there has been a bad relationship between the two villages. His son Chris had planned to take me up in a microlight aircraft but it was too windy and dangerous for flying. He showed me an ancient barn on one of his farms called 'Winspurs' farm because the spot on which we stood was where the gang from Northrepps honoured youngsters who had successfully made three smuggling trips.

Next we had coffee in a huge shed with Anthony's farm workers and with Patricia and his daughter, Sandra. It was a loud and friendly occasion as always with Anthony Gurney around. He knows and loves his farm workers and the feeling is obviously reciprocated. Afterwards I went to watch them sorting potatoes and visited his prize bull which he obtained from a friend for payment of a bottle of whisky. The friend felt the bull had outlived its usefulness but was so fond of him he did not want to send him for slaughter so sold him to Anthony for a token payment. The bull is still very active and was peacefully sitting among a group of beautiful young heifers.

After a drink at Manor Farm and a huge and delicious meal at the rectory, we drove to Felbrigg to a meeting of the Mothers' Union addressed by Anne Eames from Southrepps who gave an interesting talk about being a grandparent, which of course I enjoyed. After tea I went back to Roughton rectory and had three-quarters of an hour free to walk around the local fields.

I spent an hour with the Trunch ministry team, having a discussion followed by another enormous tea to which I could hardly do justice, and then we walked to Trunch Church for sung evensong and Bible study. About thirty or forty turned up for evensong but most left before the Bible study began. The Bible study was quite hard work, involving a difficult passage about the mission of the seventy-two but, as so often, I found my thoughts stimulated particularly by what the lay people said in discussion and so was able to reflect, I hope with some purpose, for fifteen minutes at the end.

Thursday 21 September

The wind on the north coast had dropped and it was a warm sunny day with the sea sparkling and beautiful as we drove out to West Runton for morning prayer and Bible study with clergy and parishioners. This was followed by a visit with two lay readers to a local old people's home for Communion and a chat with all the residents. Afterwards in the church hall I had lunch with an old people's luncheon club – masses of food, as always on such occasions, and for me a peripatetic meal. It was a rather more prosperous group of old people than I had encountered so far, finding myself sitting next to the daughter of a Harley Street surgeon on one side and the local Conservative agent and his wife on the other, together with the widow of a wing commander. They were nearly all incomers but on the men's table – the men always sit together – there was a lovely old Cromer fisherman with a blue jersey and windswept face.

Paul Atkins, the Rural Dean, took me back to his house for a short rest and then we drove to the splendid new Council Offices of the North Norfolk District Council on the edge of Cromer for another valuable talk with local government officers and the Chairman of the Council, Dick Broughton, whom I have known for years. The design of the offices is outstanding, the work of a local architect in competition with others, based on old Norfolk barns with a mass of indoor plants giving the place an unusual environment which those who work there clearly appreciate.

I was taken from the Council Offices by pony and trap to Cromer High School. The trap belonged to a retired sheep farmer from Walsingham who had kindly transported his pony and trap all the way for this short ride through the streets of Cromer. On the way he showed me a letter from some Somerset parishioners, Jean Batty and her husband, from Yeovil. The letter reminded me of the occasion many years ago when I heard Jean lead the intercessions at a Eucharist and I remember being struck not only by the beauty of her language but by the way in which she created a prayerful atmosphere. I spoke to her afterwards and asked if she was a lay reader. 'Good heavens, no,' she said. 'I wouldn't dream of such a thing.' But the letter said my remarks had caused her to think and eventually she went forward for training and was licensed as a reader in 1987 and has been very active since.

At the High School I met governors, parents and teachers and we had a good hour together, the teachers including the wife of Sidney Gilbert, Rector of Beeston Regis, and Peter Bower, better known to me as the wherry skipper. The Headmaster is new and a regular churchgoer which is in direct contrast to his predecessor who was rather hostile. David Hayden, the Vicar at Cromer, of course is delighted and I sensed a good rapport between him and the others there.

We walked back to the vicarage and I had a forty-five minute break which I used to walk to the cliff by the lighthouse at Cromer and down on to the beach. The walk back up was quite a slog and I felt overheated again, as I had in August, for the first time this week.

Cromer

Next stop was the splendid refurbished church hall in the middle of Cromer where we had a buffet with various representatives of the local community: lifeboatmen, Rotary, carnival committee, doctors and teachers. It was a worthwhile meeting and it was good that David, an evangelical, places so much importance on his ministry in the community at large.

Afterwards we walked to the magnificent parish church at Cromer, one of the finest in the county. Here we had a service with a packed congregation from the deanery to license David as Rural Dean and Elizabeth Bailey as a non-stipendiary curate, transferred from a group of rural parishes nearby. David preached an excellent sermon and I am sure will make a good rural dean.

Friday 22 September

Another interesting day began with morning prayer and a Bible study at the little parish church in the remote hamlet of Bradfield. For the first time this week there was sufficient time to have a longer discussion and a period of silent prayer at the end, which on previous visits people have valued. This was followed by a farm visit at Metton where Richard Harrison manages a National Trust farm previously owned by the owners of Felbrigg Hall. We had a tour of the open air pig farm, set on a hill where the soil is light and the drainage good, ideal for pigs. During the hot weather they had to make scrapes for them, filling them with water to keep the pigs cool because they cannot sweat. Helen, who is in charge of the pigs, I had met on one or two occasions previously this week because she helps with the Crusaders and is active in the local churches at Felbrigg and Roughton. Richard is not a regular churchgoer but interestingly asked if I would like to see the village church before I moved on and of course I agreed. We spent some time in the little church at Metton, of which he is clearly very proud. It was another instance of the way in which people genuinely love their church buildings and there is a real sense of commitment through that affection, which I believe goes deeper than mere attachment to historic bricks and mortar.

We had lunch at Roughton vicarage with Keith and Ginny James and one of the churchwardens, Arthur Hammond, formerly a senior policeman in the Metropolitan Police, and a chartered accountant. After lunch I took assembly at Roughton Primary School, where we had fun with the pilgrimage badges and herding a flock of infants with my crook.

The next two hours were spent with Andrew Lane at Sheringham. He was formerly an RAF chaplain and quite senior. When his wife died three or four years ago, leaving him with three teenage children to care for, he left the Royal Air Force and became a member of a slightly obscure religious community called 'The Society of St Luke', which is actually Dutch in origin. He lives by a simple rule in temporary vows which gives him an anchor and a context for his work as a non-stipendiary priest and he helps a great deal in the locality. He is only forty-six and I do not think, as I told him, that he should continue this kind of life indefinitely, but it is perhaps right until the youngest girl leaves home in three years' time, after which he really ought to tackle a sizeable parish because he is an able priest. He lent me a sweater for a walk up to the cliffs above Sheringham and down to the beach where I sketched for a while. After evening prayer together in the little chapel in his house and tea with Rebecca, his youngest, who is at school in Sheringham, the three of us talked together about what Andrew ought to do eventually. Rebecca, who is a bright and friendly child, spoke warmly of her father's preaching gifts and of how good he is with people.

'Wherever he goes,' she said, 'the old ladies flock to him and flirt with him outrageously.'

'That is not the kind of thing you ought to say to the Bishop,' said her father.

Next stop was the delightful and unusual little church at Thorpe Market, built 200 years ago. Inside was a huge group of young people called 'The Village Folk' who started as a group of young people wanting to sing together. It has grown and gradually in recent years become involved much more in the church where they organise a monthly service. The excellent leaders told me that most of the children come from homes which are deprived in one way or another, many of them with single parents. We had a singsong for half an hour and then I was taken off to another group of young people, the

Scouts and Cubs at West Runton.

There were more than sixty which is amazing, given the size of the community. There were a large number of adult helpers, and teenagers who were Rover Scouts, preparing eventually to take over leadership themselves. They had organised a barbecue for the deanery synod, which was not just sausages and beefburgers but kebabs, smoked mackerel and other delicacies. The Cubs spent their time cooking 'twists', which consisted of flour and water twisted round a stick and warmed before pouring jam into the hole made by the spike. I didn't try them but the Cubs obviously found them delicious. There are a number of mentally handicapped Scouts of all ages in this group and it was wonderful to see the way in which they were cared for by the others in a quite natural way. Afterwards the Scout Leader, himself a member of this same troop since becoming a Cub fifty years ago, told me that many troops will not accept the mentally handicapped because they find them disruptive. He said in Runton they have been a positive benefit; I can see why because they not only make a contribution themselves, in their own right, but create an atmosphere of caring through which those youngsters will learn a great deal.

The evening ended with an impromptu epilogue led by David Pierce, the curate of Cromer, in his broad Ulster accent. It was extremely well done, likening the attitude of Jews to Samaritans to that of Norwich City supporters' attitude to Ipswich Town fans. So ended a varied and fulfilling day, and we drove home through a shower of rain but so far not a drop has fallen on me.

Saturday 23 September

Today we installed Stephen Platten as the new Dean of Norwich in a splendid service devised (perhaps a little over-devised) by Michael Perham. The cathedral was full of representatives of Church and community, and Stephen preached about his commitment to cathedral, diocese and local community. During his predecessor's term of office, because he was never really happy after leaving Yorkshire, the cathedral's influence rather shrank and counted for little either in the diocese, city or county at large, but I think Stephen will energetically change all that. He is very definitely a leader and his relative inexperience will doubtless lead to mistakes but at the heart there is a spirituality which will enable him, I trust, to listen and learn, and we all have great hopes for the future of the cathedral in the next few years.

The last part of the service was conducted by me from the ancient throne behind the altar, which I am reluctant to ascend on a frequent basis but it was right today. Stephen mounted the steps, knelt in front of me as I anointed and blessed him using the words of the blessing sung by the choir as I ascended to the throne at my enthronement. It is also the blessing traditionally used by Franciscans and said to have been used first of all by St

Francis himself as he blessed his brother Leo who became his special companion. The notes attached to the service at Stephen's request stated that this blessing was intended as a symbol of the close friendship that should exist between a dean and bishop. Although there is no comparison between me and Francis, I hope that something of that same closeness and partnership in ministry will in time develop.

The day was warm and afterwards the bishops and their wives, together with John Holroyd and Hector McLean and their wives (Prime Minister's and Archbishops' Selection Secretaries), came back to the house for drinks on the terrace.

Sunday 24 September

We set off in dull, cool weather which promised rain, for Sidestrand Church where I celebrated Communion and afterwards the rain began in earnest as I drove to Beeston Regis for their harvest festival. Coincidentally this church also celebrates its 900th anniversary next year and the congregation was enhanced by the presence of pupils from Beeston Hall Preparatory School nearby. I spoke informally, mostly to the children, and afterwards one of the girls said, 'That was a brilliant speech' – a heartening if unecclesiastical comment. I then went for lunch at the rectory with Sidney and Gill Gilbert. The rain eased after lunch sufficiently to allow me to have a short walk along a country path to put some thoughts together for the afternoon service.

At Sheringham we had a Taizé style service, well attended by clergy and laity from throughout the deanery, and afterwards a cup of tea in the church before I left at 5 o'clock. At the service I met a girl from Thornage Hall, the community for the mentally handicapped I had visited some weeks ago. I told her to give my love to all my friends at Thornage. I heard later that she could hardly wait to give my greetings, and told them, 'The Pope sends his love to you all.'

11

Lothingland

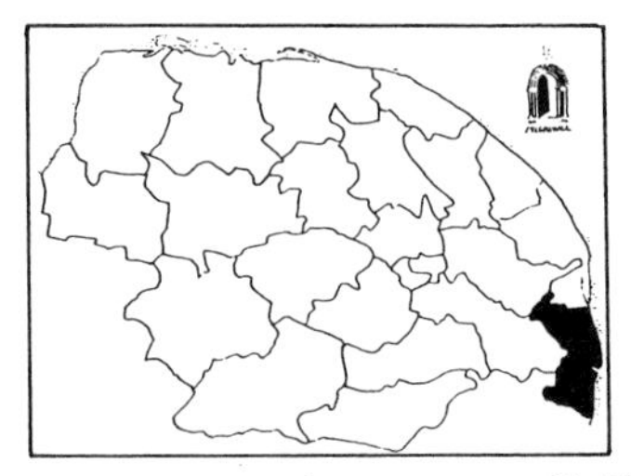

(This deanery, centred on Lowestoft, is in Suffolk. When the county was removed from Norwich to form the new Diocese of St Edmundsbury and Ipswich in 1914, this deanery refused to move. Logic might argue that it should be joined ecclesiastically with the rest of Suffolk, but loyalties to Norwich diocese and Norwich City football club remain strong.)

Tuesday 3 October

A day of contrast began at Somerleyton rectory, where I was decanted from the comfortable Audi into Jonathan Riviere's old Skoda for the journey through his rural parishes to Blundeston, where Communion was attended by a large group of parishioners. The six churches of this Group contain no less than five round tower churches in which Jonathan delights and I have no doubt his ministry is much appreciated. Among the congregation, as I expected, was Bill Somerleyton, a landowner who is most supportive of the church in his domain.

We then took Communion to two parishioners, one of them a missionary doctor aged ninety-six who had spent many years in India and Africa. She was the daughter of a Lancashire coalminer and left school at the age of twelve to work in a mill, later sorting coal because she preferred working out of doors, even though the air was full of coal dust. By dint of tremendous perseverance, various scholarships and inspiring teachers, she eventually qualified and fulfilled her childhood dream to be a missionary. A remarkable old lady, with all her marbles intact and a great talker.

At Gisleham Middle School there was an old people's lunch. This is a new venture, supported by the school and a local charity, where every week in term time old people have lunch with a large group of children, to their mutual benefit. I didn't really fancy the school dinner and was glad of the excuse to move from table to table so that people didn't notice how little I ate.

After lunch we visited another delightful old man, housebound after a stroke, who flies a Union Jack from his garden flagstaff and collects old farm implements, among them an ancient eel catcher, hanging by his front door and looking like a thick grass rake. The men who went out to catch eels used to plunge their eel catchers in the mud until they caught an eel which had mistaken it for reeds around which eels like to curl themselves.

A walk on the beach at Kessingland was rather bleak, with dark clouds threatening after a lovely autumn morning. I sat in the lee of an old boat and sketched for an hour before returning to the rectory where John Hunt took me on more visits to people's homes. Kessingland is not an easy village. There have been divisions for a century and more between the fishermen at one end and the farmers at the other. Still there are separate pubs used by each community and although retired people have moved in, and there is a large council estate, here, as always in Norfolk villages, ancient divisions tend to be inherited for generations. But at tea in the rectory I met a friendly group of parishioners and afterwards at evening prayer in the parish church a very good embryo ministry team who have prayed together for a year and are supporting Joan, an LNSM candidate, and another woman who is to become a reader. The difficulties are real, but John has achieved more than he realises and there are some fine people in the church.

We drove to Christ Church, held up for a while by the raised bridge in the middle of Lowestoft as a large oil rig service ship passed through. In the church centre at Christ Church we had sandwiches and tea and met a group of leading parishioners, not all of whom I found easy. We had some lively conversation, however, about infant baptism and Phil Moon, the Vicar, was glad I brought it up because he has been trying to persuade some of his senior parishioners to have their children baptised – they don't believe in infant baptism.

At 7.30 a large number of parishioners arrived for their weekly prayer meeting. This included a short address by Phil Moon about the passage for the day, but there was no discussion. There was more than an hour of extempore prayer led by two lay people with the use of a flip chart and headlines from the daily papers. Some of the prayer was good and articulate and occasionally even moving, but of the fifty or so people present I reckon only six or eight actually opened their mouths and there was a fair amount of informing God about the details of people's illnesses or what was in the news. I felt it was much more like a godly conversation than prayer as I understand it, but it is part of their tradition and perfectly legitimate. Certainly the people turned up in considerable numbers. I was given (a little reluctantly, I felt) the last twenty minutes and led them into silence which I think was strange for many of them.

At coffee afterwards a churchwarden and another parishioner tackled me about a curate, saying that a church as successful and large as theirs really deserved a curate. I pointed out the difficulties as patiently as I could but I was uncomfortable with their self-satisfaction. However, I have every confidence in Phil Moon, who is a good man, but he will need all his leadership skills to cope with this lively and self-confident community who have a tradition of independence close to congregationalism.

Wednesday 4 October

On our way to Lowestoft we called at the hospital in Ditchingham to visit Hugh Blackburne, the former Bishop of Thetford, who has been ill for some time and is now very frail indeed. He was opening letters when I got there, one of them a card from former parishioners, and it was lovely to hear him reminiscing briefly about some of the names he read to himself. We talked for a little while and after a blessing I left him rather sleepy.

Martin Gray, the Vicar of St Margaret's, led us on a marathon tour of Northfields First School, visiting all nine classes in turn. It was perhaps made more tiring because the children were clearly not prepared for the visit and most hadn't a clue who I was, so one had to make the running each time. Most impressive were the two remedial classes where they specialise in teaching children with learning difficulties. They were small classes, led by teachers who are dedicated and good at their work, and the children very responsive.

This was followed by another old people's lunch, this time at Harleston House which is run by the Church Army. This was different to other such lunches and visits to old people's homes for two reasons: the food was excellent and not excessive and of all the old people's homes I have visited this was the happiest, with a group of twenty-five very contented people. It is well run by John Worsfold, a former Franciscan friar, and Chris, the Matron, both of them large in body and spirit. After lunch, to my surprise, I was presented with gifts – a Church Army plate commemorating fifty years' patronage by the Queen Mother and a framed sermon with a brass plate. It was in fact the sermon preached at my consecration at St Paul's on St Luke's Day, 1977, by Father Michael, SSF. The Warden, John, had obviously done some research and knowing Michael well from his days as a Franciscan had obtained a copy of the sermon which he thoughtfully framed. It was a moving and marvellous gift and I told them some of the stories surrounding the consecration and particularly the interpretation of the ring. Father Michael had preached on the text from the story of the prodigal son, including the words 'put a ring on his finger' and ever since that day I have always regarded the bishop's ring as a sign of the prodigal's ring, that is, of the love and forgiveness of God. It was a happy time and afterwards I visited an old lady dying upstairs. A marvellous feature of this place is that people can come here and know they can remain until they die. The care in every sense is of very high quality and it was interesting that a number of people talked to me about this place as 'my home', and meant it.

We walked back to St Margaret's Church where we met the large parent and toddler group in the hall which is run by Pauline Gray and a group of helpers and is providing a much needed service to young mothers in the area. The local Press came to take photographs but children less than two years old are not always co-operative and I don't know whether any will be satisfactory, unless they are happy with a photograph of a child who took one look at me and yelled. A former churchwarden was there, a grandfather, whose grandchildren were in the group. He had made easels for them and showed me how to make them which I must do one day. He is a carpenter and made proper joints but showed me how to take short cuts.

After three and a half hours' solid talking I was ready for a bit of silence and Steven (who is driving me this week) dropped me near the promenade where I walked its windswept length with light rain driving horizontally. Eventually I found a deserted shelter and sat sketching for a while before returning to St Margaret's for the onward journey to Lowestoft Hospital where Janet Stewart, wife of Will, the Rural Dean, is chaplain. The future of the hospital is in doubt, with Trusts and various authorities in conflict, and we listened to the staff express their anxieties. The hospital itself is excellent and why they want to muck around with it I cannot think. I talked to a large proportion of the patients in various stages of illness or old age. I blessed some and gave prayer cards to everyone. They were well received except by one old lady who, I noticed out of the corner of my eye, quickly tore hers to shreds which was rather sad.

Philip Meader, the Vicar of St Andrews, came to meet us at the hospital and we walked together to his vicarage chatting on the way to parishioners. He is an excellent parish priest who knows his people well and they clearly love him, both churchgoers and non-churchgoers alike. On the way he asked me how I managed to keep going, given the programmes that I was undertaking, and wasn't I completely exhausted? I told him the truth that although it is physically tiring the pilgrimage is always spiritually refreshing and you can recover from physical tiredness quite quickly. The evening with his parishioners in the hall attached to his church proved a perfect example of what I meant. They were warmly welcoming and presented me with an icon painted by Philip, and a basket of flowers for Betty. They laid on a huge supper with a magnificent cake, decorated with the logo of the pilgrimage, and the evening was the best example of parish fellowship one could wish for. It is interesting that in Lowestoft I have met more people who are born and bred in the community than in any other place I have visited so far. Two

Plate 1 Reedham

Plate 2 River Yare

Plate 3   Breydon Water

Plate 4   East Bilney

Plate 5 Newton

Plate 6 Worthing

Plate 7 Larling

Plate 8 Longham

Plate 9 Rougham

Plate 10 Gaywood Rectory

Plate 11 Near Burnham Norton

Plate 12 Whissonsett

Plate 13 Horsey

Plate 14 Attleborough Rectory

Plate 15 Ranworth Vicarage

Plate 16 Horning

Plate 17 Bacton

Plate 18 Honing Hall

Plate 19 Hassingham

Plate 20 Mundesley

Plate 21 Kessingland

Plate 22 Kessingland

Plate 23 Oulton Broad

Plate 24 North Creake

Plate 25 Great Ryburgh

Plate 26 Near Brooke

Plate 27 Caston

Plate 28 Rowley Farm Hilborough

Plate 29 Near Wheatacre

Plate 30 Bergh Apton

Plate 31 Near Docking

Plate 32 Ingoldisthorpe

or three people this evening live still in the same street in which they were born. Sadly, growing unemployment in the area may mean more emigration because Lowestoft no longer enjoys the modest prosperity that has been a feature of this town for a long time.

On the way home we called at the James Paget Hospital in Gorleston and I went to see Jim Liddon, a retired priest who is dying. His wife Iris was there and we talked and prayed a while and then I left for home. On the way out of the hospital I walked the confusing length of corridors with an old man and his daughter. He put me right when I lost my way and we walked on together and started talking. He had been visiting his wife, who had had a stroke. I sympathised and told him who I was.

'I thought you were a Roman Catholic,' he said, looking at my purple cassock.

'No, I'm Church of England, the Bishop of Norwich,' I said.

'Oh, that's all right then,' he said rather enigmatically, and I told him what I was doing and gave him a prayer card before saying a friendly farewell. If this had been an ordinary visit to a hospital on an ordinary day, I don't think I would have engaged him in conversation, or pressed a prayer card on him. I suppose one is now so used to making conversation with strangers, and with that particular adrenalin still flowing it seemed the natural thing to do. Perhaps it is something I should do more often,

Thursday 5 October

We made our first rail journey today, travelling from Norwich station to Lowestoft. I sat in the front with the driver, which was a marvellous treat, and they explained the technicalities to me as we rode through lovely countryside across the marshes beside rivers in a perfect morning with cloudless skies. From the station in Lowestoft we drove to Carlton Colville where we had a very informal Communion service in the hall. This is a weekly celebration attended by about twenty people, with a simple but rather odd, laid-back sort of liturgy devised by a community in Northampton.

After Communion I visited a young family nearby who have fairly recently become involved in the life of the church, and we sat in warm sunshine in the back garden drinking coffee and talking. After several jobs the husband is now doing part-time work selling carpets from his garage (he used to work in a department store) and giving instruction on first aid because he is a qualified St John Ambulance instructor. It illustrated the uncertainty of life for many people these days who are in and out of work. For a time, he told me, he and his wife had swapped roles. He enjoyed being a house husband for a couple of years but was glad to be back to being the breadwinner again.

Alan Smith then took me on a tour of his parish. The small village of Carlton Colville with its round tower church has grown out of all proportion and now numbers nearly 10,000 inhabitants, mostly in new housing in serried ranks unrelated to any centre, without shops or facilities and certainly with very little community feel. Alan took me to two other wonderful churches: Rushmere, once in danger of redundancy but lovingly restored by the sixty parishioners, and Mutford, another round-towered gem – common in this part of Suffolk and south Norfolk. We returned for lunch at the rectory with two parishioners from Mutford and then I had a walk and spent a while sketching under an oak tree – in bright sunshine, in contrast to yesterday.

On my return I was confronted by the sight of a wonderful 1928 Lagonda open tourer, driven by Hamish (Alan's next door neighbour). Alan and Steven sat in the back and we had an enjoyable ride with the wind blowing through our hair through the streets of Lowestoft to Kirkley. I said how glad I was that we weren't doing this yesterday in the rain but Hamish claimed that if you drove at more than thirty miles an hour you wouldn't get wet. I took him at his word. Reluctantly disembarking, we were met by John Eyre at a parishioner's house in Kirkley for a meeting of their bereavement group. This consists of a number of bereaved people, mostly widows, with one widower. They meet once a month to talk and be together, occasionally having outings. They sometimes talk about their personal problems but not always, I gather. This afternoon there was an interesting discussion about the nature of bereavement. There were some tears and much laughter, mostly provided by the widower's delightfully eccentric, elderly girlfriend who, wearing a hat, with blonde hair, painted fingernails and much made up, from time to time launched into hilarious stories about her adventures in London and her childhood in Lowestoft.

After tea and sticky buns, we drove to the hospital at Gorleston. We had received a message during the day that one of Tim Thompson's parishioners at Caister, Richard Soanes, whom I had met on my visit in July, was dying and wanted to be confirmed. Tim and Sue Thompson met us at the hospital, together with all the equipment needed for confirming and Holy Communion, and they brought along with them the two little daughters of Richard and Julia Soanes: Katie, a very friendly child who held my hand, and her rather more reserved sister Lizzie. Katie was the 'Rainbow' from the Caister lifeboat service who presented me with a teddy bear. Richard was sitting beside his bed but looking very ill, with apparently most of his stomach now removed in addition to all his other troubles. Poor man. He managed to express his gladness that we had come and we had a very simple and moving service of confirmation, first Communion and anointing. We left them quite soon, with Tim and Sue Thompson, and the little girls taking it in turns to carry my staff. It was all very sad but they are well cared for and although they have few relatives alive, I believe the community at Caister will be very supportive of Julia and the children when the time comes.

We drove across the deanery to Pakefield where we had supper with Bob and Christine Baker and two of their three boys. We saw the rabbit in the garden, who misbehaved when Betty and I visited them in the summer. I think he is probably still not house-trained. They talked about their holiday, which begins on Sunday, when they are to visit Disneyland in Florida.

After supper we walked through the old village of Pakefield to the house of David Porter, the local MP, and had half an hour's talk with him in his study. He told us about his recent conversion – having been brought up in the Church, he had for many years drifted away, and had been brought to faith quite suddenly by a rather dramatic episode in which he had felt ill and near to death when on holiday. His story was simply told, matter of fact, and was all the more impressive for that. He is a good man, a local person born and bred in Lowestoft, who now worships at a free Evangelical church to which his wife has belonged for some years. He and Bob have struck up a friendship and see each other regularly.

We then walked back to the church hall at Pakefield for a Bible study, led by a reader. On my persuasion they agreed, a little reluctantly I felt, to study in groups rather than in a large gathering of twenty-five, and the Bible study went reasonably well. I never feel these evangelical parishes wrestle with the text as effectively as some unsophisticated country congregations have done in other places on the pilgrimage. Is it to do with the risk of letting lay people have their head, unsupervised? But maybe it was the difficulty of the text, and also I was really tired by now, and glad to spend the last twenty minutes leading them into silence before we drove home at the end of a long day full of varied experiences.

Friday 6 October

A day of easier pace began with a Holy Communion, on the Feast of William Tyndale, in the Victorian church of St Margaret's at Hopton which contains an interesting chapel dedicated to Julian of Norwich with some modern abstract stained glass. After chatting to parishioners, we went to Hopton First School. In Suffolk they have first schools, middle schools and secondary schools so the oldest children in this school are seven. We had a good harvest thanksgiving, in the middle of which I told them about the pilgrimage and herded a few five-year-old sheep around the room.

At a parishioner's house there was Bible study preceded by a house Communion. It was a good session led by John Simpson, the parish priest, who has recently joined us from the United Reformed Church and is already making his mark in the diocese, astonishingly being appointed Chairman of the House of Clergy in the diocesan synod in his first year. Afterwards we had a soup and cheese lunch, not as austere as it sounds, with delicious home-made soup and home-baked rolls.

After a brief stop at the vicarage, we moved to a group of almshouses where a small marquee had been erected because the weather was poor, and there I opened four new bungalows in this sheltered housing complex, and visited each one, blessing the houses and admiring the facilities. After cake and wine, we returned to the vicarage for a long break, which enabled me to go for a walk and sit in the lee of a large rock on Corton beach putting some thoughts together for tomorrow's service at Oulton Broad.

We drove to Gunton rectory and met the new incumbent, John Fairbairn and his wife Sue, where we had supper together. John worked first as an engineer, then as a teacher. When the call to the ministry came, he was turned down by his first Selection Conference, which he now regards as a positive experience because up until then his life had been straightforward and successful – the feeling of disappointment and failure, he said, had helped him grow. He has recently come from a working class parish in north London to which he and Sue were very committed, and they talked with some insight about their experiences. He is a humble and godly man and she is very lively and quite outspoken. I think they will do well in this parish.

Afterwards we went to the multipurpose church of St Benedict for a Bible study led by Alan Chamberlain, an LNSM candidate, to which lay people from some of the other parishes in the North Lowestoft Association came. It proved to be the best Bible study of the week, though the discussion in groups at the end was rather dominated by a strong lady who had a go at Church leadership. I realised that there was hidden agenda and tried to be reasonably diplomatic about my response without letting her have her own way entirely. But that apart it was a rewarding and lively evening, John Fairbairn expressing surprise at its liveliness.

Jim Liddon died today. He had been the much loved Vicar of Gunton many years ago and also Rural Dean of Lothingland.

Saturday 7 October

The first event today was the opening of the new church centre at St Mark's, Oulton Broad. The church was always nondescript, a late Victorian building on the main road, and the whole site looked tatty. But the addition of hall, office, kitchen and meeting room has transformed the site into an attractive showpiece which now presents a pleasant aspect and, from the Broad opposite, a notable landmark. The church was packed, and after a good liturgy there was a huge bunfight in the hall with a speech from Will Stewart thanking everyone. It has been an amazing achievement, springing from his vision ten years ago, and in the process raising £250,000 within a parish which is not at all well-heeled. His leadership, both of the parish and deanery, has been outstanding.

During the bunfight, a man gave me a pectoral cross made of a purple wood from Latin America. He had been asked by Will some time ago to make some crosses for a mission. Until then he had not been a churchgoer, but that request, and the experience of making crosses, had drawn him into regular commitment.

After a break in the park by Oulton Broad, where yachts were racing, we went by motor launch to the opposite side and joined parishioners from St Michael's parish led by their priest, Robin Pritchard. Robin is not unlike John Fairbairn, a definite evangelical, but modest, quiet, and I sense a very effective parish priest. We walked to the St Michael's Institute (a kind of church hall) where we had tea, and then a question and answer session followed by compline, which included a Bible study, while the children in another room watched a video of *The Lion King*. This was a good end to an interesting and encouraging day.

Sunday 8 October

I was rather disappointed that the programme today had not included a deanery service, which normally makes a fitting climax to the week, but I suppose the service at St Mark's yesterday counted as a deanery occasion when people came from most parishes to celebrate the opening of the church centre. In the event, the day turned out to be enjoyable and, for me, undemanding.

A family service at Pakefield was attended by Scouts, Guides, Brownies, Cubs and Beavers (but no Rainbows). It was the best kind of family service, with imaginative use of overhead projectors and a good illustrated sermon from Bob Baker. His illustrations and ideas were excellent but as I know from trying to do watercolours, he made the mistake of going on just a bit too long and trying to put in just too much detail. He could have stopped after about eight minutes instead of fifteen minutes and it would have been perfect. Afterwards we had lunch in the church hall, a friendly all-age meal, and I wandered around chatting to various people. Again I noticed the phenomenon that has been a feature of this week, that is, the number of people who have lived in this area all their lives, and those who have come to live here have usually had some connection, a wife or husband having been born here. I asked one woman at Pakefield if she was local.

'Certainly not,' she said, 'I come from Carlton Colville' (approximately one and a half miles away).

After lunch I sketched on the beach in blazing sunshine like midsummer – what a contrast of weather we have had this week. Afterwards Steven and I drove to Oulton Community Church, a prefabricated building on a housing estate, an ecumenical church shared between Methodists and Anglicans. Trevor Riess recently left here to go to St Margaret's, Gorleston, and now the Methodists are led by Valerie, a probationary Methodist minister in her early sixties, who is quite splendid, and we had a marvellous harvest service. At first it looked as if it was going to be a Methodist hymn sandwich, but it turned out to be much more imaginative and I was impressed with the way Valerie dealt with obstreperous children, treating them like a grandmother and keeping everything in order in a very relaxed way. She will be good value.

Afterwards there was a great harvest tea laid out in the hall, which looked as if it would go on for a long time. Having recently had an enormous lunch at Pakefield I did a circulation, chatting to small groups at various parts of the table and after half an hour we took our leave. I can't remember how many harvest festivals I've been to in the last two pilgrimage visits. I hope that by the time I'm on the road again the harvest season will be over because I'm becoming saturated with ploughing the fields and scattering.

Interlude

Friday 13 October

In the morning I visited Simon, the twenty-one-year-old son of Chris and Mollie Walter (Chris is a curate in Fakenham), who is in Priscilla Bacon Lodge, a hospice in Norwich. Simon has fought a critical form of lymphatic cancer for two years, very bravely, but he is now in the last stages. He was at Taizé with us earlier in the year, and courageously undertook a long cycle ride throughout England during a remission. He has a strong faith and is an inspiration to all who visit him.

I then travelled to London for a meeting between a few Church Commissioners and the Archbishop of Canterbury to discuss the Turnbull Commission report. In general it is a good report and makes sensible suggestions about the central administration of the Church, but is unlikely to affect the parishes much in a direct way.

Lambeth Palace

On my return in the early evening there was a message to say that Simon was much worse and so I went to see him again. In the morning he had recognised me, but was now in a coma. So with his parents and brother John present, I prayed the Commendation ('Go forth upon thy journey from this world, O Christian soul . . .'), and blessed the others in the room. Simon died a couple of hours later.

Saturday 14 October

Today there was a memorial service for Bill Williams in Fitzwilliam College Chapel. Bill had died aged ninety-four at his home in Appin. He was a much loved don at Fitzwilliam during its formative years and had been a good friend to me when I was chaplain there in the sixties. He was both critical and kind, always huffing and puffing about modern youth, but there was great mutual affection between him and his pupils. I remember once waiting to say Grace at high table when Bill walked to his place. Passing behind me, he pressed half a crown into my hand.

'What's that for?' I asked out of the corner of my mouth.

'Get your hair cut,' he replied.

Sunday 15 October

This was a very sad day. Our beloved sixteen-year-old springer, Carrie, died. She had a stroke in the morning, and could no longer walk properly, but still she wagged her tail – cheerful as always. However, we realised this was the end, and we had to take her to the vet. Betty, Lucy and I took her and stayed with her while the nice lady vet gave her the injection. Her heart had been bad for two or three years, and I suppose it was a small miracle that she lived as long as she did. But she was a precious member of the family, especially close to Betty, but greatly loved by us all. Tearfully we took her home and buried her at the top of the slope under the great plane tree near the garden room door, a favourite spot of hers. She was born on a hillside in the Quantocks in Somerset, and so a little hill was an appropriate resting place.

Later in the day we drove to London, because I am on duty in the Lords next week.

On this same day we heard that Bishop Hugh Blackburne had died. He had been growing weaker in recent months, having had a serious heart attack a few years ago. He was the founder of the Hilborough Group thirty years ago, and was deeply saddened by recent events, deploring the behaviour of those who sought to divide the Group. Hugh was a gifted and greatly loved priest, and an expert sailor and yachtsman. After the war, he and his wife Freda bought a derelict windmill for £210 and converted it themselves into a holiday home for their large family. He and Freda were great birdwatchers (in fact, Freda introduced him to the hobby) and in their small house in Swaffham, as in all their houses, the bird table was a focal point. When I visited Freda on my return from London she showed me the water pistol Hugh kept by him to 'shoot' starlings who kept the smaller birds away.

I talked to Tony Foottit on the phone from London in the evening and we spoke about the recent deaths of people we all knew. Tony said, 'It's good to think that Simon and Hugh and Carrie will all be arriving in heaven together. I think they'll get on well, don't you?'

Monday 16 October

Today tributes were paid in the Lords to Lord Home, who died recently, and I gave the tribute for the bishops. By chance I had met him years ago at the home of Desirée Butterwick, a Beaconsfield parishioner, who had been a friend of his from childhood, and so I was able to make a personal comment or two. I ended by saying, 'None can doubt that passing from this life he earned that simplest and noblest of all accolades, "Well done, thou good and faithful servant."' It was an apt epitaph for all those who have died during these last few poignant days.

Later in the day we heard that the Industrial Tribunal in Norwich had ruled that a priest was not an employed person. This ruling was a great relief, not just to us but to the Church at large. If clergy were deemed employed persons, it would have changed the Church considerably. Immediately we would have had to give contracts of employment, which would not be to the advantage of the clergy. In order to protect the Church, an essential clause would certainly be to the effect that if a clergy man or woman divorced, their employment could cease. Thank goodness we do not have to go down that road – yet.

Thursday 19 October

Today our annual staff outing was in London. Steven brought Mel Richardson, Vanessa and David Cole, David and Jenny Stone, Simon and Fiona Gaches, John and Una Palmer and Joan Lambert to London by train. We had a conducted tour of the Houses of Lords and Commons, then walked over Westminster Bridge to Lambeth Palace where we saw parts of the palace and walked in the garden. After lunch at Church House, the party returned to the Lords Gallery for Questions, during which I asked a supplementary about VAT on church buildings. (As usual the minister failed to give a straight answer.) The weather was fine, all the arrangements went smoothly, and everyone much enjoyed the day together.

Monday 23 October

In a packed cathedral this afternoon we had Hugh Blackburne's funeral and memorial service. Hugh had been brought to Norfolk by Launcelot Fleming to begin the Hilborough Group, one of the first of Launcelot's revolutionary new group ministries – famous in their day. Later he became Vicar of Ranworth and the first Chaplain to the Broads. I found a letter in Hugh's file, replying to a pious complaint that American visitors to the Norfolk 'Broads' would misunderstand and the title should be changed. 'I also enjoy watching birds,' Hugh replied, ' – do you think I should rephrase that?'

He was only Bishop of Thetford for a relatively short time, but became, as he was throughout his priesthood, a loving and much loved model of that ministry, too.

12

Burnham and Walsingham

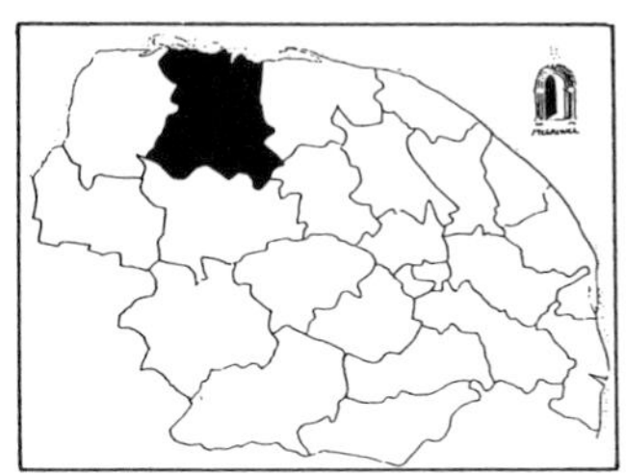

(A large rural area stretching from the market town of Fakenham through the famous pilgrimage village of Little Walsingham to the yachting and holiday areas of North Norfolk.)

Tuesday 24 October

Alan Bell, the Rural Dean, drove me from Fakenham to Wells where we arrived ahead of schedule and had coffee with Pat King, one of the churchwardens of Walsingham, who told us the results of the General Synod elections. These were mostly predictable. The only difference was that Martin Smith, the local representative of 'Forward in Faith', replaced Hilary Wakeman in the House of Clergy by one vote. I think it is a great pity that we have not got more clergy seats because Hilary will be a sad loss. In five years' time when we have new elections we should qualify for one extra clergy seat because the rate at which men and women are coming forward for LNSM and NSM means that we should have considerably more clergy by then – about fifty, we have calculated.

We rode on the narrow gauge railway from Walsingham to Wells, a delightful journey in an open carriage in warm sunshine. I chatted to Matthew Hickling, a young reporter from the *EDP*, the son of a clergyman and a history graduate from Pembroke, Cambridge. The journey was over all too soon and William Sayer met us and drove me to the Cottage Hospital. I met staff, patients and members of the Friends' Committee, somewhat anxious because the hospital may be under threat yet again. They have so far fought off all attempts at closure and I hope they succeed again because these

Wells Rectory

small local hospitals are a great boon to rural communities. We then moved next door to Heritage House, a day centre for old people, and chatted to the twenty or thirty who had come for a day of relaxation, baths, treatment for minor ailments, good food and company. They were a cheerful lot, nearly all of them genuine locals.

William drove me back to the rectory for a short break. I strolled in his acre of garden and visited his labrador puppies, recently weaned, and was tempted to make an offer for one of them but resisted, wisely I think. We then moved to the parish church for a buffet lunch with the chapter, lay readers and retired clergy. The active clergy are outnumbered by the retireds in this deanery, which sometimes causes a problem for the chapter. This time they split into two. I spent an hour talking with the large group about prayer and leading a period of silent prayer, after which the retireds were politely asked to leave and I had another hour and more with the active clergy, discussing a range of issues, particularly focusing on the tensions they felt between stipendiary and non-stipendiary clergy. There is a sense of (quite unnecessary) threat at the advent of LNSMs, and I did my best to calm their fears and talk positively about the long-term vocation of the stipendiary priest. Feelings among clergy vary across the diocese. This group has had as yet no personal experience of LNSM vocations because so far most are coming from town parishes. But it was a good, friendly and open discussion among people who trust one another, although the differences between such people as Alan Bell, a middle-of-the-road liberal, and Keith Haydon, the new Vicar of Walsingham, were obvious.

At Bishop Ingle House I met the Warden and her husband and talked for a while about its closure, which will happen soon. This has been a good holiday place for clergy for many years but can no longer keep going during the winter and is not as popular as it used to be, partly perhaps because nowadays two incomes are often coming into a clergy household and if so they can afford holidays more easily than in the past.

Afterwards we drove to Bill and Betty Tipler's home in a suburb of Wells, from where I went for a brief walk along the quay at Wells. By now a gale force wind was blowing and it began to get quite chilly, too cold to walk far. I did not want to go back to the house and talk for an hour before supper so I went into a seafront café for a cup of coffee which tasted like dishwater. The place had an end-of-season feel with labels peeling off windows and the front of the ice-cream refrigerator, and with the chairs and tables needing a lick of paint. It was one of those cafés where men keep their hats on so I sat in my old Barbour and cloth cap sketching the back of a becapped old age pensioner in front of me.

Back at Bill and Betty's house, a group of parishioners had gathered for supper – the group had deliberately been chosen to be representative of the congregation rather than just officeholders, which was thoughtful, and we had a good time together. Just before I left, their grandchildren, May and Grace, with their parents, arrived from Manchester for half term. I gave a badge to Grace, aged two, but four-year-old May refused to take the badge,

Café in Wells

politely saying, 'No, thanks.' Her father explained that she had been taught not to accept gifts from strange men.

The Bible study in Fakenham was led (I learned later – just as well I didn't know beforehand) by a lady who has a first class degree in theology. It was an excellent introduction, as one might expect, and a very good Bible study with about twenty-five people present. Many of the group had been studying St Luke from the beginning of the pilgrimage and there were some intelligent and imaginative comments on the text for today.

It has been a good first day of this week of pilgrimage with people, both clergy and laity, immensely friendly and welcoming. A full gale was now blowing, southerly, so not too cold, but John drove home more slowly than usual because the gusts were quite dangerous with debris flying off the trees.

Wednesday 25 October

The day began with an interesting prayer group at a parishioner's house in Sculthorpe – interesting because it was a benefice prayer group and most of the prayers concerned the benefice itself and the people in it. This was another example, among an increasing number I am encountering, of benefice identity, where parishes are seeing the need to work with and for each other. The group was very mixed and included a couple recently confirmed who had unusually transferred from a Pentecostal church.

One lady prayed modestly, 'Let there be just a tiny spark of life in North Creake – please, God.'

The Pentecostalist lady immediately continued, 'Coming in behind Mary's prayer, let there be a great outpouring of the Spirit upon the congregation at North Creake.'

Perhaps we should expect great things but Mary's modest prayer is more likely to be answered, I think. After this I walked next door to the church school where, during half term, a group of children, again from the benefice, meet together for games, crafts and Christian instruction, an excellent enterprise staffed by a number of women including, heroically, two schoolteachers giving up part of their half term.

At Fakenham I had lunch with the Rotary Club, a friendly gathering in the Crown Hotel, now run by a Frenchman – an enormous meal with a whole chicken breast each and friendly company. During questions after my talk about the pilgrimage they were interested to know how women priests were going down in the diocese and were obviously glad to know how well they are being received. We get the impression from the national press that there are still deep-rooted divisions but that is not our experience in Norfolk. There are still those opposed or uncomfortable, to be sure, but there is a good level of mutual tolerance and a number of those formerly opposed are now quietly coming round and living more happily with the reality.

After lunch we went to FMC, a huge factory on the outskirts of Fakenham which makes agricultural equipment, particularly enormous pea and bean harvesters, most of which are exported to various European countries and Australia. The noise inside the factory as steel plates were being punched, drilled and cut, was deafening. It was a relief to emerge into the fresh air and on to a field where I was allowed to drive, under instruction, a huge bean harvester – the biggest vehicle in which I have travelled so far. Like the tractor a few weeks ago, it was luxuriously equipped with computers, air-conditioning and stereo radio. The power steering made it easy to turn this great monster with one finger. At one stage I tried going backwards until the driver beside me told me that if I did not stop I would demolish their Social Club.

At South Creake vicarage I dropped my gear, went for a walk up the hill behind the village and watched the sun setting, before descending, rather cold, to have tea with Andrew and Pam Thomson in the study while their four exceedingly lively children watched *Neighbours* in the next-door room. They are a good couple who arrived in England from Zimbabwe three years ago. He is doing a good job, better probably than he thinks he is, but suffers from a certain amount of stress and anxiety about his pension because the pension rights he earned in Zimbabwe will almost have disappeared by the time he retires in England. They only had a week's holiday this summer, in a special place in Devon for clergy. The rest of the time was spent in the vicarage, happily, they said, but I think we must ensure they have a really good holiday. I am lucky to have a discretionary fund which makes this possible.

Supper was at the home of Jenny and Malcolm Nichol. They have lived there for twenty years, having emigrated from South Africa where they could not live with the political situation. Jenny works as a social worker and Malcolm, having taught woodwork in a secondary modern school for years, has now become a cabinet maker, doing restoration work and building furniture, especially long-case clocks. His mother, now living in Canada, was there and a fifteen-year-old daughter who wants to be a pilot. They are an interesting family, very good company, and the meal, with home-grown vegetables, was excellent but for me hardly necessary after that massive lunch.

The day ended with a Bible study at Rudham School led by Vernon Scott, a delightful widower with a beatific face. He gave a good introduction and we had another lively discussion, thanks not least to the fact that, like the group last night, many of them had been studying St Luke for some time. Alan Bell was there again, as he has been at every Bible study, and is always on hand, making sure things go smoothly. He has organised the week well and clearly has put in a lot of work in preparation and is doing so in the execution too. Vernon's population of rabbits has decreased. He once had sixteen housed in hutches, as Tony Foottit said, 'like high-rise flats' but myxomatosis has reduced them to four and he does not think he will increase the population.

Thursday 26th October

A simple Prayer Book Communion at Fakenham Parish Church was followed by coffee, not just with parishioners but with a large number of people who had come in for coffee on market day. All the churches in the town open their doors and have done for many years which is an excellent idea. I chatted at various tables and then went out with Alan Bell, meeting stallholders and shopkeepers, giving out badges and prayers to various people. In a television shop we met Simon, the son of Maurice Burrell; and as I passed a small shop selling clocks I remembered part of my conversation with Malcolm Nichol last night and on an impulse went into the shop and asked if it was he who was making long-case clocks with Malcolm, and it was. He was delighted to see me and there was another couple in the shop who introduced themselves as old friends of David Conner from Oxford days.

We then visited an office where I met a man who lived in the Brisley and Elmham deanery. 'All I heard about you in our deanery was that you rode a horse, which I thought was a bit of a gimmick,' he said.

I replied, 'Well, you mustn't believe all you read in the papers. I was actually spending an average of ten or twelve hours with parishioners as well.'

'Well, I didn't get to see you,' he said.

I reminded him that there were Bible studies every night open to everyone.

'Oh, I was far too busy in the evenings to attend,' he said.

'Well then,' I insisted on reminding him, 'we had an all-day pilgrimage walk on Sunday.'

'Oh that's not my kind of thing,' he said. 'The trouble is,' he said, 'Norfolk people are difficult to understand.'

Getting more than a little irritated by this time, I replied testily that Norfolk people weren't half as difficult to understand as some of them thought they were. I slapped a Pilgrimage Prayer and badge on his desk and was glad to leave this representative of Norfolk with its least attractive face.

We walked across the town to the Citizen's Advice Bureau, housed temporarily in prefabricated accommodation, soon though to move into the fine Community Centre. This has been founded by Alan Bell and is doing excellent and important work. After a prayer meeting with the Methodists, we continued walking through the town and saw a fair amount of new housing and, indeed, of new businesses near the edge of town. Like so many places, Fakenham gets a bad press and there is a Norfolk tendency to talk oneself down which does not help. But there are a lot of forward-looking, hopeful people and surely a good future for the town if everyone pulls together, because it is in a strategic position serving scores of villages in the surrounding countryside.

After lunch at the rectory with Alan and Valerie, we visited Cranmer House, a residential home and day centre for the elderly. Here again I met old Billy, aged ninety-nine, whom I had met at Heritage House on Tuesday. But he was a chicken compared with Hilda whom I met upstairs, a sprightly hundred-and-five-year-old, reputedly the oldest person in Norfolk.

We drove a little way down the road to some sheltered housing where we celebrated Communion with half a dozen residents and the Warden – lovely old people full of fun, and they produced delicious cake. One of them noticed that my cassock was splitting at the seams and said that if I had got ten minutes she would mend it for me, but I didn't as we had to leave at that point, so the split will have to stay until the end of this pilgrimage week.

The day had dawned grey and drizzle merged into more serious rain as the afternoon drew on. I went for a damp walk by the riverside and sat under a tree trying to sketch the interesting view of the church from the river but it was hopeless. So I walked back into the town and spent a happy hour mooching round the second-hand bookshop.

After a cup of tea at the rectory, Pat King drove me to Walsingham vicarage where I had supper with Keith and Kathy Haydon and their son, Kevin. Kathy, recently out of hospital, looked tired but cheerful and relieved that the prognosis was good. It was a happy meal with people I have known since the beginning of my time in Taunton when Keith was a curate in Wells.

The Bible study at North Creake Hall was led by Freddie Hetherington-Sims, a lay reader and retired diplomat. It was scholarly but comprehensible and a very interesting discussion followed on the topic of anxiety. I overheard one lady talking about her daughter who had joined an evangelical community twelve years ago and from whom she felt very separated. When the discussion was over I talked to her in the kitchen as she made coffee, because I had an instinct she wanted to talk a bit more about it. This made my departure rather later than usual but it had been another fulfilling day and extremely well organised, which has been a feature of this deanery visit so far.

Friday 27 October

At the posh new day centre in Burnham Market (nearly everything is posh in Burnham Market) we had coffee with local worthies and churchwardens and were shown round the centre with its facilities for the elderly. Then I walked with the two lady churchwardens through the centre of this impeccable little town, which has become very fashionable and expensive, to the Hoste Arms Gallery to see a watercolour exhibition by Hugh Brandon-Cox, an artist blind in one eye whose first wife was Finnish. He spent much of his life in northern Scandinavia and Iceland where he wrote and painted. All this I heard from his charming second wife to whom he has been married for eighteen years but she said he still misses his first wife who died young. Later he himself, with tears in his eyes, told me the same thing – rather sad really. His pictures were fascinating, painted free and fast and he explained some of his techniques which I found instructive.

I was collected by David, another churchwarden, in his Porsche and driven to the Sutton Lee estate which is a group of bungalows for the elderly. I met the residents in their own day centre and had friendly conversation with them all. Afterwards I visited two housebound residents, first a lady with multiple sclerosis, aged about sixty, and serenely beautiful – a happy person, full of peace, and a delight to spend time with. I learned afterwards that her husband had deserted her soon after the onset of the disease thirty years ago. Next I visited an old man known locally as Tom Thumb – indeed, he had a sign in his window proclaiming the fact. He is a delightful old boy, contented and busy in his wheelchair, a CB radio fan who spends a lot of time talking with farmers in their tractors and lorry drivers. He used to work on a farm and I think perhaps was crippled by a farm accident.

The Porsche was waiting outside Tom Thumb's humble bungalow and I was driven to Crabbe Hall, the home of another churchwarden, Anthony Stilgoe. I had lunch with Anthony, his wife, Lyn, and the new Rector of the Burnhams, Jonathan Charles, and his attractive wife, Penny, who is disabled and walks with a stick. Jonathan reminded me that I had met him years ago when he was chaplain of Denstone and I was the Archbishop's Adviser to the Headmasters' Conference. He seems a good chap and knows this part of Norfolk because they have had a house at Burnham Overy Staithe for many years. Crabbe Hall is a large Georgian stone-flagged farmhouse which I guess is freezing in the winter but was warm today with bright sunlight shining through the windows. We had a good lunch together and then I was decanted into the Porsche once more for the journey to Fakenham.

On the way I visited Reg Baldry, a former postman and churchwarden who is dying of a brain tumour. He was delightful, accepting and unafraid – like the lady this morning, an inspiration to those who visit him. (He died the following Tuesday.)

En route to Fakenham I learned that David and his brother, both bachelors, own the bookshop in Burnham Market – they were solicitors who gave up their practice in their mid-fifties and love their new life, though they don't make great profits; probably they don't need to. The road to Fakenham hardly gave me a chance to discover what the Porsche might do, but there were one or two nice surges of power as we overtook slow vehicles which gave a promise of things that might have been.

In the Salvation Army Citadel we had an hour and a half's discussion with leaders of the local community, heads of schools, doctors, social services and voluntary agencies. It was an interesting and stimulating discussion which could have continued, but I was now ready for a break and Alan drove me to the home of Tony and Tessa Gent at Barney where I had a walk through pretty woodland near their home.

Tony offered me the possibility of a shower, jacuzzi or turkish bath, all of which apparently are installed in the house, but I declined and settled for a cup of tea. Supper was just the three of us which was nice with a good Australian dry white wine.

After supper Tony drove me to the hall at Hindringham where John Denny led a Bible study, the largest group so far this week with thirty people present including teenage girls. Like all the Bible studies, this again was of a high standard with intelligent and serious wrestling with the text – a difficult one about the Second Coming. As usual, I eavesdropped on each small group in turn and was particularly fascinated by the contribution of one of the teenage girls talking of her experience of being a Christian in her comprehensive school. She said interestingly that her contemporaries, most of whom are not Christians and are totally ignorant of the Christian faith, are nevertheless curious and take a full part in discussions during RE lessons, often posing questions which floor the teacher. Last year, she said, they didn't even bother to take an interest but this year they are obviously asking themselves serious questions. That was one of many enlightening comments made this evening.

After a short general discussion, I led them into silence and left after a short chat with Philip and Elizabeth Tower, due to move next year to a rather grand old people's home near Salisbury. He is a retired general and former gunner whom I remember from my days as a subaltern as a dashing young major in the Royal Horse Artillery. He has always been immensely friendly and encouraging during my time in Norfolk and a most loyal supporter of successive parish priests. Both Philip and Elizabeth are rather frail now and, having no children of their own, feel it is unfair to ask nephews and nieces to come all the way to Norfolk, so they have decided to live more centrally in Wiltshire where Philip will be near scores of old army friends.

Saturday 28 October

On a perfect crisp autumn morning with bright blue skies we drove to the Slipper Chapel where the Roman Catholic priest and a dozen of us prayed for unity and then walked the 'Holy Mile' to Walsingham, passing groups of pilgrims on the way. At the village hall we had coffee and I blessed some kneelers made by ladies for the church. Keith Haydon thrust a silver cylinder into my hand just before I performed the ceremony. 'It's a portable asperger,' he explained. 'In Walsingham they don't think things are properly blessed unless they are sprinkled,' so I duly did as I was told. Afterwards we had a Bible study, led by Sister Alma from Trinidad on an exceedingly difficult passage at the end of Luke chapter 12 about Jesus' saying about bringing fire on the earth and causing families to be divided. She dealt with it well and we had a fruitful discussion, but I was glad not to have had the job of leading it.

The Mothers' Union served lunch of sandwiches and hot tomato soup in plastic cups. The tomato soup was particularly good and I went back for a second helping, congratulating the ladies in the kitchen. 'Well we added some alcohol,' I was told, 'to give it some zip,' which it certainly did. In contrast to the pilgrimage in Lothingland, which was totally dry, I have been consuming alcohol at least twice a day in Burnham and Walsingham. Perhaps it is something to do with churchmanship.

After lunch we strolled up the village street to meet brother Leon, an Orthodox, at his icon shop. He took us through back streets to his workshop which is fascinating. He uses traditional methods, making his own gesso, using gold leaf, and mixing his own egg tempera paints. His icons are in great demand in Roman, Orthodox and Anglican churches, not cheap but certainly beautiful.

At the Shrine fifty or sixty pilgrims from a London parish were gathered for the service of sprinkling in which I took part. After a good introductory address from Martin Warner, the Administrator, I led a procession down some steps to the Holy Well, still inside the church, where priests gave us Holy Water to drink from a ladle, then put a cross on our foreheads and finally emptied water into our hands. A crook in one hand and water in both palms made for a slightly awkward exit and I got rid of the water on my face and cassock which must have looked stained for a while.

Back at Martin's house I changed into my old Barbour and cloth cap and walked into the Abbey grounds. At the entrance there is a little kiosk where they take money and sitting inside was Nora, whom I had met an hour before after visiting Brother Leon, when I was dressed in a cassock, and I had chatted with her for a while. This time I put my head in through the door and said, 'Hello, Nora, nice to see you again.' She looked rather blank, and I said, 'You don't recognise me, do you?'

She said, 'I know I've seen you somewhere before but I can't think where.'

Then to her embarrassment I let out the secret and walked on into the grounds and sketched in the fading sunlight.

Nora came round eventually and explained that they were closing the grounds. She said, 'I'm so sorry I didn't recognise you, but when I saw this figure in a rather scruffy coat and cloth cap I wondered who on earth it was.' We had a laugh and then she said, 'I'll take you out a different way,' and showed me through the grounds to her little cottage attached to the Abbey with a beautiful cottage garden. I went inside and greeted her husband and then walked back to the Shrine.

I had tea with the nuns who were all very friendly except one who sat in the corner looking distinctly uncheerful. She is probably very much opposed to the ordination of women and disapproves of me, but we had a good talk with the rest, and then on the dot of 5.30 Patrick King arrived to take me off to my next engagement. He marched into the room and said, 'Bad news, I'm afraid – England have lost the Rugby League final.' The Sisters looked bemused, so I gave them a blessing and we drove off to Great Ryburgh.

At the home of Mary Plumbley, one of the churchwardens, half a dozen friends had gathered for supper – sausage and mash with inevitably more wine, and sherry of course beforehand. We had a lively conversation over the meal about the Group, the argument raging about which deanery they should be in, and with questions about when they would get a new vicar. I said I really hadn't a clue because I was not very much in touch with what was going on at the centre, spending all my time in the parishes. I hadn't attended a pastoral committee for months, and was not due to go to a staff meeting until January. This amused them greatly, especially when I told a story, which I think is probably apocryphal, that someone had complained the other day that I was never available in Norwich but always seemed to be out in the parishes. Again I came across one of the most encouraging phenomena of this pilgrimage – the newly formed benefice is really working well and there is a genuine benefice identity growing up. Tomorrow I shall be at a benefice Eucharist; the churchwardens meet regularly and they are planning for secretaries to meet in the same way. This does seem to be a growing feature, particularly in the countryside, which I guess is going to make deaneries less and less relevant.

Alan Bell arrived after supper to take me to Hempton church hall to meet some young people. Twenty or so were gathered, led by Kate Clodd, a gallant schoolteacher who seems to be giving up most of her half term to caring for young people of all ages, and we had a good talk together. Included in the group were no less than six children from clergy families who talked about the difficulties they had at school concerning their fathers' jobs. I encouraged them by saying that it would be much worse if their fathers were undertakers, and then told them the story of the school run in Beaconsfield. My son Andrew's school was nine miles away and we were involved in daily complex school runs which I did on Mondays, my day off. One Monday evening I collected the eight or nine small boys on my list and got half way home when one of them said, 'Tincknell's not here.'

I said, 'He's not supposed to be here on Monday. He's got some club or other.'

'No, he hasn't,' they said, 'it's cancelled. He should be with us.'

I jammed on the brakes and swore, 'Bloody hell.'

All the little boys fell silent.

As I drove back, fuming quietly, I heard one of them say to the other, 'I didn't know parsons swore.'

Another whispered, 'It's all right because it's his day off.'

Sunday 29th October

Another crisp autumn day with cloudless skies and the church at Great Ryburgh looking beautiful in the early morning sunshine. A benefice Eucharist was well attended with about sixty people. The old priest who was here for years used a Roman liturgy which Martin Smith, his successor, modified but continued, though he did sterling work in drawing the Group together before leaving to become Vicar of St John's, Timberhill. There was not an *ASB* to be found until someone came from one of the other churches in the Group and I borrowed it for the collect and lessons and slightly changed the order of things to make it more Anglican. But the singing was good and the fellowship afterwards in the church school warm and friendly. Afterwards I walked in the recreation ground next door and chatted to two boys playing football.

'I expect you'll be watching Norwich City on television this afternoon,' I said.

'No, we won't, they're rubbish. We support Manchester United,' they replied in broad Norfolk accents. Oh dear.

Talking of local accents, I remember meeting a priest in my first days in Norwich who came to see me about moving. At that time I was unfamiliar with the Norfolk accent, with which he was well endowed. When I asked him to talk about aspects of his ministry he found rewarding, he replied, 'I really enjoy gropes – not big gropes, Bishop, but little gropes, you understand.' I didn't, and thought I was faced with my first pervert priest, but everything else about him seemed normal. However, I slowly realised that he was talking about 'groups', because in Norfolk they drink tomato 'soap' and wash their faces with 'soup'.

Alan Bell drove me to the rectory at Fakenham where we had a buffet lunch with nearly all the deanery clergy, their wives and deanery officers and their wives, too. I spent a short time in the churchyard after lunch putting some thoughts together and then went to the final service in Fakenham Parish Church. It was a good liturgy with excellent music and attended by about 150 people. Afterwards they presented me with a large bunch of flowers for Betty, a typically thoughtful touch from this deanery who have been unfailingly kind, lively and extremely well organised. Finally after the service, the choir sang a Celtic blessing which was very touching and I then left, very satisfied with one of the most enjoyable weeks so far.

Tonight we had been invited to a concert and dinner at Chequers in honour of the French President. We had to refuse, of course, because of the commitment to the pilgrimage – perhaps just as well – there was a demonstration which invaded the grounds to protest about the French nuclear tests in the Pacific.

13

Depwade

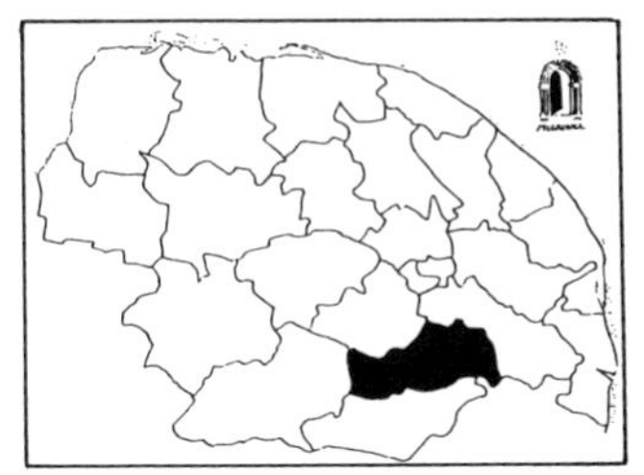

(In the south of the diocese, apart from the large village of Long Stratton, this deanery is very rural, and farming predominates, largely arable as in most of Norfolk.)

Tuesday 7 November

The week began with a meeting of the chapter at the home of Ian Bishop at Tasburgh with a Bible study well led by Peter Halls, the Rural Dean.

After an hour I was taken to Tasburgh First School for an assembly with the children, then to Saxlingham for school lunch of sausages, cabbage and rather hard carrots, and afterwards a round of the classes. There followed two more schools, Carleton Rode Primary and Aslacton, a new building opened in recent years by John MacGregor. In all the schools the children were lively and friendly as always, but four schools on the trot were a trifle much. These were capped by a visit to the 'children's church' at Aslacton, a club which meets after school one Tuesday in each month. This is a small village and much credit is due to the initiative of the women who organise this group. About twelve or fifteen children came and some young mothers too.

Next stop was the home of Dr David Money and his wife. David is an elderly doctor who has kept the church going in Tibenham. He is a most interesting old boy who spent many years in Africa ministering to lepers and also in general practice in England. In retirement he studied theology to good effect and is an excellent and interesting preacher. It was 4.30 when we arrived, and getting dark, and although pretty tired by now I went for a walk through the farmyard and beyond. David had set aside a room for me and supper was laid out, surprisingly, for me to eat alone, which I did and then joined David, his wife and daughter, Sue, for coffee. Sue Pennell, their daughter, is a remarkable woman who runs the farm. She has three children of her own and adopted two more from the village when their mother died, their father having died a few years before. They were all interesting and delightful people and we had a good talk together.

After coffee we drove to Tibenham Church for an evening of Remembrance. This has been taking place for three years now and is a curious occasion but well attended, organised by one of the locals, formerly in the RAF. People read poems and we sang songs from the First and Second World Wars, interspersed with one or two hymns and prayers. After the cold weather of last week, the evening was mild, but not the church at Tibenham which was like a refrigerator.

Wednesday 8 November

The day began with another school visit, this time at Seething, and then at a parishioner's home we had a Bible study led again by Peter Halls. Following this we went to Brooke School, where senior children who had been elected to the school council gave me a tour of the school, proudly showing me all its facilities, including the new adventure playground in memory of a child who died, and the conservation area which seems to be a feature of a number of primary schools these days.

Lunch was with Peter Halls at his house together with Martin, a young graduate who is spending a year working for Norwich Youth for Christ. We then drove in Peter's 1948 Triumph Roadster through the tortuous lanes of this part of Norfolk to Bunwell where the Church Guild was meeting. I listened to an interesting, if over-long, talk from a young Baptist minister and then answered questions which focused in a useful way on the meaning of establishment and questions of unity.

Sam Read, the local vicar, came to collect me and took me back to his house at Earsham. By now it was 4.30 and getting dark but I needed exercise and so walked for nearly an hour and then returned for tea with Sam and Barbara. They are a good couple and Sam has, in a modest but very effective way, drawn together his large group of parishes.

At Ditchingham village hall a great number of parishioners from the whole benefice had gathered and a huge amount of food was laid out which, after a delicious stew of steak and kidney at the Reads', I could not face, but discovered to my relief that a number of those present had already had supper as well. I went from table to table talking informally and then for the last half hour answered questions which began rather aggressively with, 'Why did we have such a long interregnum?' but continued with more interesting and positive questions. The whole atmosphere of the evening was very friendly and at the end Sam said, 'We all wanted you to know how much we have admired your stand over traditional values of marriage and family life and how strongly we support you in the difficulties you have experienced.'

It was a good day but again not well planned, with no less than four hours scheduled to be spent with Sam and Barbara Read alone. I like spending time with the clergy but this was not a good balance.

Thursday 9 November

A better day began with a school assembly at Ditchingham and a visit to the classes, followed by a Bible study in a house in the village. A number of the group were retired teachers and so the level of study was high and there was a very good discussion. But being Ditchingham and independent they had irritatingly chosen to continue their year long study of St John's Gospel and not to study St Luke, so we looked at verses from St John, which was okay but not a good use of my time. Sam Read was present and made a good and typically self-deprecating contribution. His mixture of natural humility and wily assumed dimness have clearly endeared him to the sophisticated people in Ditchingham, and without noticing it I think they are being rather effectively and cleverly led.

There was an old people's lunch at Hempnall, in the church hall made from a converted mill. I sat opposite a lady whose father had been the miller many years ago and she told me stories of her girlhood; how she used to be woken by her father in the middle of the night when there was a good wind to go and grind flour. After a short walk in steady drizzle, Ernest Green, Team Rector of the Hempnall Group, drove me to the church at Great Moulton. Originally a Saxon monks' church, it was heavily Victorianised but expensively so, by a rich rector in the nineteenth century, employing the same architect who built Osborne House on the Isle of Wight. They didn't fiddle around – they transformed the entire building, wall-paintings, furnishings, the lot, with just a Saxon arch in the tower and one or two remnants outside to show its origins. English Heritage at first refused to give them a grant for repairs because they said the Victorians had vandalised it, but I guess it now ought to be listed for its Victorian additions alone, which I normally dislike. Whatever one's taste, one has to admit this was well done.

The 'King's Club' at Bunwell is an after-school group for younger children, one of a number of such meetings I have come across in country parishes. This is clearly developing into an alternative to Sunday schools which work in very few places nowadays. A good number were there from the village and it was well led by three women with the children alert and responsive. They even had a prayer meeting, which I thought could be risky. Their leader asked if anyone wanted to say a prayer. One said, 'Yes, please pray for my foot which hurts like anything,' and another little voice said, 'And my duck who died yesterday.' She started weeping quietly and it was touching to see her fellow seven-year-olds gently stroking her back and comforting her as other prayers went on. My journey is often punctuated by beautiful moments like this.

Selwyn Swift took me to Bunwell, a large and interesting single aisle church which looked as if it might have been a priory. Like Moulton, it was expensively restored in Victorian times, though not as extensively, obviously by Tractarians with six candles on the altar, space for a tabernacle and a huge rood-screen. Selwyn is the first vicar for many years even to wear a coloured stole, conservative evangelicals having been appointed without much sensitivity to tradition.

Selwyn drove me away in his Lada, the car stuttering badly in the now persistent drizzle, but eventually, after almost stopping several times, we drew up at the rectory. After a short and rainy walk, Selwyn, Glenys and I had supper together and a good talk. Selwyn is a fine country parson, very sensitive to people's feelings. He put forward an interesting analogy for my pilgrimage as it might apply in multi-parish benefices, suggesting that the incumbent could spend a week in each parish and then a week at home catching up. He has longed, but never found time, for the more leisured contact with parishioners that he believes to be so important and this just might be a way – worth an experiment anyway.

We did not want to risk the Lada again so Peter, the Headmaster of Carleton Rode, collected us for the long drive to Hempnall for an evening meeting of the deanery synod. I seem to have traversed this sausage-shaped deanery several times each day, and it takes three-quarters of an hour to drive from end to end. But the evening in Hempnall was excellent. It was an open meeting of the deanery attended by sixty people and we had the Bible study for the day led by Pat Crowley, the Lay Chairman, and then the usual pattern of groups with me coming in at the end. It was a cheering and encouraging evening because the people were so interesting and responsive. The planning for this week has been uneven but there is no point in moaning about it; I must just go with the tide and appreciate the people who, as everywhere, give one great hope and encouragement.

Friday 10 November

Cygnet House in Long Stratton is a brand new residential home and respite care centre for those suffering from senile dementia. The environment is homely, the staff dedicated and very professional – all of them experienced in nursing the mentally ill. There are a number of illnesses which come under the heading of 'senile dementia' including Alzheimer's and a condition resulting from frequent small strokes. The care of such patients is exhausting and the staff themselves paid tribute to the heroism of those who care for such people at home. I tried, with limited success, to communicate with some of the patients but Peter Coley, the local Rector of Long Stratton, is a frequent visitor and has obviously managed to create a relationship with some of them which is impressive. We got smiles from one or two and the sister-in-charge said afterwards that that was their reward for the day and perhaps the only reaction they would get. The staff have to work with the satisfaction of very small responses like this.

A short distance away is Long Stratton Middle School, a huge church school consisting of 350 pupils. I visited all twelve classes in a fairly rapid walkabout, dishing out pilgrimage badges like a benevolent Victorian gentleman scattering pennies to urchins in London streets.

At the church there was a time of prayer with a group of parishioners who meet every week, before a buffet lunch with about twenty parishioners at the rectory. Afterwards I walked up a nearby hill among lovely autumn coloured trees in rising mist with a chill in the air. It was only 3 o'clock but evening was drawing in, dry, however, in contrast to yesterday's miserable drizzle.

Peter and I talked on the way to Saxlingham. He seems to have settled more happily and to have got over the culture shock experienced by everyone who becomes a vicar after being a curate. He tends to lack self-confidence but his people are affirming and more than one told me how much they appreciated his ministry. Sometimes this was said deliberately in his hearing. He knows he is well supported, so hopefully this will help him when he goes through a dark patch.

At Saxlingham Church I was met by Verena Hemmant, a lay reader dressed in a Roman soutane, and I visited the children's school, attended by about fifteen children. This is another after-school club like others I have seen recently. Again it was a well conducted, enjoyable affair and I had already met these children at their school a couple of days before so we met as old friends and they all qualified for a second badge.

Afterwards we returned to the rectory where Verena and her husband are living for a period of three years. John Hemmant is the son of a farmer at Sisland who, I discovered, was the farmer churchwarden I met on a visit there a few years ago. John works for National Westminster and is away a great deal, at the moment on secondment in the Isle of Man. They have two children, aged seven and four, both of them full of energy. John was at home for a long weekend and it was good to meet and talk with him. On his father's farm he has planted a vineyard of grapes for champagne and we tasted some at dinner, not bad at all.

After the meal we drove through winding country lanes to Tharston, a tiny village difficult to find, where there was a meeting in the Church Room to talk about parish strategy. Before the meeting I looked around the church with the ninety-two-year-old churchwarden, Harry, who first became a warden in 1926 in another parish. Next year he celebrates his sixtieth anniversary as churchwarden of Tharston. He was stooped, but with a strong and handsome face, mentally completely alert, and he told me in detail about recent repairs to the tower and roof. In the Church Room the four parishes of the benefice met for the sixth of a series of meetings about parish strategy. They are in the hands of an able young incumbent, Ian Bishop, and I guess the place will prosper in his hands. They delayed the start in order that I could have a time of informal chat and were just beginning to get down to business as I left at 8.30 pm.

Saturday 11 November

To Wacton, a tiny village in the Long Stratton Group, for lunch at the home of Edward and Georgina Jewson at the Manor House. Fifteen or so from the village, all committed churchgoers, were at lunch and we had a good time together talking about the problems of country parishes, and then went over to the parish church for a short act of worship. Wacton is slightly unusual insofar as the line between church and community is quite clear. A large percentage are commuters to Norwich and take little part in village or church life. The fifteen or so present were planning an imaginative approach to the community to raise funds for their parish church which, as in so many other parts of the diocese, can be something which actually unites a village and draws people into the life of the church.

There had been intermittent drizzle during the morning and I wondered if the proposed flight from Tibenham aerodrome was going to be possible in the afternoon, but as we drove from Wacton it was evident that, although there was rain, the cloud cover was high and so we hoped a flight would be possible. Tibenham is a former US Army Airforce base where the film actor James Stewart was once in command during the war. It is now a gliding club with one or two powered aircraft, a Tiger Moth and other light aircraft, used as tugs for gliders. I went to the clubroom where there was an assortment of members, including Selwyn Swift, the local Rector, who, by a marvellous providence, had qualified as a glider pilot many years before. He is very much part of this club. Also present was the ubiquitous former RAF pilot with a handlebar moustache, now in his seventies, still managing to qualify year by year to continue to fly his glider. A tall Norfolk man called Mr Bean took me up in a powered glider with a little engine in front. It was a peaceful, very enjoyable flight and we flew round the parishes of Selwyn's benefice, floating down and circling churches to take photographs before climbing again, and then I had the thrill of taking control and learning the basic elements of flying. In some ways it is not unlike sailing or steering a boat, where you have to be sensitive on the tiller, and when making a turn start centering before the turn is completed. It was immensely enjoyable and I was quite sorry to leave the aerodrome.

Selwyn drove me in his Lada, now firing on all four cylinders, to Tasburgh

Barns at Tasburgh

rectory where I spent some time with Ian Bishop, his wife, Sue, and their three boys, Joe aged four, Daniel two, and baby William. First I went for a walk and then played with Joe and William, and afterwards went to the computer where I was shown an educational video featuring Noddy, and another which was a flight simulator. At Joe's bloodthirsty request, Ian crashed his Boeing into the Statue of Liberty. Afterwards I had a time of quiet, wrote some letters and then, just before leaving, listened to Joe reading his latest reading book. He knew most of the words but I suspect that he is rather like my youngest daughter Lucy who at primary school, to her teacher's amazement, got through reading books at a huge rate, and the school thought she was a genius. One day I read with her at home and sure enough, she read through the latest book fluently. Then I said, 'Let's read it again,' and held my hand over the pictures. She couldn't read a word. Similarly, I think young Joe may have been memorising with the use of pictures but at least that shows intelligence.

We went to Shotesham for an evening of old-fashioned entertainment and fish and chips, in a large hall adjacent to almshouses owned by the Mercers' Company. The whole evening was due to end at 8.30, but predictably everything went on longer than anticipated. It began with a very long sketch about a railway station, and then livened up with a Stanley Holloway monologue and a delightful Norfolk story from Derek Bunkell, the churchwarden. There were sixty or seventy people in the room and Derek, before the evening began, introduced me to each one by name. He is an impressive, friendly man and the epitome of what a churchwarden should be. In fact, next week he is going to Papworth for a triple heart bypass, but was very casual about it when I spoke to him. He is the kind of loyal, friendly, and enthusiastic man who makes one proud to belong to the same Church. The turns continued, including a rather risqué act about wedding preparation from Ian Bishop which is the kind of thing which goes down well at theological college but not in a Norfolk parish, and a wonderful dance routine called 'Crimewatch' from teenagers in the congregation. Eventually fish and chips were served, with salt and tomato sauce, and very good they were.

Sunday 12 November

The little church at Topcroft in the Hempnall Group was packed with sixty or seventy people for a Remembrance Day service at which one of the team, Conal Mahoney, formerly a Roman Catholic priest, preached well. It is a rare treat to listen to someone else preach for a change. Remembrance Sunday in Norfolk is always a major festival, but this year especially because of the fiftieth anniversary of the end of the war, and the links with the armed forces are strong here.

After the service we drove to the old USAAF airfield for another short service which is held every year to honour the American airmen who died and who were based here in Liberator Squadrons. During the silence an old Tiger Moth biplane flew over and dropped poppies. Significantly, this year instead of the normal 500 there were 510. Topcroft has just twinned with a village in Brittany called Mellé. Some parishioners went to Mellé earlier in the year and visited an American Cemetery nearby. By chance they found the graves of ten crew members of an aeroplane from Topcroft airbase which had been shot down in France, so we remembered the ten men by name at the moving little ceremony today. Afterwards we gathered in the former Officers' Mess, which has been lovingly restored by the farmer who owns the land, and had a buffet lunch attended by parishioners, villagers and a large number of people who keep alive the commemoration of American airmen.

We drove back to Hempnall rectory where I sat in the garden to put some thoughts together for this afternoon's service, and then drove to Long Stratton for a deanery Holy Communion attended by at least 150, with a huge choir from a number of parishes. It was a good occasion and afterwards people thanked me for my sermon. I am never very confident because the whole thing is so ad hoc, but evidently people managed to pick up things which spoke to them, for which I was thankful.

14

Hingham and Mitford

(Dereham is one of the four main centres of population apart from Norwich [the other three being King's Lynn, Great Yarmouth and Lowestoft] and it lies geographically at the centre of Norfolk. The charming small Georgian town of Hingham and large village of Mattishall apart, the deanery is rural and contains the largest rural group in the diocese [eighteen parishes].)

Tuesday 21 November

A day in the Barnham Broom Group began at Barford Church where I was met by Heather Potts' brother who is the manager of the AA in Norfolk (Heather is an ordinand in the Group), and given an AA Land Rover Discovery as my vehicle for the day. It was driven by Mike Simmons, a delightful man and member of the Baptist Church at Hethersett. Photographers were there and tried to get Mike to open the bonnet of the Land Rover, but we both felt this would be wrong for the image of the AA, so they contented themselves with a picture of him holding a spanner which we hope will not be misunderstood.

After prayers in the church, we went to Barford School where I opened a new extension consisting mostly of indoor lavatories, which must be a great relief (!) for the children who thus far have had to cope with an outside Victorian loo. I visited the classes and then went to Barnham Broom Primary School, which has also recently had a modern extension. The senior class presented me with a book they had compiled of what they think a bishop does, which should prove interesting reading. At Barford Church there was an exhibition of local industry. In this village of 400 people there is a small industrial estate with an astonishing variety of work going on and I was given a pot of honey and a honeycomb produced locally.

At Garveston village hall there was a monthly lunch club for all ages and the food was very good. I circulated from table to table and talked to everyone. Interestingly, at least seventy-five per cent were born and bred locally. This group of villages feels very remote because they are small and scattered but in fact they are only about fifteen minutes from the outskirts of Norwich.

After lunch Pat Hopkins, the Team Vicar, took me to two old post offices, first in Garvestone and then in Reymerston. They are village shops and post offices in the old style, both of them run by eighty-year-olds, selling everything, a focus of the life of the village and information centres. What happens when these two old ladies have to give up, one dreads to think. The probability is that both shops will close and something very precious will go from those villages.

I had an hour's break and walked until the rain started in earnest, when I returned to the rectory and had a long talk with Pat Hopkins. She was disappointed because she was not selected as the Team Rector (that is, the Team leader) recently. She talked about her feelings openly, and I think I was able to reassure her, not least about our own high opinion of her ministry. Her own five years' experience in this very good Group will be a valuable experience to take elsewhere, and I hope to keep her in the diocese if possible.

We drove through narrow lanes to Westfield, to the farm owned by Peter Riches. There we changed into wellingtons and tramped through the mud of the farmyard to visit his ninety sows, in old sheds but looking very comfortable in straw, which is the old-fashioned way of keeping pigs. There were scores of piglets at various stages of development, some born only three days before, scrabbling for a meal from their enormous mothers who were kept caged so that they did not roll over on the tiny piglets – a tragedy which happens all too often, I understand. In another shed twenty or thirty sows were lying down fast asleep in a thick straw bed, together with the huge boar who was snoring loudly – worn out after lovemaking.

Rather late we arrived for evening prayer at Cranworth Church, led by Gordon and Angela Reynolds, a lay reader and NSM ordinand in training. Like all the churches at this time of year, Cranworth was beginning to take on the character of a refrigerator and I shall soon have to think seriously about wearing long johns.

Supper was at Letton Hall, an enormous Norfolk mansion designed by John Soane, taken over by Peter Carrol who has turned it into an evangelical conference centre, successfully so far, but the cost of upkeep must be enormous. We had supper with members of the ministry team and good conversation. This is the oldest and strongest rural ministry team in the diocese, and much has been achieved. I suppose there is some danger of complacency, but I found them lively, searching and looking all the time for new initiatives. This was followed by a Bible study on the passage for the day from Luke and, with a ministry team which included eight lay readers, it was predictably of a

Farmyard near Mattishall

high standard. At the end I led them in a little meditation on Luke's words about the Pharisees watching Jesus closely and talked about the three ways of watching. First, as those Pharisees watched, critically, looking for fault; but also of the watching that a shepherd does, leaning on his crook guarding the flock; and of the watching which is loving, close to adoration and the prayer of contemplation; all three applying both to our relationship to God, and to other people. Then tucking up the skirts of my cassock, I donned a crash helmet and drove a go-kart from the house down the long drive to the gate. It was raining hard again and mud splattered up from the wheels, but it was an interesting experience. Someone drove in front to guide me, but I wish they hadn't because I couldn't put my foot down as far as I wished.

Wednesday 22 November

Last night in bed I read the book which had been produced by Class II of Barnham Broom Primary School. Each child had been asked to write a piece about what a bishop was and then to put a question which the child wanted to ask me when I visited the school. The best was this one: 'A bishop is a person who looks after all the churches in Norfolk. I think a bishop should be responsible, experienced, happy, careful, understanding, peaceful, know about problems, sensible and clever. How did you become a bishop? Love from Nicole.'

After coffee and meeting some parishioners in the church at Mattishall, the Rector, David Pearson, and I went to Mattishall First School for an assembly with the children and then to a church hall to open a day centre for the elderly. There are plans for a fine modern centre and church hall, but this is in the future when they can raise £200,000. For the time being the old hall is used and on David's initiative, with the assistance of social services and local voluntary organisations, a weekly day centre has been established. There was a homely atmosphere with about twelve old people and double that number of local worthies and helpers present.

We went to the house of Colonel Mike Hodges for sherry and a talk with parishioners. Mike and his wife live in a charming former pub, decorated with military memorabilia. Mike's brisk, cheery manner belied the pain they are suffering following the death of a beloved daughter. Given that, their warm hospitality was the more remarkable.

We then proceeded for a brief visit to Welbourne Church, a little gem with a curiously large transept which, I expect, used to be a family pew at one stage in its history. Lunch at the house of the curate, Ian Bentley and his wife, a mercifully simple meal, was followed by a walk through country lanes nearby before visiting the school at Yaxham for another assembly. Afterwards the children clung to the wire netting in the playground like monkeys in a cage and waved as I set off in a pony and trap to Yaxham Church a mile or two away. This is another simple country church restored by a Tractarian benefactor in Victorian times complete with rood screen, six candles and tabernacle on the altar – hardly necessary now since the patronage is in the hands of evangelical trusts. A dozen or so parishioners had gathered and we had a good talk before returning to the vicarage where the leadership team and members of the PCC were assembled for a buffet tea.

The day ended with a service of Youth Praise back at Mattishall Parish Church. This is an annual event for which a huge number of Rainbows, Brownies, Guides, Beavers and Scouts had gathered, together with other young people. This service originated from an initiative by the Mothers' Union and had been called 'The Mothers' Union Children's Service'. It was felt that in this modern age that title might not have enormous appeal so now it is called 'Youth Praise'. It had all been well rehearsed and was performed with no hitches apart from the tearful exit of a Brownie overcome by the responsibility of reading a sentence from a piece of paper in front of a microphone.

Mattishall is a large village – a small town by Norfolk standards – and both church and community life are well supported and strong. It was interesting to contrast the confidence of the leadership team at Mattishall with the much more reserved group of parishioners I met at Yaxham. But at Yaxham they have raised enormous sums of money for their church and there are good and hopeful signs, with one or two young couples supporting Yaxham when their inclination would have been to join the more youthful congregation at Mattishall.

Thursday 23 November

The assembly at Hockering Primary School was unusual because the children had learnt the modern version of the Lord's Prayer by heart. This is the first time I have encountered it. In every other school where they have said the Lord's Prayer it has been in the traditional form. Also they had learnt the Pilgrimage Prayer by heart so were obviously well prepared for my visit. We had coffee in a parishioner's house and afterwards we went to Ailwyn Hall Old People's Home at Honingham where we had a service of Holy Communion and visited the residents in their new extension. The old building is to be used for a new influx of senile dementia patients. Roger Dawson (whose relationship with both the children and the old people is very good), told me about the visit of the former Archbishop of York, John Habgood, to a home for old people where some of them suffered from dementia. He went up to one lady and said, 'Do you know who I am?' and she replied, 'No, but if you ask the Matron she will tell you.'

Lunch was at The Lodge, which on the programme I thought was someone's private house. It turned out to be a pub in North Tuddenham where parishioners from the benefice gathered – a mixture of farmers, housekeepers and retireds – and we had a good time together talking about farming and the rural Church.

After lunch I went for a walk in Hockering and visited the parish church, which was being cleaned by a very tall man with a beard wearing thigh-waders. His family had kept the local pub for many years but now they were retired and he was looking after his old mother and father – a male version of the dedicated unmarried daughter.

Back at the rectory the ministry team were assembled for a Bible study on the day's passage from St Luke, led by John, a lay reader, and a good group of people. After tea and scones we drove to the chapel in the village of Honingham, which had been given by Lord Ailwyn to the parishioners because the parish church was so far away. It was a rather cold building with ineffective heating, and we said Prayer Book evensong with two hymns but it was shortened because nobody had thought of bringing a Bible, and none could be found in the church.

We returned to Hockering rectory where a crowd of twenty or so people from the deanery, clergy and readers and their spouses, arrived for supper – all of whom I either knew quite well already or had met during the week.

Friday 24 November

The day began quietly in the Lady Chapel at St Nicholas Parish Church, Dereham, with prayer and a talk with the churchwardens and Andrew Todd, who is based here half time and is half-time Director of Studies at the East Anglian Ministerial Training Course. He is a good priest who was a curate in Norwich some years ago and then became chaplain of King Alfred's College, Winchester. St Nicholas is beautiful, well restored, and with imaginative interior alterations which make it adaptable for liturgy, concerts and more informal meetings. The Lady Chapel is a peaceful place with a good atmosphere. Facing us was a beautiful bronze statue of St Withburga which had been made by Sister Benedicta, aged ninety-one, who lives as a solitary in a house near the church.

The visit to the First School in Dereham was so relaxed as to be almost a non-event at first. We briefly saw the Headmaster, who handed me over to three tiny children to take me round the school. The first class we visited were just exiting for playtime and then we saw two more, neither of whom had been prepared for my visit. As this is a church school I thought it a wasted opportunity. I then said to one of the teachers that I would prefer to see the next three forms all together, which I did, and was able to make something of it with my normal assembly performance. But I had to work hard to make the visit worthwhile for the children.

We walked over to Church House, an old building which serves as a hall. It was market day and coffee was being served, as in Fakenham, except that here it was mostly church people who came. We then walked through the town to the market place and visited the stalls. Dennis Rider, the Vicar, was in hospital with heart trouble so could not take me round the market. He probably knew the stallholders, which Andrew did not, and so again I had to make the running.

We walked back to the church, where a fire engine provided an interesting drive through Dereham to the neighbouring village of Scarning where we had a Eucharist followed by lunch in the village hall. The Bible study which followed was attended by twenty or thirty parishioners and was the best this week, which was interesting because the other Bible studies had been attended by ministry teams and this was a more open invitation. I thought the whole standard of Bible study was actually better, though perhaps not a little was due to the fact that we had all had lunch together beforehand, and people had started talking to one another.

We drove back to Andrew's house from where I had a short walk, but it was very cold by now, and so I soon went back to the house for a cup of tea and then we left again for the church for evening prayer in the Lady Chapel. Afterwards I went over the road to meet the junior choir who were practising carols. Andrew and I took the male parts, not very expertly, but we enjoyed ourselves although I think the choir mistress was quite relieved when we left after distributing badges and prayer cards, and the serious practice could resume.

Back at Andrew's house I met his three delightful children: Benedict, who has just won a place in the choir at Ely Cathedral, Harriet, aged six, and

Lydia, aged three. We watched a tape of *Narnia* on the television for a while and the little girls, together with a big black cat, curled up with me on the sofa, which was all very restful.

Once more we crossed the town to the parish church and briefly met the senior choir before joining the youth club, called 'The Searchers', a lively group of eleven- to fourteen-year-olds led by Andrew and two or three other adults. We played games and then they asked me innumerable questions ranging from the usual, 'Do you like being a bishop?' to, 'What kind of music do you like?'; 'What books do you read?' and, 'Are you into heavy metal?' They presented me with a homemade metal badge, making me an honorary 'Searcher' and a baseball cap with 'Searchers are cool' on it. After more games I left and on the way home visited Dennis Rider in hospital. He is really quite ill, and will remain here for a week or ten days before going to Papworth for a thorough examination and possible surgery.

Saturday 25 November

The new Rector of Shipdham, Beryl Wood, greeted me at the church. She was instituted just two weeks ago, having been appointed in competition with two able male candidates. This is the third or fourth woman priest in recent months who has been appointed in competition with men, which is an encouraging illustration of how quickly the ordination of women to the priesthood has been accepted in this very conservative diocese. Shipdham Church has been marvellously reordered with a large glassed-in side chapel where we had lunch with thirty or so parishioners followed by a Bible study and discussion. It was a good fellowship and the individuals I talked to spoke warmly of Beryl, and were sensitively aware of some of the difficulties she will be facing in the future.

The discussion focused on the young and there were three young people present, including David, an interesting seventeen-year-old doing 'A' levels. He feels he might have a vocation either to the Church Army or to priesthood. A few weeks ago he was badly beaten up in Dereham for no apparent reason by a young man who, he subsequently learned, was on drugs and on a weekend's leave from a detention centre. David showed no bitterness or anger but admitted it had shaken his confidence very considerably. But he himself is determined to do something for his generation and with another young girl who was present (the daughter of the local publican) is making plans to open a youth club, which ought to be viable in this large village of 2,000 inhabitants. Like so many places, the village is plagued with vandalism by a few, and the older people present all spoke of their longing 'to do something for the young'. I believe the key is to understand that there is very little that we can give to the young, but that we need to discover what they have to give to us. Young David, in the nicest possible way during the general discussion, said that he found his contribution to the discussion constantly being side-tracked or blocked out by the contribution of adults. To be fair, they listened sympathetically to what he said and I sensed a very good group of people, open to new ideas and adventurous thinking. Beryl's predecessor, Frank Irwin, built good foundations and I believe this parish, with its neighbour Bradenham, could really take off in the future.

After lunch I was driven to Bradenham, three miles away, in a wonderful Bull-nose 1925 Morris Cowley Tourer in impeccable condition. It was the first model with front wheel brakes, as well as in the rear. Apparently there used to be a sign on the back of this new model warning following drivers that the brakes operated on all four wheels and therefore would tend to pull up more quickly than a vehicle behind which would only have brakes on the rear wheels. I had not seen one of these old cars for years but remember a photograph of my grandfather and grandmother Nott in a similar car, which must have dated from the late twenties. I seem to remember my grandfather in a cloth cap and long coat, and Granny Nott in a hat with a motoring veil. I wonder if that picture is still around somewhere.

Bradenham was holding its St Andrew's-tide fair in the village hall with a sale of books, pictures, bric-a-brac, cakes, plants and raffles. I had no money on me so borrowed £5 from Beryl. With my first pound I bought four tickets from the bottle stall and to my embarrassment won a bottle of claret and a bottle of beer. Towards the end of the afternoon, when there were just two or three bottles left, I bought two more with my last fifty pence and won a bottle of whisky. To compensate, I helped the caretaker clear up, putting away chairs and tables until John fetched me just after 4 o'clock. We drove back to Norwich for a break before the evening engagement.

In the evening we had an amazing feast in Easton Church – a lovely, medieval church which had been converted into a banqueting hall with long tables set out with linen, cutlery, candles and glass all around the church. We had splendid food, lamb carved on the spot, huge baked potatoes and fresh vegetables with St Catherine's pie and ice cream afterwards (today is St Catherine's Day). About sixty people were there from the three parishes of Easton, Colton and Marlingford: old, young and middle-aged, and also Tony, a traveller who lived in a caravan across the road from the church and who had been invited at the last minute by Jonathan Lumby and brought in. These are for the most part middle-class commuter parishioners, with a few old Norfolk country people thrown in, but everyone got on well together and there was a genuine sense of community. Some of the children had met me earlier in the week at their school and proudly wore their pilgrimage badges. An altogether enjoyable evening which ended with a few words from me about the pilgrimage and a blessing. I kept John waiting half an hour because it went on far longer than anticipated, but he was patient and uncomplaining as always.

Sunday 26 November

The 'all age' service at East Tuddenham proved to be mostly middle-aged, with only two young people present. However the village is small, only 300 and without many young families, so for the size of village the attendance was good and the informal liturgy went well with a carefully prepared sermon by Roger Dawson on the readings for the day. This is the parish he likes best and it shows, both in his attitude to them and their affection for him. The tall, bearded man who was in waders in Hockering Church was there and I was glad to be able to talk to him and give him a prayer card. They kindly presented me with specially commissioned mugs, with tops shaped like mitres, made at the local pottery which I was told uses the same technique as Ming.

Graham Reardon and his wife had attended the service and drove me to Kimberly Hall, where Ron and Phyl Buxton held a lunch for people in the Barnham Broom Group. Phyl, many years ago, was secretary to the Bishop of Truro before I took on the job temporarily in 1958 when Phyl's successor left suddenly. So I have known of Phyl for nearly forty years and she was particularly delighted when at my enthronement she noticed I was wearing the cross and carrying the pastoral staff which had been given to me by Bishop Edmund Morgan, a saintly man who lived until his nineties.

It was a friendly occasion, meeting mostly people I had encountered before on my visit to the Barnham Broom Group. When I see faces on the final day it often seems that I first met them weeks ago, but in fact it is only days. I suppose, because so much happens during the week, time telescopes. There is a magnificent organ above the central staircase, which was played during the meal for most of the time. There were lots of young people there as well as their parents and grandparents, a genuine cross-section in terms of age and social group. A twelve-year-old showed me a small orange cylinder with a kind of wick sticking from one end. He told me he had brought several back from France.

'It's a firework,' he said, 'a miniature stick of dynamite. You have to light it, chuck it and run fast, or it blows up in your hand. They're illegal in England. They call it a "petard".'

Now I know the origin of the saying 'hoist with his own petard'! This is basically a very good Group ministry which needs and deserves first-class leadership. There are still difficulties to be overcome but much potential to be realised.

15

Loddon

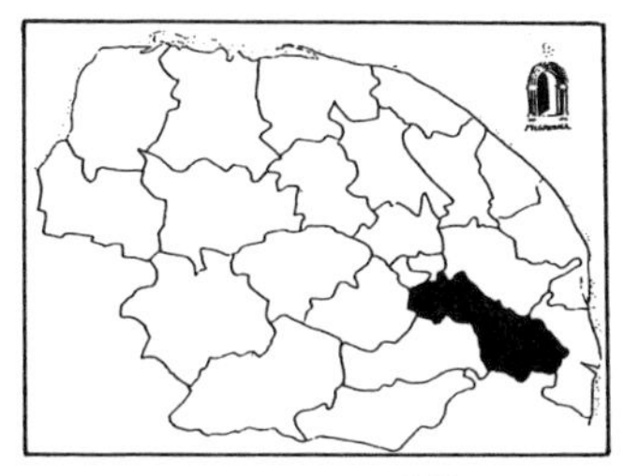

(The sausage shape of this deanery straddles one of the main roads from Norwich to the south. From the commuter villages in the north the area becomes rapidly rural with tiny communities and a number of large multi-parish benefices. One attraction of the city of Norwich is the proximity of deep countryside.)

Tuesday 5 December

After an almost sleepless night, I felt very groggy with an extremely heavy cold and set out for Seething airfield wondering how I would get through the day. It was bitterly cold with a biting easterly wind and snow flurries. Chris Chapman, the Rural Dean, met me at the airfield where the gale force wind was rocking the small Cessna aircraft in which it had been planned that I would view the deanery from the air. Standing on the airstrip I was immediately hit by the icy gale. It was so cold I felt physical pain in my face. I can only remember feeling this cold once before in my life, on a night exercise in midwinter on the North German plain. Beside the plane was a man clearly in his seventies.

'Who's that?' I asked.

'Your pilot,' said Chris. 'He's the treasurer of our church,' giving the impression that this was ample qualification for piloting an aircraft in these conditions.

Four of us clambered into the aircraft and were strapped in. After waiting for a snow flurry to pass, we took off and flew around the deanery. The flight was in fact quite pleasant with sun shining through the cloud and I was re-assured when the pilot, Jocelyn Buxton, a shy and charming man, told me that he had been a Fleet Air Arm pilot during the war, spending most of his time on Atlantic convoys, flying Seafires (the carrier-borne version of the

Spitfire) on convoys to Murmansk. I reckoned that if he could take off from an aircraft carrier in an Atlantic gale he was perfectly capable of taking us safely in a Cessna from Seething airfield. On our return flight the wind blew us this way and that but he made a perfect three-point landing and we ran back to the small club-house for welcome hot cups of coffee.

Framingham Earl High School has a high proportion of intelligent children and the visit to the junior form was easy. The Deputy Head then took us to another class and just before we entered he said, 'You'll find this lot difficult – the senior year, rather bolshie and anti-church.' Very comforting. In the event I found the children lively, intelligent and not so hostile when I challenged some of their own assumptions. We talked about a range of subjects from creation to Sunday trading and it was all very stimulating. Despite feeling rather weak, the adrenalin levels were high so I managed to cope.

Lunch was with the new Roman Catholic Bishop Peter Smith and his chaplain at his home in Poringland. Fortified by a medicinal pre-lunch whisky, I found the occasion most enjoyable and friendly.

From Stoke Holy Cross, David Broome, the Vicar, large in body and spirit, took me first to two house-bound parishioners for Communion, and then to Dunston Hall, a refurbished hotel and country club, to meet four young people working for Youth for Christ in the Operation Gideon team in which young people spend a year between school and university or post-university helping in parishes. These were high calibre young folk whom it was good to meet. We then went to a farmer's house for supper followed by a highly organised Bible study at Stoke Holy Cross Church, led by a lay reader. He had clearly been preparing this Bible study for a very long time and I felt a heel saying I wanted to leave a quarter of an hour early, but I didn't think I could last longer than 8.30.

Wednesday 6 December

I felt even worse today and the weather matched it – bitterly cold and driving sleet all day. At All Saints, Chedgrave, I asked David McPherson, the Vicar, to do most of the celebration and I simply said the thanksgiving prayer. At Langley School, the Headmaster, who has done a marvellous job in the last five years, apologised that all the children were taking exams. This was a great relief to me but I didn't tell him, and so we toured the school's facilities and just met one pupil, a delightful boy, working on his 'A' level pottery project and producing imaginative and wonderfully artistic work. I asked him what other 'A' levels he was doing.

'None because I'm dyslexic,' he replied, without any sense of embarrassment.

We then visited the lovely church at Langley filled with treasures and, strangely, glass from Rouen and other medieval glass clearly imported from

Chedgrave

somewhere – stolen most likely at some time by the rich landowner who used to live in the big house before it became a school.

Lunch was at the All Saints Centre, a fine annexc to the lovely medieval church at Chedgrave, where a large number of parishioners had gathered. David is one of the 'awkward squad' as far as senior staff are concerned, and a member of the clergy trades union, but he is a good parish priest with a varied and lively congregation of all ages. I fell asleep in his study after lunch for half an hour and then was taken to the Waveney Group where Chris Whiteman, the bright new young vicar who was a curate in the diocese, seems to have settled well.

After visiting Gillingham First School we went to the tiny Women's Fellowship at Ellingham and Kirby Cane – tiny, I guess, because of the appalling weather – where I chatted for a while before going to Geldestone Memorial Hall to meet a group of villagers, again not a large group and mostly elderly. Chris then dropped me at Kirby Cane Hall where I was welcomed by Major Simon Crisp, formerly of the Horse Guards, and I had a pleasant hour with him. He lives in his beautiful house alone with a housekeeper and butler, a strong supporter of Chris and beneath the bluff, grandee, heavy-smoking exterior is a good and sensitive man who thinks about his faith.

At the Wherry public house a group of parishioners gathered and, wilting by this time, I was glad of some whisky before driving through appalling conditions and sliding along country lanes to Norton Methodist Chapel in the sticks, miles from civilisation, it appeared. There we had another Bible study, well conducted by Chris Poulard, the Rector of the Raveningham Group. But I was greatly relieved when John came to take me home.

Thursday 7 December

The wind had dropped and the snow fell intermittently through the day in pretty flakes. We began with Communion at the pretty little church at Yelverton, followed by coffee with parishioners and the Vicar, Gordon Jessup. He is still recuperating from a serious operation, so he wisely kept at several arms' lengths when he heard I had a cold. I had woken feeling awful and dreading the day, but strangely and wonderfully, as I celebrated Communion, I began to feel better by the minute.

At the Old Rectory next door, which is now an old people's home, there was another Communion and talk with old people. Afterwards I went to Alpington First School for lunch, which was beef lasagne, despite the county's ban on beef in schools which was imposed yesterday. I suppose it was too late to change the menu. The children were all very chatty, but most of them, I noticed, were having packed lunch.

An hour's break was taken at the home of John and Maria Phillips. John is a retired priest who used to be Vicar of Eaton and Maria, who is Czechoslovakian, escaped from the Russians in 1949 and came with her parents to England. We then went for the rest of the day to Brian Hems' parishes. It was just as well I was feeling better because we had an intensive programme beginning at the large junior school in Poringland with a visit to every class and an assembly with the senior years. Then to the Good Companions Club, where I just missed bingo but was present for drawing the lottery, an auction and tea.

Then we drove up a narrow lane to the isolated church of Bixley and met Herbert, a churchwarden and a cowman who used to be the deanery Lay Chairman of Lothingland, a delightful man. Nobody else was in the church but we had a good look round by torchlight (no electricity here), before going off to visit parishioners – an old man of ninety-three, who used to be a ship's cook and still cooks for himself, and then a former senior executive with Norwich Union who had a stroke five years ago. This was followed by a visit to the glorious church at Howe, which has one of the oldest Saxon towers in the country and is a very beautiful, much loved church with super churchwardens. Next I was taken to a swimming pool run by a local lady, who is also the church treasurer. It is a heated indoor pool in the back garden, which is leased to families who pay £200 a year for half an hour a week and it works very well. Actually, despite the oddity of such a visit, I was quite glad to go there because at least it was very warm, the churches having been freezing.

Then off to visit the 'Rainbows' in the Octagon, which is the church centre attached to Poringland Parish Church. They had arranged for me to read the 'going home story' to the little children, which was an original idea and I much enjoyed the experience with these little girls not much older than my own grandchildren.

Poringland calls itself a village but it is really a suburb of Norwich straggling for a mile along the main road to Lowestoft, linked with Framingham Earl, the neighbouring parish, and divided only by the main road, together comprising about 5,000 inhabitants. The two villages are indistinguishable but one is still reminded tenaciously of the ancient parish boundary, as when I asked the local shopkeeper how long he had had the post office in Poringland.

'We are not in Poringland,' he said firmly, 'we are in Framingham Earl.'

After a meal at the rectory with Brian and his wife, I returned to Poringland village hall, where I chatted for an hour with more parishioners, before being whisked off to Stoke Holy Cross to visit the 'Cross Bar', which is a young people's club run by a dedicated layman called Stuart, a recent convert, and the four young Gideons whom I met yesterday. At the end of a long and tiring day it was not a prospect I relished, especially as I approached the hall where a group were smoking outside – inside it was no smoking, no alcohol.

In the hall they looked at this strange apparition in a purple skirt with suspicion. But then one lanky youth with an earring unwound from a chair in the corner where he had been listlessly watching a game of pool. He took pity on me and said he'd play darts with me. 'Ever played before?' (Honestly, what do they think bishops did when they were young, read the Bible all the time?) He got a bit worried when I was on to double 5 when he still needed 70 points. Of course he beat me in the end, but that little act of kindness was as touching as it was surprising. The young man in question is Dominic Pearson, a young Roman Catholic whose mother is dying, I learnt afterwards. The darts were terrible and I decided to present them with a decent set.

Friday 8 December

The day dawned bright and sunny and so it remained throughout the morning for a delightful walk with parishioners through the village of Surlingham surrounded by white fields and snow-decked trees, looking very pretty. We assembled at the village shop which still thrives, thanks largely, I guess, to the holiday trade in the summer from the nearby river. Unlike its neighbour Bramerton, which is a rather wealthy suburban village without much community feel about it, Surlingham is a more mixed community with a school. After a long and most enjoyable walk we arrived at Broad Cottage, the home of one of the churchwardens, for coffee and a talk with parishioners.

I was then driven to Loddon where once again I met up with the Rural Dean, Chris Chapman, who, like Alan Bell a few weeks before, has been attentive and caring and has organised an extremely well-balanced and helpful week.

The rest of the day was spent in Loddon, walking the streets and calling at various shops. This is a large village, or rather small town, with a strong community sense, and Chris is clearly well known and much liked by everyone. We visited two old-fashioned shops which sell everything, one doubling as a funeral parlour, and another also providing a furniture removal service. The shopkeepers were all glad to see me, one large owner behind the counter saying, 'It's very good you're spending time with the little people.'

Lunch was at a day centre in the fine new Jubilee Hall where we had an old people's lunch. Again, as so often in such gatherings, the men sat at a table on their own. They included, unusually, a Cornishman who has lived here for twenty-five years, his wife being a Norfolk girl. It is extraordinary how many husbands and wives I have met where the wife, whose roots are in Norfolk, has managed by hook or by crook eventually to bring her husband home. To be fair, I have not met any foreigners who have resented that strong homing instinct.

From there we walked to a pub, the Loddon Swan, one of three flourishing inns in the town, run by a devout Christian couple who gave us coffee though offering us something stronger if we wished. I went for a walk afterwards, did a quick sketch and took some photographs of the now waning sun and rising mist before returning to the rectory where Chris was waiting to take me on another tour.

We called at various shops and had an interesting tour of a telecottage industry established by the South Norfolk District Council. The young man who was running it used to work for Radio Broadland and told me he had interviewed me at the beginning of my pilgrimage. Here sophisticated computer facilities are provided and one or two offices let to provide facilities for people using computers in the area, of which, of course, there are an increasing number, one man having recently leased one of the offices to carry out his accounting business. It is enterprising and typical of the liveliness of some of the district councils in Norfolk, whom I find impressive, caring and frequently visionary. They provide a good argument for subsidiarity, allowing decisions to be made at the most local level possible. So often they have the vision but power is focused elsewhere, more centrally.

I was given a tour of the headquarters of Anglia Produce, in a fine Georgian mansion on the edge of the town. This is a large concern for marketing potatoes; having started as a local farmers' co-operative, it has grown to a major business with national connections. We had a long discussion with senior members of the staff, whom I cross-examined about their policy regarding fertilisers, organically grown vegetables and marketing policy. So much is controlled these days by large retailers. For example, Anglia Produce produce potatoes for Macdonalds throughout the country, who demand long, thin potatoes so that they can be made into chips of uniform size and

Loddon

taste. On the whole they do good work for local agriculture but admitted that they could not deal with anything much less than a fifty-acre production. This means that small farmers, that is the most vulnerable ones who are often on the margin, are not really helped by such big marketing firms. But the public relations man was good, and not complacent about some of the ethical issues.

We next went to the McIntyre Care sheltered housing complex for those with learning difficulties, that is, the 'mentally handicapped', and I had tea in one bungalow shared by four residents with their care assistants and then to a next door bungalow with the more severely handicapped. An impressive place – we could do with many more of these facilities.

Finally, we had evening prayer in the Methodist church led by Gordon Spittlehouse, the local Methodist minister. I really enjoyed today, in contrast with the first days of the week when I felt quite ill. Getting through the visits then was a matter of sheer endurance, only made possible by the very good planning and Chris Chapman's sensitive caring.

Saturday 9 December

Another bright and very cold day began early with a men's breakfast at Bramerton, attended by thirty or forty from the Group, and after boiled eggs, cereal and hot rolls we had a question and answer session which was good, though at one stage I almost had to referee an argument between two men about the place of church buildings, one wanting to do away with them, the other thinking they were of very great spiritual importance. On the whole I have found that there is a very positive attitude towards medieval church buildings, and less resentment or anxiety now than there used to be about the time and money spent in maintaining them. This may be because in scores of places they are now beginning to see the results of their labours after years and years of effort. Certainly I have tried always to encourage them, and have made clear my own strong commitment to the churches of Norfolk.

A deanery Bible study at Thurston village hall was well attended and we had a full two hours which gave ample opportunity for a good discussion followed by a period of silent prayer at the end. At one stage we got on to the subject of sexual morality and I told them about the very good article by Hugh Montefiore in yesterday's *Church Times*, in which he urged the Church to make clear the distinction between moral principle on the one hand, and pastoral care on the other – which must be offered to all, whatever their circumstances. At the moment the Church is getting these two things muddled, a prime example being the recent report *Something to Celebrate*.

Chris Poulard drove me to Haddiscoe village hall where they dressed me in a chef's hat with the pilgrimage logo sewn on the front and an apron and I dished out hot soup. Afterwards I had a good walk in country lanes hard-packed with snow and ice. In this part of Norfolk four or five inches have fallen and the snow is quite thick and freezing still. Chris then took me on a tour of some of the other parishes in his large Group, beginning with a Christmas Fair in the village hall at Burgh St Peter where young people presented a very amusing and well-written Christmas drama comparing the commercialism of Christmas with the gospel. A feature of this group of parishes is the presence of numbers of young people and there is a good youth group which was begun about a year ago.

Next we went to the village shop where a sixteen-year-old left in charge was rather nervous because of the number of break-ins which had happened – a sad feature of life for some owners of village post offices these days. This was followed by a visit to Charlie, an old churchwarden, and his wife, Elsie, their grandson and his girlfriend who was in a wheelchair as she suffers from multiple sclerosis. It was a delightful visit, sitting in the tiny parlour with a roaring fire while Charlie told us stories of the old days with threshing machines and ancient tractors.

After a brief visit to a market garden shop, we returned to the rectory for tea and I had a long talk with Chris Poulard. He is an able priest, ordained late, who has done a marvellous job during the last six years. When Chris arrived, the morale of the parishes was at rock bottom following years of unsatisfactory ministry. He has part-time help now in the shape of Mair Talbot, and they make a good team. Chris has developed lay ministry and from what I saw today the whole spirit of the Group has lifted and people are positive and forward looking. Chris suffers from mood swings partly because, with his urban evangelical background, he hopes for too much too quickly. I hope he'll stay because I sense that after his hard and faithful work he will very soon be reaping the rewards of his ministry.

We returned to Norton Methodist Chapel for an evening Service of Praise with a keen choir dressed in an original uniform of blouses, skirts and coloured silk scarves. Here again there were young people present who did a mime and there is a thriving youth group consisting of twenty-five or thirty people, which is quite remarkable – something I have rarely encountered in country parishes. The service was led by Gordon Spittlehouse, the Methodist minister, and in conversation with parishioners afterwards I asked one couple if they were Methodists or Anglicans.

Their reply was polite but firm: 'We don't really take much notice of that. Actually we were both brought up as Methodists but we all belong to the same church here.'

I also met a churchwarden from Fritton in the Somerleyton Group who used to live here and comes back for this Service of Praise once a month or so when eighty people regularly attend. He told me that they had started something similar in Somerleyton during the interregnum and it had proved to be a point of growth. I said how much I had enjoyed my visit to his Group some weeks ago and that I thought things were going well.

'Oh yes, it's not bad really,' he said – a typical Norfolk reply which actually means that things are going exceedingly well.

At this Praise Service they take a collection which they give away and never use for Group funds. They raised £3,000 last year, which puts into perspective the difficulties people express about raising sufficient money for the parish share.

Sunday 10 December

At Stoke Holy Cross a family Communion began with the procession of clergy and servers entering the sanctuary accompanied by the familiar hubbub of a charismatic church as people chat and guitars are tuned. Eventually they realised we were there and the service got under way. It was a good and catholic liturgy with a twenty minute break in the middle for choruses and free prayer which was well done but this was followed by conventional *ASB* intercessions which seemed unnecessary – it would have been quite appropriate in such a setting to have extempore prayer for the diocese of South Carolina, the Queen, Northern Ireland and the sick.

Lunch was in the church hall nearby where I had met the youth club a few days before. I met Dominic Pearson's father. His wife had died the day before, after a long illness. He said Dominic had enjoyed his game with me, and was grateful for the gift of darts and a prayer card which I sent him. It had been kind of Dominic to play darts with me and it had made me feel less out of place. Apparently he is a young man who has not always been easy and his kindness to me was the more touching for that. I talked to several parishioners and at a young people's table met Charles, aged fifteen, with spiky hair – a tough looking customer who told me that he had come to church for the first time through James, the Vicar's son, with whom he had stayed for the weekend. James had taken him to church and he thought it was quite good and never stopped going from that day. He then got his two younger sisters to go and another friend or two. Although his parents are not churchgoers, the three children are now all very much involved.

'I seem to be quite good at getting people into church,' he said. 'Some people say I should be a vicar.'

I hope he will be.

In the afternoon we had a deanery service in the great parish church at Loddon. It was full of people from the deanery muffled in coats, scarves and gloves – with good reason because the church was icy cold in spite of the fact that the heating had been on, ineffectually, since 8 am. Chris Poulard had devised an excellent Advent Service of Light during which I gave an address and at the end there was a musical version of the Pilgrimage Prayer which had been composed locally in antiphonal form, with the congregation singing parts. At the end the entire congregation, singing 'Walk in the Light', processed out of the church and across the main street to St John's Methodist Church for tea in their hall. We were all frozen to the bone by this time and the warm fug which greeted us was very welcome, as were the steaming cups of tea and the very good fellowship which followed. In the winter months both congregations use this Methodist church for worship, and in the summer all transfer to the parish church, which is a very sensible arrangement.

Despite my terrible cold at the beginning of the week, it has been a good pilgrimage, due not least to the leadership of another excellent rural dean. There is a real engagement of the parishes with the local community in this area and a surprisingly strong showing of young people, not least in the very rural parishes of the Raveningham Group.

16

Breckland

(Apart from the small towns of Swaffham and Watton, this is a large and very rural area, with hundreds of square miles of heathland, tiny villages, scattered hamlets and a large army training area.)

Tuesday 12 December

The primary school at Caston is in an idyllic setting – a small Victorian building on the village green facing thatched cottages and the church. Sadly, it is soon to go because there are too many children for the building and the site does not have room for sufficient expansion, so they will have to move up the road. After assembly and coffee with the staff, Hedley Richardson, the Rural Dean and Vicar of this Group, took me to a pig farm where they also grow vegetables. I spent an hour in the farm shop with the owners Beryl and Marshall Warren, and talked to the few customers who braved the rather dismal weather to come to buy vegetables. The snow went overnight as the temperature rose but the day, though warm, was damp and drizzly.

After leaving Stow Bedon, we drove to Breckles for lunch at the home of Margaret Morfoot, whose husband was away shooting. A group of parishioners gathered and we were joined halfway through the meal by her enormous, cheerful, ruddy-faced son.

There was only a twenty minute break today because Colin Chinery, a columnist on the *EDP*, came to Caston rectory to interview me for an article on my tenth anniversary as Bishop. We talked for an hour but I did not feel on particularly lively form and of course he wanted to talk about Hilborough, which I find increasingly tedious as a subject of conversation. I just hope the resulting article won't be too bad.

At Thompson more parishioners gathered for tea at the home of the fragrantly named Lavender Garnier, sister of Lord Walsingham, and we had an interesting talk about the ministry team in this group of parishes. Hedley is a bustling, energetic Midlander who surprisingly has taken to rural ministry in Norfolk like a duck to water and his enthusiastic vision has proved infectious. For four or five years parishioners have been studying *Moving Forward* and most of the parishes have now adopted my vision that there should be an act of worship in every parish on every Sunday. Hedley has formed a ministry team which is remarkable for its ordinariness in the best sense. They are enthusiastic about the team, are being well trained through courses arranged by the diocese, and congregations have increased, in some cases dramatically. It is a fine example of what can be done in small, rather traditional parishes with a typical mixture of Norfolk parishioners. A side effect of increasing congregations and regular worship has been a transformation in their finances, and they now pay their parish share regularly and without difficulty in a way that has not happened before.

After Thompson we drove to Thorpe House at Griston, an old people's home where most of the residents are in a poor state mentally. Entering the day room I was greeted by an old lady in a chair shouting obscenities. Hedley tried to engage her in conversation, while I chatted to another lady and her son who had come to visit her. We then moved on to visit an old man, a former farm labourer, who was delightful, and another old lady, a little confused about where she was. We finally left, with yet more obscenities reverberating down the corridors, to visit a factory nearby, the home of 'Norfolk Labels'. Intricate machines were producing coloured labels for food packaging, mostly the products of Bernard Matthews, I noticed. It was Eric, a churchwarden, who showed us round the factory. He was one of those who was unfortunately turned down at a Selection Conference for LNSM – I think he had been put forward too early by the ministry team, but has recovered and is now exercising effective leadership in the local parishes.

Tea was at the home of another parishioner, Pearl Church, at Great Hockham where she had invited a group of friends who were not churchgoers. This was an interesting gathering which included an arable farmer who was very articulate about the countryside and its problems, the wife of an American pilot based at Lakenheath, two other ladies and a retired Welshman who talked about the aversion he felt towards Margaret Thatcher, to the extent that he had to switch off the television every time she appeared on it. It was a lively tea but soon it was time to drive to Watton for a Bible study with the chapter and readers. After talking to strangers for most of the day, which is always quite a mental effort, and not having had my usual break, I was glad to be among people most of whom I knew quite well and we had a helpful Bible study on that most difficult of passages in Luke, the story of the unjust steward.

Martin Down, the charismatic Vicar of Ashill, has curiously hit the

Caston

national headlines because of a controversial scheme to take out some Victorian pews. Quite why, I cannot understand, because it is an extremely boring subject and at any one time there must be thirty such controversies going on in the Church of England. The juicy bit for the Press, I suppose, is the allegation that he is removing the pews in order that people will have room to fall down when hit by 'The Toronto Blessing'. I shall be in Ashill tomorrow evening so perhaps I'll hear more about the truth or otherwise of that statement.

Wednesday 13 December

The tiny school at Carbrooke is desperately overcrowded, with ninety children in a school designed for thirty, no assembly hall or staff room and a number of temporary classrooms, with no imminent hope of improvement either. I wonder what the policy in the county is, because some schools with fewer needs have had improvements, as I have seen on my pilgrimage. The Headmaster, David Saunders, is very good and we had an excellent assembly with the children. They told me that if only they could use the church next door for their assemblies a lot of their problems would be solved. They were apparently told by the Diocesan Education Committee that they were not allowed to do this since assemblies in voluntary controlled, as opposed to voluntary aided, schools had to be in non-denominational buildings, which seemed to me the height of bureaucratic nonsense. I told them to go ahead and use the church and said that if necessary I would write a letter of authority for them to do so. If anyone attempts to rap me over the knuckles for this I shan't in the least mind.

At Watton Methodist Church we had a period of worship and a Bible study with a large group of local people, all of them retired. We focused on Luke's statement on the law of marriage and divorce, which is the strictest in the Gospels, and then went on to talk about divorce in the Church in general. As at Thurston, I shared with them the substance of Hugh Montefiore's article in the *Church Times* which I found immensely helpful, making the distinction between moral principle and pastoral compassion.

We then walked up the High Street, where I presented the prize for the best Christmas window display to Kings the Chemists, sang carols with some girls from Watton High School and then switched on the Christmas Lights (not very sensational at 12 noon). This was followed by lunch with a group of friendly old people at the community centre, an ecumenical Christian initiative which serves lunches five days a week at £1.60 – very good value. We then went upstairs for coffee in the same building to meet local councillors and had an interesting talk about the town and its problems. In Watton there are reasonably high levels of employment, and the large number of small shops seem to manage to remain viable but there is a growing problem with young people and drugs. Richard Bowett, the new vicar, is working with other people to try to tackle the problem and is hoping at some time to employ a Church Army officer to assist. This would be a good idea if they could get someone of the calibre of young Darren Thornton at Yarmouth.

After a short walk, I dictated some letters in the rectory and was then driven to the parish of Ashill with Saham Toney, now a quite famous charismatic parish in the middle of the countryside. Martin Down is an experienced, highly intelligent and sensitive priest who is managing his commitment to renewal with considerable skill. He took me to a remarkable complex of buildings called 'The Old Barn'. A Christian couple had bought these derelict buildings, set up a second-hand car business and let the other buildings to three interesting Christian enterprises, which I visited in turn. First there was the office of 'Living Water', which organises the annual Renewal Conference at the Norfolk Showground – it takes a whole year to organise. The office is staffed by a part-time secretary and Stephen Mawditt, an NSM candidate. In another room I met 'Action Workwise', dedicated to helping the unemployed. They give advice about CVs, writing letters of application and interviewing. But above all they help people in this position to value themselves because so often, of course, there is a loss of self-esteem which makes worse the experience of being unemployed, and with that lack of confidence it is more difficult to get another job. We had a most interesting discussion about the future of work and the evil of short-term thinking and action is a such a feature of life these days in politics, the world of commerce and industry

Watton

and which is also infecting the Church. The final visit was to 'Outlook', a new initiative in evangelism to the over sixties, run by a former missionary. She started from scratch and has clearly touched on an area of major importance and, given the changing age structure of society, a definite area for growth. I had to watch my language somewhat because she was very sensitive about ageism.

We drove back to Ashill rectory and with Maureen, Martin's wife, the three of us walked over to the church for evensong – straight *ASB*, with no frills. We had a delicious supper with a very good white Burgundy (they have a son who lives near Macon) – a gracious, enjoyable meal and I would like to have spent longer with them at the table but we had to move off to visit two houses in the parish. The first was quite remarkable. In a stone-floored cottage a couple in their thirties, who moved two years ago from Southend, live with their three children. The wife, Jan, has befriended young toughs from the village and beyond who come to the house night after night. Nearly all of them are in trouble with the police in one way or another but she somehow manages to relate to them.

'They all came to the Lord,' she said, but added, 'that doesn't mean their problems are over.'

They started arriving while we were there, most of them taking one look at me and diving into the next room. Jan told us about her plans to open a centre in an old pub in Watton, in which she is co-operating with Richard Bowett and others. Certainly they cannot go on using their house like this because there can be no private family life and Martin told me that it is putting great strains on them, which I can believe. We joined them in the next room where six of them sat, most with baseball caps back to front. Jan's husband said a prayer and handed out Bibles. Also present was Neville, a young 'Youth for Christ' worker who is working at Norwich Prison. He led the Bible study and, remarkably, they listened well as one of them read the entire twelfth chapter of Romans, though Jan at one stage had to remove a Walkman and earphones from one of them. Jan said she wished their conversion would have done something about their non-existent social graces but she added, 'The Lord doesn't seem to be working on those parts yet.'

We left that amazing household with its super couple and went to a more conventional house group at Saham Toney where a tidier and more respectable group were gathered with a guitar and Bibles for worship and a Bible study which was good and down-to-earth. These are people who are well taught and well led, loyal also to the Church of England, I think. Certainly one family, who live in the Hilborough Group and worship at Ashill, now support Graham Drake at Hilborough which is heartening.

Thursday 14 December

Peter Taylor, the Vicar of the Necton Group of parishes, dropped me at Keepers Cottage on the edge of the village for a meeting called Thursday at Ten. This is a group of young mothers and toddlers who meet every week, nearly all of them regular churchgoers. Eleven of us, with approximately the same number of children aged between six months and three years, crowded together in the sitting room and drank delicious non-alcoholic mulled wine. We then sang Christmas songs and hymns, ranging from 'I'm Dreaming of a White Christmas' to 'Hark the Herald Angels Sing', interspersed with talk and prayers about Christmas. It included a little play in which I was given the part of an angel called Tom. The leader of the group then drove me to North Pickenham for a Bible study in a parishioner's house, led by Jeffrey Platt, a retired priest and widower who is full of exuberant energy and is flying off tonight to Kenya to spend several months helping a poor diocese set up training schemes for clergy and lay people.

Lunch was at a farmhouse in North Pickenham, the home of John and Jenny Blackburne. John, whom I had already met once or twice, is the son of the late Bishop Hugh Blackburne. They farmed in Zambia until ten years ago and now keep several thousand pigs. We were accompanied by another churchwarden and his wife who came here from Sussex seven or eight years ago and have done great work in restoring the almost ruined church of St Mary, Houghton-on-the-Hill, which had been neglected for many years and had been used for occult purposes. Since the work of restoration and with careful guarding of the building on days when Black Sabbaths are held, this

Near Holme Hale

dreadful misuse has ceased but, as they said, they have to remain vigilant.

The tiny school at North Pickenham consists of less than thirty pupils and I spent an hour visiting both classes and talking to the children, a high proportion of whom are not very bright, but they were friendly and we had fun together until a churchwarden arrived to take me to my next port of call which was Paddock Farm in Holme Hale. This is the home of Eric and Olga Evans. Eric is a retired colonel in the Royal Artillery and a neighbour of General Robert Broke, my former Commanding Officer in Germany, who was sadly away in London today working for a charity with which he is much involved.

In my first year in Norfolk, when I went to take a service at Holme Hale, I met Robert Broke, after a gap of forty years, and couldn't stop myself saying, 'Good morning, Sir.'

'You must never say that again,' he replied. 'The roles are reversed now.'

Eric and Olga were warm in their welcome and had set aside a comfortable sitting room and bathroom for me to have my break. I went for a brisk walk through nearby woodland but by now a stiff northerly wind was blowing and it was very cold. Back at the house I wrote a letter or two and then chatted to my hosts over tea.

We drove to Necton Church for *BCP* evensong led by Peter Taylor with the churchwardens and two or three other parishioners present. Yet again when talking to the churchwardens I was impressed with the amount of restoration work that has been done and in a few years' time they will have completely restored and renovated this church to a high standard. I was glad to leave early to return to Norwich and catch up with some letters and prepare for the long day tomorrow in the Hilborough Group.

Friday 15 December

I knew that this day in the Hilborough Group was going to be one of the longest and most demanding days of my pilgrimage and so it proved to be, but with more positive experiences and a sense of God's grace than I had dared to hope for. I visited all ten churches in the Group and in each one we had a Bible reading and prayers, and in most of them, a talk with parishioners.

We began at Cockley Cley. I had chosen to read the Beatitudes in every church. One of the churchwardens of Cockley Cley, Geoffrey Crisp, faithfully says morning prayer in the church each day and at the end of our time together said that it was quite extraordinary because that morning in his lectionary the reading for the day was the very same I had chosen and pointed to the lectern Bible which was open at the beginning of Matthew chapter 5. The churches were nearly all pretty cold and Geoffrey Crisp, an old man, thin on top, asked permission to wear a woolly hat. I said I wished I had a purple one and would gladly have worn it too. Even in the so-called 'rebel churches', loyal parishioners were present; at Oxborough there was Eileen and the stalwart farmer, Ian Monson. At Didlington, a small 'rebel' church miles from anywhere, there were no cars so Graham and I walked up the path and prepared to pray alone. At that moment three American tourists turned up by marvellous providence and gladly joined us in our prayer and were quite thrilled with the coincidence of the Bishop and Priest-in-Charge arriving at the same moment.

We drove to Mundford Community Centre where the old people were preparing to have their Christmas lunch. 'Mundford Over Sixties Club welcomes Bishop Peter' proclaimed a poster over the door. 'Oh well,' I thought, 'another hour with the old dears.' And then I remembered I was over sixty, too, and qualified to join their club as one of the 'old dears' myself.

I left with Graham for a drink at the Twenty Churchwardens public house at Cockley Cley. This is a pub founded by Lady Judy Roberts, the widow of an MP for Sheffield, and Hugh Blackburne when he was the first Rector of the Hilborough Group. She was there and so was a photographer and reporter from Radio Norfolk. Two 'rebels' were seated at the bar, whom I greeted cheerfully, and Lady Roberts interposed herself between us and we had a very friendly conversation. She may have sensed they might cause some trouble in front of the camera – but she is not a politician's wife for nothing, and so we had a good time in the pub before driving off to Rowley Farm, the home of Margaret and Sam Steward, for a light lunch with this hospitable, loyal and courageous couple.

Graham and I set off again across the benefice to W. H. Knights, the huge vegetable packing factory at Gooderstone which employs 8,000 people, and I had half an hour talking to workers on the assembly line. They are remarkably cheerful in view of the repetitive work and long hours, standing all the time. The workers travel long distances to begin work at 7 am, a few, they told me, commuting daily from Sheffield. I called in at Gooderstone School to see the children before they went home, dished out badges and talked about the pilgrimage.

We drove on to four more churches, all with parishioners present except Threxton, where we arrived in darkness. It is only a tiny village with twenty-nine inhabitants, so Graham and I prayed by torchlight in the tiny church. By the time we returned to Graham's house we had travelled sixty-five miles during the day.

I was pretty tired by now, but had to face the most difficult part of the day, the meeting with the rebel 'churchwardens' back at Gooderstone rectory. We had an hour and a half together. I began with prayer and let them have their say. We went over a great deal of tedious old ground. We made no progress, but I managed to keep my cool and I trust managed to keep the lines of communication open, hopefully persuading them that I was not the cruel, vindictive dictator their mythology had created. Some of them are so entrenched as to be impossible. I prayed again at the end of the meeting and they all shook my hand as they left, some with surprising warmth.

I felt completely exhausted by this time and parishioners were arriving for supper. I escaped to the kitchen where Betty and Steven had arrived and had a glass of whisky and a ten-minute break before meeting the other parishioners. It was a very good evening, warm and friendly and full of parishioners appreciative of Graham's ministry and thankful that he is their priest. I am not hopeful about a solution being reached for a long time, but in the short period that Graham has been here he has made a considerable impact, and is clearly much loved by the parishioners who have met him. It is a fact, seldom reported, that the overwhelming majority of local parishioners have remained steadfastly loyal. I met many of them today: stalwart, loyal, sometimes saintly people, too numerous to mention by name, but one is deeply thankful for these people of whom 'such is the kingdom of God'.

Saturday 16 December

A day in Swaffham began in the marvellous parish church where parishioners were decorating for Christmas and putting lights on an enormous Christmas tree. I spent the rest of the morning with two parishioners who took me on a tour of Swaffham market which is one of the best known Saturday markets in Norfolk, to which people come from miles around. It filled the main street, selling everything, and we wandered through the stalls. I greeted a man selling Barbours and various coats, clearly doing a roaring trade. He was a stallholder I met in Fakenham, who told dirty jokes, and was surprised but delighted that I remembered him. How could I forget the man. There was a bitter east wind blowing and I was glad after an hour to be taken to the Methodist church for coffee, which they serve each Saturday to visitors to the market. After half an hour we set out again on more tours, including a visit to the outside auctions of flowers, plants and ironmongery of various kinds. We met a number of parishioners and also bumped into George Newton, the saintly former churchwarden of Little Cressingham who had prayed with us yesterday, here today with his daughter.

By 12.30 I was frozen stiff and glad to be taken to the home of Rachel Wilson for lunch. She was there with her brother, a retired prep school master, and a friend. There was a roaring fire, sherry waiting and it was marvellous to have the opportunity to thaw out. Rachel's family used to farm on Henry Birkbeck's estate, and she regaled us with amusing stories about those days. It was altogether a friendly and restful break which I much appreciated.

Sheila Nunney, the curate of Swaffham, soon to become assistant chaplain at the Norfolk and Norwich Hospital, accompanied me to the community hospital – a fine modern complex which is served by local GPs and is extremely well equipped and comfortable. We met the new charge nurse, Mark, son of David Adeney, our diocesan secretary – a tall, capable and friendly young man, whose previous job by contrast was in the East End of London.

I spent an hour visiting all the twelve or fourteen patients. Following visits to two men, five minutes later their parish priests, Peter Taylor and Stuart Nairn, came to visit them and afterwards said to me their visits had been quite superfluous because the men were full of having had a chat with the Bishop. I was amused that the parishioner from Narborough told me his vicar was 'a Presbyterian'. Stuart is indeed a Scot by origin, but also a good catholic Anglican, who would have been amused by the description.

I was glad to learn that the afternoon Bible study was to be at the Methodist Chapel Rooms. The Methodists always keep their churches and halls warm, so the twenty or so people who had gathered spent a comfortable hour in good discussion followed by a cup of tea.

Before leaving for home, I went to see Freda Blackburne, the widow of Bishop Hugh who died recently. We had a drink together and talked. She was tearful and cheerful at the same time, still very angry about the Hilborough rebels. She told me she used the Pilgrimage Prayer each night and that it helped but she longed to join Hugh. But after Christmas she will go off to Spain to visit her son and is very grateful for the support of her many friends.

Swaffham

Sunday 17 December

After getting lost in country lanes, we arrived at Stow Bedon Church five minutes late. I was greeted cheerfully by a churchwarden who, when I apologised, said, 'That's OK. We've been doing some hymn practice.' This sounded slightly odd until I looked at the register and discovered that the service was scheduled to begin a quarter of an hour earlier than the time written on my programme. So no wonder, with twenty minutes to fill, they had a practice. This is actually the first time that such a mistake has been made which I suppose is not bad in fourteen weeks of pilgrimage. We had Prayer Book Communion sung to Merbecke which brought back old memories, and then we drove to the beautiful church at Great Hockham, set in a park and with wonderful wall paintings. Here we had *ASB* and instead of a sermon I read them John Betjeman's poem about Christmas, which I love and which I think people enjoyed.

This was the end of the pilgrimage in the Breckland deanery because, as it is the Sunday before Christmas, the rest of the day in these parishes is full of carol services and it was impossible to arrange a deanery service in the afternoon. Given the exhausting week and my cold, which is still hanging around, I was very grateful.

On the way home I called to see the artist, Enid Clarke, in Carbrooke. She paints miniatures and I have always admired her work which I first saw at an exhibition at the Norfolk Show nine years ago. They are exquisite, small still life paintings of flowers and fruit in the classical tradition. She now exhibits regularly at the Royal Academy and is becoming well-known and much respected. I don't know what I expected when I met her. I suppose I imagined someone wearing a rough shawl, ethnic beads and woollen skirt in an untidy house littered with canvases, brushes and paintings all over the place. In fact she lives in a modern bungalow with her husband Jack, a former Royal Marine, and is herself a neatly dressed lady, her sitting room giving no hint that she is an artist. She is Norfolk born and bred and has lived in Carbrooke most of her life. She has very few paintings of her own there, just half a dozen kept in a drawer which she showed me. She is now in such demand that many of her paintings are away at exhibitions and there is a considerable call for her work. She very kindly gave me a small flower painting and I bought another.

Her husband Jack brought us coffee and we talked about his service life. He served throughout the war as a marine on board ships, from the North Atlantic and the Murmansk convoys, to the occupation of Japan at the end of the war. I asked if I could see Enid's studio and she said she didn't have one, just a small spare bedroom which she showed me.

'Painting miniatures, you see,' she said, 'I don't need much room.'

But I was fascinated by the ivory paper she showed me, and the brushes.

'I've just had to buy some more of these small sable brushes. They are terribly expensive, you know. They cost more than five pounds each.'

Professional watercolourists think nothing of paying between fifty and a hundred pounds for a large watercolour brush and her remark was typical of the delightful modesty of this charming, self-effacing and very gifted lady. I could not have had a more pleasant ending to this week of pilgrimage.

Interlude

Christmas and New Year

The cathedral services at Christmas were packed to the doors – there seemed to be more people than ever this year. In my Christmas sermon I read a poem by John Taylor, who used to be Bishop of Winchester. Called 'To a Grandchild', it is both beautiful and telling:

> *Over the swinging parapet of my arm*
> *your sentinel eyes lean gazing. Hugely alert*
> *in the pale unfinished clay of your infant face,*
> *they drink light from this candle on the tree.*
> *Drinking, not pondering, each bright thing you see,*
> *you make it yours without analysis*
> *and, stopping down the aperture of thought*
> *to a fine pinhole, you are filled with flame.*
>
> *Give me for Christmas, then, your kind of seeing,*
> *not studying candles – angel, manger, star –*
> *but staring as at a portrait, God's I guess,*
> *that shocks and holds the eye, till all my being,*
> *gathered, intent and still, as now you are,*
> *breathes out its wonder in a wordless yes.*

On Boxing Day I went to Carrow Road to see Norwich defeated by Southend. They are having a miserable time, and there were demonstrations against Robert Chase, the Chairman. He has done much for the club in recent years through his business skills and has created a ground and facilities that are excellent. But he is blamed for not buying players and feelings run high. The local press is plastered daily with stories of the controversy, but Robert remains unmoved.

House of Lords

The weekend after Christmas was spent, as always, at Sandringham. It coincided this year with my birthday on the Saturday and New Year's Eve on Sunday. I missed being with my family, but I enjoy this weekend each year, which is a privilege enjoyed only by Bishops of Norwich. For the five weekends after Christmas a bishop is invited but normally only once in his period of office. This was my eleventh visit.

On Saturday 6 January, after a few days in London with the children, we went to Winchester for the enthronement of the new Bishop, Michael Scott-Joynt. His father, George, was at Westcott House with me – an older ordinand who had been a professional oratorio bass. Sadly, both Michael's parents have now died, but I think he was glad to have me there as a link with them. When I first met Michael he was a polite schoolboy who called me 'Sir'.

The next week was spent on duty in the House of Lords. The duties were light and I was able to use some time to catch up on correspondence (a constant uphill task during this year of pilgrimage) and hold meetings with the suffragans and the new Dean, Stephen Platten, who is settling into Norwich with great energy.

17

Norwich (first week)

(The city contains a quarter of the population of the entire diocese, and is a regional capital for most of East Anglia, at one time in the Middle Ages being considered the second city in England. A centre of commerce and light industry, it has through the centuries remained prosperous with high employment levels until recently, when the recession has begun to cause serious problems. It remains a beautiful city, but contains areas of deprivation with problems of homelessness increasing.)

Tuesday 23 January

St Catherine's, Mile Cross, was built in the 1930s like a fortress standing on the intersection of busy roads. It serves a large council housing estate which has recently been given a major grant by the Government for regeneration and this has caused great hope and encouragement locally. We walked to the junior school, a long low building with six intersecting classrooms, where I visited the children and then held an assembly. Although a state school, it has close relationships with the Church and there are a number of Christians on the staff. Its facilities are nothing like as good as I found in many of the village schools and suburban areas. It seems that deprivation and lack of resources in such schools mirror the deprivation of the area, but they have a dedicated staff and friendly children, though predictably many of them are from families with problems of one sort or another.

Donald Salway then drove me to the old parish church of St Mary in Sprowston which used to be a village but now is part of suburban Norwich. There I had coffee with a group of parishioners and was given a conducted tour of the church by a knowledgeable churchwarden; it is a very fine medieval church with interesting memorials and well cared for. Afterwards in the warm vestry, in contrast to the freezing church, we had midday prayers together, which happens every Tuesday here. Michael Stagg, the Vicar and Rural Dean and also my former chaplain, then took me to the Adult Training Centre, one of two such large institutions in the city, which caters for those with learning disabilities. As always in such places, it is staffed by dedicated people and the hundred or so 'clients' are well cared for and involved in a variety of stimulating activities. My general impression is that care for the mentally handicapped is far superior to that given to the mentally ill, where 'care in the community' often has a hollow ring.

At Sprowston Fire Station I met a team of fire-fighters who had just returned from RAF Coltishall where a jet fighter had crashed, killing the pilot. They had been called because they are specialists in accidents which might involve chemicals or radiation. I had a most interesting time with them, trying on breathing apparatus and chemical protection suits which made me resemble an astronaut. The fire-fighters are a tough and committed team who take great pride in their work. I asked them about the effects of witnessing horrific accidents and how they are debriefed. Although they have a specialist unit at headquarters in Norwich which deals with stress counselling, they make little use of it, finding their sharing with each other after incidents more beneficial.

After a freezing walk from the vicarage up to Mousehold Heath, I returned to Mile Cross vicarage where Donald Salway took me on a round of visits. First we went to the Norman Community Centre where they are very excited by the grant of a single regeneration budget and are making imaginative plans to use the money wisely. Donald Salway then took me to three homes on the estate. First we visited David and Teresa who have a fifteen-year-old boy who is severely mentally handicapped, an older teenager with learning difficulties and a little girl, Melissa, aged four. A teenage daughter died six years ago. David does not work any more but spends all his time looking after the handicapped son who needs constant attention. Their faith and cheerfulness was moving and impressive. Next door I met Cliff and Sue. Cliff has multiple sclerosis and Sue has muscular dystrophy. Once more we were with a loving and deeply Christian couple who cope, with impressive acceptance, with their sufferings, made more poignant now because their daughter has inherited Sue's genetic disability.

A street or two away we visited Roy, another man with multiple sclerosis, who used to be a professional footballer, and his wife Margaret who is gradually becoming totally blind. All three families were uncomplaining and grateful for the help they receive in grants, but it was humbling to spend time with people who are suffering as they are. Is it true, I wonder, that there is more suffering among the poor than those well off? I don't know, but I can understand the Latin American theologians' insistence on 'Christ's preferential option for the poor'. I believe it is not so much that Christ loves the poor more than anyone else, but that he is present with the poor in a special way. That is why it is such a privilege to be with them, because to be with the poor is to be close to Christ.

Donald drove me back to Bishop's House for a two hour break which gave me time to catch up on the day's correspondence and write this diary. Normally I do this in the car on the way home from a far-flung deanery but in these city visits I am never more than fifteen minutes away.

The evening Bible study in Hellesdon was attended by sixty or seventy people and was well led by Rosie, a young schoolteacher whom I shall meet again at Horsford tomorrow. When I arrived home there was a message from Phillip McFadyen to say that SPCK had accepted his commentary on St Mark, written along the same lines as the Luke commentary which has been a marvellous help and stimulation to the Bible studies throughout the year.

Wednesday 24 January

Morning assembly at Old Catton Middle School was followed by the weekly Mothers' Union Communion at St Margaret's, Old Catton, and coffee in the church hall with parishioners. Afterwards Jonathan Boston collected me in his thirty-five-year-old Land Rover. It was the kind I used to drive in the army, with individual motors for each windscreen wiper, and Jonathan had installed various home-made electrical devices in the cab including an ominous notice against one part of the dashboard: 'Danger – Live Earth'. He took me on flying visits to the three schools in his parish where I distributed hundreds of badges and talked to the children.

After lunch with parishioners in the church hall at Horsford, we returned to the rectory at Horsham St Faith's – a huge Victorian house with four and a half acres and a cottage in the grounds. The grounds are littered with old caravans in various states of decay, Land Rovers and other vehicles in states of either decay or repair (it was not clear which), leftover tree houses from the time when the children were young, and a home-made assault course for the Army Cadet Force of which Jonathan is chaplain, as well as a rough driving course, laid out to teach cadets to drive. The house is filled with cluttered memorabilia, piles of books and papers, fine paintings, sculptures and odd collections such as Victorian truncheons. Jonathan is a genuine eccentric and an admirable priest, whose good relationships with his parishioners were very evident, particularly with the young, with whom he has great gifts.

Keith Crocker collected me and took me first to Blyth-Jex School where I had an hour with a group of a dozen sixth formers, which was hard work but stimulating. None of them would describe themselves as Christians but there was intelligent and positive discussion ranging from the Church's place in politics and ethical issues to the meaning of a relationship with God. They talked of their respect for Christians, but said that aggressive evangelism was repelling because it was not a dialogue. They were willing to listen to the Christian view but reckoned they had views worth hearing, too. Interestingly, some of them found a short discussion about prayer gripping. Afterwards, three or four stayed behind to talk. This is an aspect of mission which is very important and to which I sense I should devote more time in the future.

After the school visit we briefly visited an old people's fellowship meeting in Christ Church hall, a far smaller group than one finds in most villages – I suppose because in the city there are more facilities for old people, and many of them live within easy reach of relatives.

A welcome break back at Bishop's House was followed by a Bible study at St Luke's, New Catton. This new church has good facilities and we spent a profitable evening together – when we eventually got down to the Bible study. It was preceded by a kind of warm-up session during which the Vicar, Derek Dolman, told a series of clerical jokes which would have had him booed off the stage in a northern club, and then a period of singing choruses. This latter is an interesting phenomenon. Just as in the 1960s and 70s the Church of England could do nothing unless it had a Eucharist attached, so now in many churches you cannot have a simple discussion group or Bible study without a considerable period of singing beforehand. Derek could never make his living as a comedian but he is no mean theologian and he produced an excellent and scholarly introduction to the study. I spent most of the time with one group and found it very rewarding.

Thursday 25 January

William Noblett, the chaplain, met me at Norwich Prison and we walked outside to see the new secure block being built. Despite two pullovers, long johns, a cassock and Barbour I was soon chilled to the bone by the east wind – the wind factor taking the temperature down to −12°C today. We were finally admitted to the prison where my crook caused much amusement and predictable jokes from the warders. We then crossed prison yards, locked and unlocked numerous doors and eventually arrived at a secure wing for prisoners who have caused trouble. There are two such units here, one for so-called 'vulnerable' prisoners, mostly sex offenders, and one for those who have been disruptive and have to be isolated. We talked to a huge man with no shirt on, covered with tattoos, who was clearly on very good terms with William, who afterwards told me that he was a real villain who had no intention of leading anything but a criminal life, but despite all that, he said, 'There is something likeable about the man.'

Next we visited another prisoner in his cell – a pleasant enough personality though obviously unstable. There were religious books on his shelves and he asked me to pray with him which I did and then we went back to the prison chapel and talked in the chaplain's office for a while. A little while before, the Deputy Governor had told me that they very much appreciated William's ministry and were dreading the fact that, because he was so good, he would be grabbed to go elsewhere before long.

Peter Howard met me in his tiny car and conveyed me to the Heartsease estate where we drove round to get a Fiat's eye view, and then went to the church. Imaginative alterations have been made and I spent the rest of the morning talking to parishioners who had come for coffee, and a group of mentally handicapped people from the Sprowston day centre who go there every week. It was all warm-hearted, friendly and relaxing.

At Thorpe St Andrew's church centre a marvellous lunch, cooked by Alan, the head server, was attended by churchwardens and their wives. Stephen Collier, the curate, then drove me to St Andrew's Hospital, an early Victorian psychiatric hospital, where we walked round the outside of the buildings in the freezing wind and then visited the old abandoned chapel. This is a vast classical building, seating about 500, with at one end a special entrance for men and at the opposite end an entrance for women. Afterwards we visited patients on a ward, all elderly, the younger patients now having been transferred to Hellesdon Hospital. The people here were mostly suffering from various depressive illnesses and for some there was hope that they would eventually return to their homes. They were interesting and mostly quite articulate, not different in many ways from the kind of old people I have met before at old people's lunches in rural parishes. The difference is that these people, almost without exception, have been living alone, and have no close family to care for them which would be the ideal answer. One dreads the thought of what might happen to them if they return home unprotected to fend for themselves, with only the aid of so-called 'community care'. Included in this gathering was a priest's widow, a former music teacher, a farmer, the widow of a commando who had fought in almost every action during the last war, and a lovely old man from King's Lynn who told a long rambling story about his friend the Methodist minister. He spoke beautifully, using old-fashioned phrases, both his voice and language reminding me of broadcasts by John Betjeman.

The Bible study this evening at St Matthew's, Thorpe, was small with only about ten people – not perhaps surprising given the Siberian weather. But there were perceptive and sensitive contributions from people without pretensions, who were well led by their lay reader.

Friday 26 January

Last night the wind chill took the temperature down to −17°C and it felt no warmer this morning as I made my way to Costessey in light snow flurries.

An enjoyable and leisurely morning was spent, first playing with children at St Helen's play group, and then talking to people in the community centre who come there each week to a group organised by MIND. They all have mental problems of one sort or another but, like the people at St Andrew's Hospital yesterday, were friendly and happy to talk. Some were knitting while others talked or played pool. After a while I joined another group to play whist in a foursome including a delightful young man who cheated outrageously, and a lady who insisted, before laying down a card, on showing us all her hand and asking us which was the best card to play.

Andrew Good drove me to the Bowls Club at Spixworth where a large group of parishioners had gathered for lunch, followed by a good and lively 'Any Questions?' session in which, among other things, I was called on to defend the Church Commissioners and the House of Bishops' stance on homosexuality. I was collected by John Clark who drove me to Taverham Middle School in a blizzard where I took a large assembly and then presented gifts to their retiring cook.

The Chairman of the Governors, also a churchwarden of Ringland, drove me to a factory in the old church school where for many years they had been making 'antique' furniture. They use old materials, mostly now collected from France, producing furniture for film companies and owners of stately homes both in England and on the continent of Europe. We then visited the delightful parish church of Ringland, which is a gem with its beautiful angel roof, all in very good condition, and the parishioners who gathered there were very proud of their building. The congregation has recently doubled, thanks, they believe, to changing the time of service from 11.30 am to 9.30 am and having a service each Sunday instead of twice a month.

We then made our way in the continuing blizzard to the Scout hut at Taverham where I attended the Brownies' tea party and was presented with a pot of honey from John Clark's bees and a knitted woollen bishop with a flatteringly large amount of hair. A churchwarden then drove me back to Bishop's House. It was a nightmare journey, taking nearly an hour and a half, and I walked the last half mile or so.

There was just time for a hot toddy before setting off to St Mary Magdalene for a Eucharist and prayers of healing, which happens every Friday evening. It was an excellent liturgy with a good address by Richard Woodham, attended, remarkably, by twenty people who had braved the appalling weather.

Saturday 27 January

Despite more overnight snow, we made our way to Norwich Airport for a visit conducted by Trevor Eady, the Commercial Director and Richard Kennan, the deanery Lay Chairman. Although we were unable to visit places like the control tower because of the weather we had an interesting tour looking at security arrangements, duty free, offices and talked to lucky passengers awaiting a flight to Alicante. We watched incoming passengers arriving, nearly all of them older people who were sensibly dressed. Trevor remarked that if this had been a holiday flight from Benidorm they would have been walking across the snow-covered Tarmac in shorts and sandals.

Sunday 28 January

The main roads were clear but the surface became hard-packed snow as soon as we turned off into the country lanes on our way to Felthorpe. We drove to the pretty church, on a slight rise in the village, where twenty or so parishioners had gathered for Prayer Book Communion. It was icy cold in the sanctuary and I was grateful for the kind parishioner who had brought a flask of hot coffee so that I was able to warm my hands afterwards. It took me back to the well-remembered occasion in my first year and one of my early experiences of the refrigerated character of Norfolk churches. After the service I walked to the back of the church, my hands totally without feeling, and a churchwarden thrust a mug of coffee in my hands. I thanked him profusely and said, 'My goodness, your church is cold.'

'Oh yes, Bishop,' he replied, 'that is cold – but you should be here when we don't have the heating on.'

Philip Harrison, the Vicar, drove me to the main parish church at Drayton where a large mixed suburban congregation had gathered for a family Communion. The church was much warmer and the service the best of such parish occasions with its mixture of informality and good liturgy, children and young people present, clearly at home among the older members. Afterwards we all went to the village hall for lunch, a delicious beef stew, which was followed by an entertainment given by the City Treasurer playing a guitar, a lovely old man playing the violin and Lizzie, who works at the SPCK bookshop, playing the harmonium. Lizzie was the youngest child at a confirmation I conducted here ten years ago, when she sat on my knee for the group photograph. They took another photograph of us together today, but this time I put my arm around her shoulder – to repeat the pose of a decade ago was perhaps not appropriate. It was a marvellous entertainment, the three of them walking among the tables in the style of some 1930s café players.

In the late afternoon I went to the Sports Village on the outskirts of the city. This visit had been arranged by Gill Bridges and she and the Duty Manager, Pat Raven, gave me a tour of this vast complex with its scores of tennis and badminton courts, football pitch, gymnasium, saunas, restaurants and the Aqua Park – a lush tropical extravaganza with five pools and equatorial heat which made a wonderful contrast to the temperature outside. They kindly put a bedroom at my disposal in the hotel for a wash and brush up. In the Village Centre – a place normally used for aerobics – 200 people had gathered from the deanery for a lively act of worship led by the Hellesdon Music Group and conducted by Michael Stagg. I spoke of some of my experiences during the week, particularly the time spent with people who were disadvantaged in one way or another which had moved me deeply. This was a memorable day to end a week of pilgrimage which has been much more leisurely than most but very welcome because it has not been easy getting into the pilgrimage mode again.

Interlude

Friday 2 February

This afternoon I licensed Sheila Nunney, the curate at Swaffham, as assistant chaplain at the Norfolk and Norwich Hospital. Canon Maurice Green, her vicar, and a number of parishioners came and she was warmly welcomed by the hospital staff. She herself was formerly a senior nurse and starts with a good background for this ministry. Not long after I returned home, there was a phone call from the hospital to say that Maurice Green had had a cardiac arrest in the hospital car park and was very seriously ill. I drove back to the hospital where Margaret, Maurice's wife, had arrived. Doctors and nurses were working on him all the time and it was 11 pm before I could go with Margaret to pray and lay hands on Maurice. A kind consultant talked to us during the evening and warned Margaret that there was very little hope of him surviving.

Saturday 3 February

I visited the hospital this morning and was greeted by the sister in charge of the intensive care unit who told me that the Greens' four children had arrived from various parts of England. 'We think he only has a few hours to live,' she said. 'So if there are things you would like to do, you'd better do them now.' I gathered the whole family around the bed and we said prayers and then finally I spoke the beautiful commendation, 'Go forth upon your journey from this world, O Christian soul. Go in the name of God the Father who created you. Go in the name of God the Son who redeemed you. Go in the name of God the Holy Spirit who sanctified you. . . .' It was a beautiful moment and of course very tearful. I left the family weeping quietly and returned home.

John Taylor, the recently retired Bishop of St Albans, was lecturing in the cathedral about the Royal Maundy. He is the Lord High Almoner who organises this event each year. This year they are coming to Norwich Cathedral and, as is customary a few months before the event, he gave a lecture, after which we invited him and some others to dinner. Two or three of our children were at home for the weekend which is always a good time for a dinner party because they are very good at serving and washing up. I told them I would be getting a phone call (indeed I was surprised I had not already received one) and that they were not to say, 'The Bishop's out,' or, 'Can I take a message?' because it would be from the hospital and I wanted to speak to them myself. But no phone call came.

Sunday 4 February

I visited the hospital again this morning and was met by a smiling Margaret. 'He has survived and more than that, he seems better.' We went to see Maurice and his eyes were open and he clearly recognised us. That night I heard he was sitting up in bed and drinking soup.

On Sunday afternoon there was a great gathering of the family and friends of Bishop Launcelot Fleming to dedicate a memorial to him. He was Bishop here from 1959 to 1971 and pioneered a number of rural teams and groups. In earlier years he had been an Arctic explorer and always had a great gift for friendship. Late in life he married Jane, a widow with a grown-up family, and they lived happily in Bishop's House until they moved to Windsor, where he became Dean in the last years of his active ministry. I had known Launcelot slightly over the years and when I was a parish priest we had corresponded about the nature of teamwork. He and Jane came to visit us a few years ago and we had a most enjoyable day together. Our views about the Church in the countryside and its development were identical, and I had a strong feeling of continuing his work, which I think he felt also.

A fine sermon was preached by Richard Hanmer, now a residentiary canon and formerly Launcelot Fleming's chaplain.

As we walked away Steven Betts, my own chaplain, said, 'I suppose in about thirty years' time I shall be doing the same thing' – a comforting sort of chap to have around.

18

Norwich (second week)

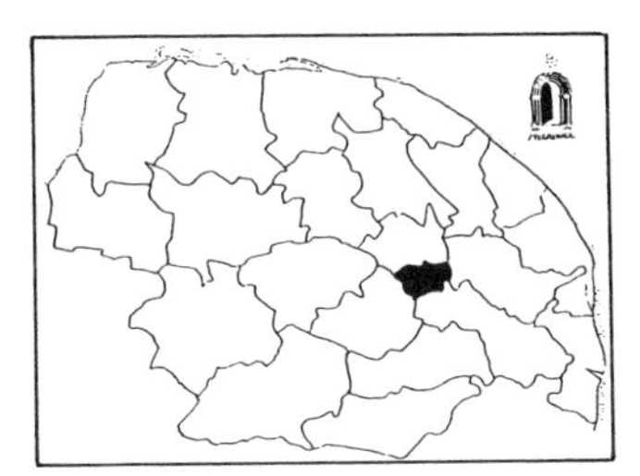

Tuesday 6 February
Another bitterly cold day began with a group of us huddled cosily in the back of St Anne's, Earlham, for morning prayer. We then went next door to the Area Housing Office which controls the large Earlham estate. This is a good estate, but the only new housing is that being built by housing associations. They are hoping that a new Government will allow them to use capital from the sale of council houses to build more accommodation, which the present Conservative Government will not allow. There is still an enormous shortage of housing, which directly contributes to homelessness in the city. Across the adjacent ring road, at the District Health Centre I visited the offices and spoke to groups of dedicated health visitors, psychiatric social workers, school nurses and others whose morale is high despite some confusing changes of regulations by central Government. It seems to be the complaint everywhere that detailed regulations are issued which it would be better for local authorities to decide.

We recrossed the main road to the church hall where a mother and toddler group was meeting and I met a series of young mothers with their babies, a father and two professional baby minders.

The Co-op Dairy nearby is a 1934 art nouveau building, still, apparently, with its original decorations inside, and it will soon, I guess, be due for listing. The roundsmen were a cheerful group who regard themselves not just as people who deliver milk but as those who perform a social service, particularly for the elderly and the single. The workforce is shrinking as more and more people buy milk from supermarkets. They were a friendly and very interesting group of men. Paul, one of the roundsmen, then drove me in his milk float to UEA, en route stopping for a photographer who made me pose with a bottle of milk on the back of the float. The Chaplaincy Centre at UEA was full for their weekly bread and cheese lunch and I had an hour with them talking about all manner of things, including an interesting talk with a man with cerebral palsy doing a PhD on the subject of 'The disabled in India'. He was in India recently and said they found it almost impossible to understand that someone as disabled as he is could also be a professional academic. After lunch I had a short chilly walk down to the lake; the grounds of UEA are beautiful in contrast to the severe Denis Lasdun concrete campus.

Hereward Cooke, the industrial chaplain, took me to the Bally shoe factory where I had a walkabout after a short talk from one of the directors. After being in the doldrums seven years ago the firm is now thriving, thanks to new work methods. Instead of assembly lines, or assembly rooms as they used to be, they now work in teams rather along the lines of Japanese models. The workers were all friendly, cheerful and seemed to be happy with the firm. Hereward, an Old Etonian, walked around the factory with me, greeting people rather like an old-fashioned squire talking to the workers on his estate. But they all knew him and clearly liked him very much. Nearly all the people are old Norwich families and I chatted to a number of them including the marvellous Jenny who trains new entrants and is a kind of pastor/mother figure. She wanted me to meet two men in particular who were atheists and I had an interesting talk with each of them. One believed we all came from outer space, Mars to be precise, and I recommended that he read C. S. Lewis' *Out of the Silent Planet*.

'I hope it's not a religious book,' he said.

I assured him it was just a good story, which it is, but also full of good, subtle theology.

I could have spent many more hours in the factory because the people were so interesting, but I was whisked off to County Hall where I met the Chairman, Chief Executive and senior officers, including members of the Christian Fellowship at County Hall. The Chairman soon left the meeting, explaining that he had to go and pick up his wife from school, and we then had a very good conversation about a whole range of matters particularly focusing on the partnership between the Church and local community. The senior officers at County Hall are without exception high calibre and we had some stimulating exchanges.

After an early supper of Chicken Maryland at Old Lakenham vicarage with Latham and Elaine Bewley, we went to the church for their weekly Eucharist with prayers for healing and I gave a short exposition of the Bible study for the day. Like the service in Mary Magdalene two weeks ago, this was an excellent liturgy with about forty participating. This was a good first

Earlham Cemetery

day of this pilgrimage week but I could have done with a little more free time.

Wednesday 7 February
Bignold Middle is a large old school near the hospital with a mix of children from the varied housing in the area, from a tower block to well-to-do housing. Among the children I met the granddaughter of Bishop Eric Cordingly who died many years ago and was formerly Bishop of Thetford. After an assembly and visiting the classes, we went to the Great Hospital where we had a Eucharist in one of the sheltered homes in this marvellous complex, founded by one of my predecessors in the Middle Ages, originally for 'poor and decrepit clerics'. It now has a village atmosphere where old people are cared for in independent accommodation, sheltered flats and finally a nursing home. Some say it was a model for Hiram's Hospital in Trollope's novel *The Warden*. Afterwards we assembled in the old church for coffee with Lorna Wood, who is the chaplain, and residents.

Nick Garrard, the new Vicar of St Thomas', Earlham, took me to Parkside School for lunch. This is a special school for those with learning difficulties and was a most rewarding experience. They have good resources and a high staff/pupil ratio. All the children come from schools where they have been unable to cope, particularly because of literacy problems, but there is also a large number with associated behaviour problems and some Down's Syndrome children. Both staff and pupils were delightful and notable was the politeness of the children, more pronounced than in any school I have visited so far. There was a lovely gentleness about them, as well as an openness and vulnerability. They were unselfconscious and easy to talk to, and everywhere there was a well-ordered atmosphere in the small classes with no apparent discipline problems. One wonders how these children will get on in the harsh world which they will enter at sixteen when they leave, and indeed how they mix now with their contemporaries with more ability. The staff are very conscious of this and so arrange work experience, training and interviews, generally trying to prepare them for a society which will not value their gentle and important qualities as it should.

I walked for a while in the large cemetery which geographically forms half of Nick's parish and then went to the West Norwich Hospital where Leslie Ward took me to the new gastroenterology unit where I was shown all the latest technology – space age stuff and most impressive. At the ophthalmic unit I met a number of patients who had just had cataract operations and were waiting to go home having only been in the hospital a few hours. As in the gastroenterology unit, most here are outpatients and very few have to stay overnight. I visited a number of old men on a general ward, which I always enjoy, and then we drove across the city to the Larkman estate.

This is probably the most deprived estate in Norwich, though Mile Cross must run it a close second. John Panting is a dedicated person (almost recovered now from ME) as is his wife Harriet, a Labour City Councillor and crusader for the needs of the deprived. We were joined by a parishioner and a lodger for supper, vegetable curry, and then went to the youth club in the church hall where about forty children between the ages of eight and twelve were gathered with a number of leaders. It was noisy and cheerful and I so much admire these people who struggle, often against very difficult odds on this estate, to bring the love of Christ to young and old and to the many who are not just indifferent but actively hostile. ('Nothing personal, Vicar, but we don't want anything to do with the Church.')

The day ended, by contrast, in the luxurious new complex at Holy Trinity, the central evangelical church in Norwich, where I met the new Vicar, Alan Strange, and about seventy or eighty parishioners gathered for singing and a Bible study. The Bible study was led by John Valentine and it consisted simply of an exposition by him. I was disappointed that there was no opportunity for discussion in groups which would have drawn more out of the text than was possible through the exposition of one man, however able. But the people were warm and supportive and at the end I led them a little further in the Bible study and talked about the pilgrimage. Alan and his delightful young American wife will need some support in the next couple of years. As I told him, and he clearly recognised, you cannot exercise leadership and win a popularity contest, and this parish needs firm and sensitive leadership which I think Alan will give to them. An interesting but long day which left me exhausted having once again been allotted too little free time.

Thursday 8 February

Bowthorpe is a vast modern estate of mixed private and local authority housing with good facilities and the remains of a small medieval village. The church here is a Local Ecumenical Project, led for many years by Ray Simpson who is soon to leave, to live in his cottage in Lindisfarne. He has dreams of forming a small religious community and whether or not it proves to be viable remains to be seen. Ray is undoubtedly a holy man and through his enterprise has built up an interesting array of workshops around the church at Bowthorpe, where the disabled and those with learning difficulties are able to produce toys and various items of carpentry which are beginning to sell well. The future is a little uncertain because so much has depended on the personality of Ray himself, more than he realises. The church itself is very independent, but with an interesting theological and liturgical mix between Pentecostalism and Taizé.

After prayers in the church, we visited the workshops and then the local church aided school. There seemed to be some lack of communication because Ray thought that I did not wish to take assemblies but to visit informally, and that special arrangements for my visit should not be made. This was a pity because it did not give all the children the opportunity to meet me but I did manage to visit four classrooms. Interestingly, this is a church aided school and the children hadn't a clue who I was. When I gave them a hint that my job began with 'B' it provoked a series of answers ranging from 'Bridegroom' to 'Butcher'. But I left them with 300 badges in the hope that the teachers might use them to give a little more information about the Church to which they are theoretically so closely affiliated.

Back across the city at Radio Norfolk I had a fifteen-minute interview live with Tony Mallion, a well-known local broadcaster whom I have known for years and who was part of an ecumenical pilgrimage to the Holy Land I led many years ago. If he can persuade the producers to give the space, Tony wants to do a full length hour's programme at the end of the pilgrimage which might be interesting.

David Abraham, the Vicar of St Giles, took me to the YMCA. This is a large institution with accommodation for a hundred people and is extremely well run by John Drake, a large, bearded, devout Christian, who introduced me to staff and showed me the facilities. These included not only accommodation but a training centre and a job centre which is doing excellent work in placing young people in jobs – a centre which is going to be closed soon unless the relevant government department changes its mind. This seems a mad policy since it will simply result in more people being on benefit instead of in work, because the YMCA is able to encourage young men towards work who do not fit in easily with the conventional job centre routine. John is a strong leader but clearly a sensitive man who keeps a firm but light touch on the tiller. Crossing through a glassed-in corridor we looked across at a bedroom where two young lads were sitting in the window smoking.

'You see,' he said, 'they've got the window open; they're smoking pot and letting the air in to clear the fumes. What do they think I am, a complete idiot?'

Across the road the YWCA is a much smaller institution and quieter, with about thirty residents and again a caring and efficient staff. The clergy of the city centre from all denominations meet every other month and today they had gathered for lunch and Bible study after which David Sharp, the Vicar of St Peter Mancroft, took me to the Mancroft Advisory Project.

MAP is one of the most important of such projects in this part of England, indeed in the whole country. It was started with the aid of a trust fund for youth, which was part of a legacy from a former parishioner many years ago. With proceeds from the sale of land they built this new centre and installed Justin Rolph, an experienced Christian youth worker, as its leader. The facilities are excellent and contain three elements: a counselling service for young people where trained counsellors give advice on a whole range of subjects; a job advice centre where they are given help with application forms, CVs and general advice on seeking work and how to apply for places on courses; and thirdly, a rest and refreshment area where people can come in for coffee and snacks for a couple of hours each day. Mothers are regularly allowed to bring young children and I chatted with a group of mothers and toddlers, a number of them with their fathers present – none of them, I think, married. This is a superbly run project doing significant work, and is fully used because they are trusted by the young. Homelessness is an increasing problem and they are soon to employ a full-time worker, dealing with the problems of homelessness in the city, to supplement the advice they already give on finding suitable accommodation.

Much credit for MAP is due to David Sharp's vision and his administrative effectiveness in bringing it all to fruition. There have been many great vicars of St Peter Mancroft. In recent years Bill Westwood, recently retired as Bishop of Peterborough, is the best known and most affectionately remembered because he was an outstanding personality. He is still spoken about warmly and, I guess for David Sharp, with maddening regularity. But David's achievement in the church and particularly, perhaps, in this project will have provided the city and its young people with a service which is the envy of other places and I hope he will be given the personal credit he deserves. It reminds me rather of a biography of Archbishop Geoffrey Fisher which I once read. Before becoming Archbishop of Canterbury he was an outstanding headmaster of Repton but the biographer remarked that when he was there nobody said, 'Geoffrey Fisher is a great headmaster,' but during that period everyone said, 'Repton is a great school.'

After a walk through the market talking to stallholders, and a brief break at Bishop's House, I met David Newton, the friendly and dynamic General Manager of Castle Mall. We had drinks with senior members of his staff and some lay people from St John Parmentergate who are beginning to consider how the parish might make links with the shopping area. We walked through the mall and had an interesting time with the Manager of Argos who is called John Rutter. I told him that he was the namesake of a famous twentieth-century composer of church music and thought it would be a good idea for him to buy a CD and play it to customers at Christmas. It turned out that years ago he was a choirboy in Cheshire. It is interesting how these church links come out in conversation and could perhaps be built upon. The Security Manager also revealed that she was a former churchwarden.

Hereward Cooke dropped me at the Night Shelter where we were greeted by a phalanx of reporters and photographers. I was slightly dubious about this because I wondered how the residents would feel about being photographed, but the local Press were sensitive and asked their permission first. I talked to groups of them with the local vicar, Hilary Wakeman, who goes there once a week and is much liked and trusted. They all had rather sad stories to tell, and it was interesting that two or three of the people I spoke to suffered from epilepsy, which perhaps accounts for some of the problems of the unemployed and homeless. As with my other encounters in the city with the poor, I found it a moving and humbling experience, with people who are at the bottom of the pile in society, but who still try in little ways to keep their dignity and self-respect. The staff, as one would expect, are heroic.

I asked two of the residents what they would buy, not for themselves but for the Night Shelter if they had some money to spend. After a long discussion they thought they would like to have a video recorder so that they could watch films. The management tends not to ask for much but depends on the goodwill of people to provide their needs. So I shall make sure that from a Trust I have they will have a video recorder soon. Interestingly, Jimmy, a bright and talkative Liverpudlian, wanted above all a Scrabble dictionary, so perhaps we can find one of those for him, too.

St John Parmentergate vicarage is in a side street off Rouen Road, not far from the Julian Shrine, in the red light district of Norwich. Martin Smith, the Vicar, has redecorated the house sensationally with Spy cartoons, expensive wallpaper and holy statues. He is a jolly Friar Tuck kind of figure, already much loved by his people and my credit rating has gone up considerably since I appointed him. The people of Parmentergate, fiercely opposed to the ordination of women, have always been very suspicious of me. A group of forty or fifty parishioners had gathered for a party – a most enjoyable evening ending with compline, devoutly said, which begins with the words, 'The Lord Almighty grant us a quiet night and a perfect end.' It was indeed a perfect end to another full day.

Friday 9 February

There was a surprise for my granddaughter this morning as I made an unplanned visit to Sunningdale Nursery School, a well-ordered group in the charge of Mrs Woolsey-Brown. A week ago the children had a visit from a fireman and were told that someone else in a uniform was coming this morning. The children stared as I walked in and Mrs Woolsey-Brown said, 'Who do you think this is?'

'Grandpa,' shouted Alexandra in delight and I had fun with the children for fifteen minutes before going to a ladies' Bible study. This efficiently led group had obviously been together for some time and were uninhibited in their comments. Many of them had been involved in Alpha Courses and it showed, so I felt it right to tone down slightly some of the fiercer comments about judgement; but it was a good and fruitful hour.

I was to have visited Hewett School but sadly the head of science died suddenly and his funeral was today. So instead I visited the Breast Cancer Support Unit in St Alban's church hall. This is a relatively new group where women are giving important support to one another with the help of outside experts who give advice and lead physical exercises. They came from a variety of backgrounds and there was a wonderful honesty, as well as cheerfulness around. I don't know how many of them were churchgoers but they all received a copy of my Pilgrimage Prayer with genuine appreciation.

At the City College I was greeted by Angela, an attractive blonde, the cousin of Ted Longman, a very old friend from Westcott days, who she told me has gone for the last few years to be Vicar of Cerne Abbas, a good place for the last years of one's ministry. I then went upstairs to meet the new lady Principal and in the suite of offices was greeted by two other female executives, charming, good-looking and power-dressed – not a man in sight. After coffee together we had an interesting tour and met several students. This is a vast college which offers 900 courses for 16,000 students. They have recently been trying to gain a higher profile in the city and had their most recent prize-giving in the cathedral for the first time. The college has been around for about a hundred years and is one of the city's most important institutions but has not yet achieved the place in the public mind that it deserves.

After a buffet lunch with senior staff I went in pouring rain to Trowse First School where I was met by John Wilson, the local parish priest. The school is a county school but very Christian in its ethos. John goes there often; the children all know him and clearly love him. They all greeted 'Father John' and told me that 'Father John said this' or 'did that'. I visited all the classrooms and then held a short assembly. In one of the classes the children asked me what my stick was.

'What do you think it is?' I said.

'A walking stick,' one answered.

'No, it isn't, it's something to hit people with,' said another.

And then a little girl called Kim said, 'I think it's a stick which a shepherd uses.'

'You are absolutely right,' I said. Kim is a Down's Syndrome child, the only one in the school, and it was a highlight of the day to see the beam on her face and the delight of the teachers present that this child should get it right when others got it wrong.

John took me to the offices of Eastern Counties Newspapers where Hereward met me and we visited the newsroom where I talked to Peter Franzen, the editor, and a number of others whom I already knew. We then talked to Clare Gillingwater, the editor of the *Eastern Evening News* who is shortly to leave for a senior position with the *Daily Express*. I was reminded of City College as she is assisted by two able women in the most senior positions. The *Eastern Daily Press* and *Evening News* have been particularly helpful throughout the pilgrimage and have provided good coverage. This week there seem to have been more pictures than ever. I have long got over my reticence about having my photograph taken in all sorts of strange places because I believe such publicity is genuinely good for the Church. I think most people do not see it as publicity for a personality, but it cheers them that a church leader is noticed, and therefore that the Church itself given good notice.

After a short break at home, I had supper with Alan and Maggie Beardsmore – baked salmon and salad, quite delicious. (The food this week has been excellent.) Alan used to be a naval chaplain and was in the Falklands during the war there. His love of the sea is evident everywhere with some fine seascapes on the walls and naval memorabilia in his study.

In the evening we had a Taizé service in St Andrew's Church, organised by Janice Scott, the curate, and attended by more than a hundred people. It was extremely well done and very peaceful. At the end I told them a little about my day and its highlight, seeing the face of Kim and her teachers. I asked them all to think of some small thing that day for which they could thank God as we sang the final chant *Confitemine Domino* – 'Give thanks to the Lord for he is good'. I listened to the radio on the way home and heard the tragic news of the IRA bomb in Canary Wharf. In the Taizé service there had been a period of intercession when people came to a table and lit a candle saying for whom they offered prayer. One man prayed for Ireland and its people and for peace, obviously not having heard the news. One prays that this won't wreck the whole peace process.

Saturday 10 February

I slept badly, as I often have this week. I was up before six, trying to tackle a mountain of work waiting for me on my desk. This has been a real problem during this pilgrimage year for, despite secretarial help, there still seems to be an enormous number of matters which must have my decision, letters which I must personally write or dictate, and literature to read. Apart from our holiday in the summer there have been no days off and hardly even a chance of an evening free. Despite my gratitude for the marvellous experience of this pilgrimage, at times like this I long for the end.

I had a second breakfast with parishioners at St Paul's, Tuckswood, followed by a question and answer session. As I had been warned, the first question was, 'When are we going to get a new vicar?' I managed to turn this into a profitable discussion about team work, so we had a good and positive exchange. Latham Bewley was there and soon Gill Bridges will be joining the team which I think will begin to give new confidence to the people of Tuckswood who feel a bit demoralised.

I visited one of the houses of the St Matthew Society, formerly the Carr-Gomm Society, a large nationwide organisation providing housing, both hostel-type accommodation and independent flats. It was founded by Richard Carr-Gomm whom I vividly remember talking to us when I was a student at Westcott. He was a Guards officer who resigned and went to work as a home help in Bermondsey, and eventually founded the Abbeyfield Society. The St Matthew Society now has hundreds of houses all over the country. There are seven in Norwich alone. I spent time with the residents, Warden and members of the committee. All the residents come from difficult backgrounds but are clearly happy in their home and many have lived here for years. There are two houses next door to each other, one with small flats and the other with six or seven residents who have single rooms, a common room and eat together. These people need special help managing their lives. I asked them if they had problems getting on with each other because they are a very disparate lot. They replied that the experience of living alone was for them so awful that the irritations of living together were as nothing compared to that isolation. This is a very well managed project where people are given security and confidence.

Cynthia Elias, the Lay Chairman, drove me across the city to St Stephen's Church in the city centre, which has a glassed-off area in a side aisle where we had a buffet lunch and a good discussion. Cynthia has been a constant and cheerful presence this week, though sometimes disconcerting, for she is

Bishop's House Garden (pencil)

an amateur photographer who fancies herself as one of the paparazzi. She leaps out of bushes with a camera as I arrive at various places, and she must have a number of photos featuring a bishop with a startled expression.

The afternoon was spent with the Norwich Fire Brigade. Like the visit to Sprowston two weeks ago, this was most enjoyable and it was a privilege to be among these tough professionals. The sense of teamwork is tangible, not just when they are at work on an exercise but when relaxing together. They dressed me in a firefighter's kit and I took part in an exercise with them – a simulated road accident – filmed all the time by Anglia Television. (The BBC have not taken much interest in the pilgrimage, but Anglia have been often on the scene.) We put Hereward Cooke and a dummy in the front seat of an old banger in the yard outside the fire station and I was taught the procedures for cutting free a trapped passenger. I was paraded with the Blue Watch and with the others leapt smartly to attention on the command of the officer in charge (I haven't done that since I was in the army). We then proceeded to tackle the car and rescue the injured passengers. With the aid of the amazing cutting gear we took the car apart, cutting through the roof and peeling it back like a tin of sardines, then demolishing the doors and sides of the car. It was a vandal's dream of heaven. We then lifted Hereward gently out and placed him on the floor. The exercise did not go as far as giving him mouth to mouth resuscitation, for which I was grateful, and we then proceeded upstairs to their restroom for a splendid meal cooked by one of the fire-fighters who is a super chef. The Blue Watch manage to do extra duty for him in order to leave him behind to cook food for when they return from an incident.

Afterwards they presented me with a photograph that one of them had taken only an hour before and amazingly had got developed and framed. Included in the White Watch was Peter Johnson, the son-in-law of Dean Paul Burbridge and formerly a verger in the cathedral. What a change. I said farewell, warmly thanked them, and went into the yard where a lorry was loading the remains of the old banger, now just a heap of scrap metal. It had been a memorable and privileged afternoon.

Sunday 11 February

On my way to St George's, Tombland, I took a short cut through the cathedral, dressed as usual for the pilgrimage in my increasingly tatty old cassock, shoulder bag and stick. People were arriving for the cathedral Eucharist and gave me very odd looks, no doubt thinking I was some peculiar kind of tramp. I said hello to them but many still averted their eyes. At St George's I dedicated the new tower and conducted an old-fashioned High Mass with all the trimmings which I much enjoyed. The excellent NSM Priest-in-Charge, John Minns, has done much to restore morale and give the congregation a sense of purpose.

After a glass of wine with the congregation, I went to lunch at the home of Hereward and Diana Cooke with the other Rural Dean who has been sharing this week, Paul Oliver, another fine priest and excellent rural dean, and the Lay Chairman. I visited the Cookes' daughter, Frances, who is in bed with glandular fever. I had confirmed her a year ago and she was pleased to receive the laying-on of hands.

After lunch Paul drove me to the Earlham estate where I boarded a bus. This was driven by Malcolm, a parishioner, who, at his own expense, hires a bus every Sunday to tour the estate and take parishioners to church. We had a jolly ride picking up parishioners and I had fun being a kind of bus conductor dishing out badges instead of tickets. A big congregation gathered in the small church of St Mary's, Earlham, near the university where we had evensong followed by another bus ride to the centre of the estate and tea in the church hall. This has been a good week, very full and tiring but immensely varied and rewarding.

Interlude

Monday 12 – Wednesday 14 February

Today Keith Sutton, the Bishop of Lichfield, and I introduced Michael Scott-Joynt, the new Bishop of Winchester, to the House of Lords – a quaint ceremony at the beginning of the day's sitting, which involved much bowing, sitting, rising and doffing of mortarboards. We took it all very seriously but were slightly put off by a small group of bishops sitting on the steps of the throne who were not yet members of the House of Lords, and who had come along to see the fun. They were all grinning broadly which made straight faces difficult. Wait till it's their turn.

This was followed by two and a half days of meetings of the General Synod to take the Turnbull Report the next step forward, with minor alterations. It is a good and necessary piece of legislation to help the Church at the centre work more effectively but will not cause great excitement in the dioceses.

There was a lively debate concerning stipend differentials. Every five years or so someone proposes a motion to do away with differentials which gives the opportunity for a certain amount of bishop bashing because we earn almost twice as much as incumbents. A hundred years ago we earned sixteen times as much, so differentials have been whittled away somewhat. The fact is, as the Bishop of Chester bravely pointed out, that the cost of living for bishops in our large houses means that we are mostly no better off than incumbents and often far worse off because a bishop's wife usually works full-time around the house, offices and gardens without pay, whereas a high proportion of clergy wives these days work full-time outside the home. A young clergyman once complained to me about bishops' lifestyles and I asked him to come and talk to me. I explained to him how our money was spent and then asked him what his wife earned and pointed out to him that his family income was precisely double mine. He hasn't commented on the subject since.

House of Lords

Friday 15 February

This evening I attended the annual dinner of the Strangers Club for business and professional men in the city of Norwich. It is a good club which meets in a lovely old house in Elm Hill. The food and friendly atmosphere are excellent and I just wish I had more time to spend with them. I generally make a visit about once a year and every two or three years attend their annual dinner. This is a huge affair with 300 people present. It was a good occasion but, like so many annual dinners, it was somewhat marred by speeches of excessive length and dubious wit.

19

Humbleyard

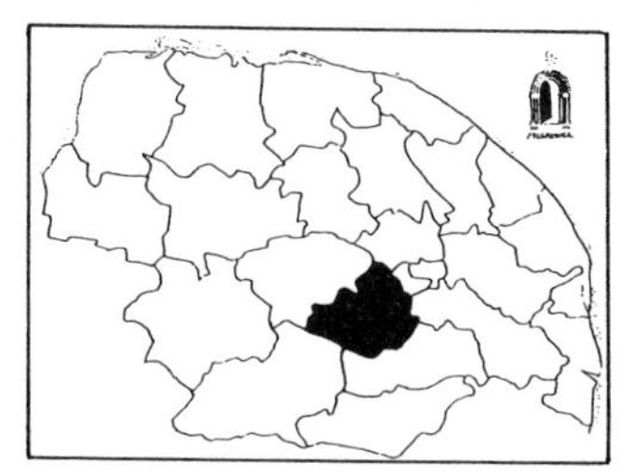

(Like many deaneries which abut the city, the character of the countryside varies from suburban villages to small rural parishes, with the town of Wymondham, and its famous Abbey Church, at its centre.)

Tuesday 20 February

The weather took a turn for the worse again at the weekend and last night there were falls of snow and gale-force north-easterly winds which blocked several roads in the county. However, we were able to make our way without too much difficulty to the church at Wicklewood where Peter Stephens and parishioners met me for a Mothers' Union toddlers' service. A surprising number of young mothers and their children braved the elements and we had a good time together, and ate pancakes afterwards. From the church I was then due to ride on the front of a forklift truck. Mercifully, I was allowed to ride in the cab though that was still very cold.

We drove the short distance to the Ashcroft Project, sheltered accommodation for young women, most of whom have a history of mental illness or breakdown. The accommodation ranges from single bedrooms through flatlets, where they are semi-independent, to four bungalows where they can live almost completely independent lives if they wish. In this very caring atmosphere the women thrive and I talked to many of them individually. It is clearly well funded and certainly well staffed by dedicated people but caters for only fourteen patients or clients. I have seen some excellent facilities for the elderly, homeless, mentally ill and those with learning difficulties, but I sometimes wonder how many of the total in need are actually cared for by these places.

Peter then drove me to the Morley Research Centre where the Deputy Director, Andrew Thurston, drove us round the extensive farmland and

Bawburgh

showed us offices and outbuildings. This is a major agricultural research establishment which has been going for more than a hundred years, originally inspired by the modern farming methods pioneered by Coke of Holkham. They do important work testing varieties of seed for arable and root crops as well as insecticides and fungicides. They are keen on conservation and the farmland, which was converted to prairie for arable use some years ago, is now being re-hedged field by field.

After home-made soup at Morley rectory, we drove to Bawburgh for a service to commemorate St Walstan, their patron saint. Walstan is a great figure in East Anglia, a devout rich young man who became a farm labourer. When he died his body was drawn by an ox cart, eventually passing through the walls of the church at Bawburgh (so it is said) where he was buried. A well sprang up nearby with miraculous healing powers. It is a beautiful Saxon church set on a hillside in this very pretty landscape. Afterwards we walked down to the well in the valley though I did not fancy a drink of the water which looked rather stagnant.

We then said goodbye to the cheerful, welcoming parishioners and drove to Colney Church. This is another delightful small building, well restored, with some of its Norman origins still evident and including a wonderful, probably sixteenth-century, font. The acoustics are perfect and I should quite like to preach here one day – indeed, I half promised to return in 1997. Again, it was a friendly, happy group of parishioners. We left for a brief call at the BUPA hospital and then went next door to the old people's home where chair-bound residents were throwing a ball to each other, sometimes quite violently. I talked for a while and gave them a Pilgrimage Prayer before leaving for Cringleford church hall. Here we had a cup of tea and a good question and answer session on a variety of subjects. Afterwards I was presented with a delightful watercolour by one of the parishioners, Sheila Sewell, who is a member of the Royal Society of Miniature Artists and actually taught Enid Clarke whom I met before Christmas.

We returned to the vicarage for supper with Clive and Shirley Blackman and then scrunched through the ice to the church next door which had been heated since last night's choir practice so was comfortably warm. There the lay reader, Charles, led a Bible study – the most scholarly introduction I have yet heard, full of references to Josephus and learned commentaries. Clive is also a fine teacher so I guess this is a well-taught congregation and there was a good discussion in small groups. Afterwards I led them into a period of silent prayer which I think they appreciated – I certainly did after a long, interesting and talkative day.

Wednesday 21 February (**Ash Wednesday**)

The wind had dropped slightly and there were only snow flurries so it was comparatively warm at −2°C! On the wall of the church at Wreningham is a memorial to a former rector, ending with the simple ascription, 'Jesus, Mercy', in contrast to some of the florid eulogies I have seen in some churches. In one (I forget where) there is a memorial to a local squire which reads something like, 'He cared much for his estate, his workers respecting him as a generous and fair master; an indulgent and affectionate husband and a father whose children revered and loved him. He was a devout and loyal servant of his church, an examplar of Christian virtue, who will be mourned by all who knew him.' He had apparently composed the wording of his memorial himself.

At another of Simon Stephenson's parishes, Ashwellthorpe, we joined in a coffee morning which happens every Wednesday – an extremely popular initiative undertaken by the church for the village. It was started six years ago as a result of a discussion following *Moving Forward*.

After chatting to parishioners and villagers, I was taken to a farm at Forncett St Peter where they have what is called an adult adventure playground. Here there are all manner of vehicles for adults to play with, including two tanks, both of them today unfortunately frozen to the ground, a Sierra Cosworth, a Honda Pilot which is a very powerful beach buggy, a Fiat where the controls are reversed – that is, if you turn the wheel to the right you go left and so forth – and go-karts. I had great fun trying out the Cosworth, the beach buggy and the reversible Fiat, driving around a cinder track for half an hour. 'Adult playgroup' would be a more apt description for this fun event where you can live out all your fantasies. It has proved a profitable bit of diversification for the farmer and his wife who started it a couple of years ago.

Afterwards we returned to Simon and Pauline Stephenson's home at Tacolneston for lunch. Simon, despite his urban evangelical background, is deeply committed to rural ministry and loves the open landscape of this part of Norfolk. He was constantly waxing eloquent about it as we drove around, which was good to hear.

After a short brisk walk, Peter Stephens, who had been with us most of the morning taking pictures with his video camera, drove me to Wymondham vicarage where Brian Gant took us first to an old people's day centre, one of hundreds now springing up all over Norfolk and doing marvellous work. I found them playing a game, throwing woollen balls at plastic bottles, which is good exercise. In so many old people's homes there is no kind of physiotherapy, and these day centres are often the only place where old people can have the kind of stimulation, mental and physical, that they so need.

We then drove across Wymondham to a new centre in the buildings of the former prison, the Wymondham Bridewell, which by all accounts was a tough old place. It is a fine local initiative which now contains a Red Cross Centre, Citizen's Advice Bureau, town museum, flats for former prisoners in one part of the building complex, and flats for former mental patients in another. It is marvellous to have this mixture of offices, voluntary organisations and living accommodation. Around the building we saw the remains of the old prison, which must have been grim. It was one of the last to chain prisoners and was thoroughly condemned by the Howard Reforms of the nineteenth century. However, following that criticism it was transformed and became a model prison – it is so typical of Norfolk to take a long time to be persuaded about change, and then to change more radically and quickly than anyone else.

After evensong in Wymondham Abbey, we had a meal back at the vicarage with Brian and Diana Gant and the Armstrong family. A sung Eucharist in Wymondham Abbey in the evening was well attended, not only by Wymondham parishioners but by people from the deanery also. It was nice to see Sue and Carol there, who live in the cottage next to ours in Burnham Thorpe. Again the faithful Peter Stephens was present with Angela his wife. It was a long service, including the Imposition of Ashes, but very good and prayerful.

Thursday 22 February

It was snowing again as we left for the Lotus factory at Hethel where we had an interesting tour, first of the engineering offices where bright young

Tacolneston

graduates were sitting at screens designing bits of engine and making complex calculations about stress factors. We then moved into the large, airy assembly plant where the cars were being assembled – it seemed at a fairly leisurely pace. Practically everything is handmade. There is no need for quality control because the workers are all so proud of their work that it is, without exception, good. After looking at the prototype of a new small sports model, Ultralight, interestingly using a Rover engine because it is the lightest that is made, I posed for photographs beside a yellow Lotus and felt rather like a model at a motorshow. Afterwards I was given a short drive in a Lotus by the test driver, the weather conditions being too bad to go on to the racing circuit. It also meant that I could not borrow a car for the day, as had been planned, but they promised to let me have a car for two days whenever I wanted it, so I must plan this for a time when the family is at home, perhaps after Easter.

We then proceeded to a totally different kind of factory, this time a mushroom farm, and watched manure being processed from stinking heaps to sweet-smelling fibre for growing the mushrooms. I can't remember the figures but they produce several tons every day. We then saw staff cut and sort the mushrooms which are grown in large trays stacked nine feet high. Again, it is a place which is well run, with high morale and worker commitment. Jess Stubenbord, the Rector of Mulbarton, accompanied us on these visits and he has evidently built up a good relationship with both these firms; another fine example of an evangelical who takes seriously his ministry beyond the bounds of his congregation to the community at large.

After a light lunch with Jess and Anne-Marie, I attempted a short walk on Mulbarton Common, but it was snowing heavily by this time and I was soon driven indoors. Peter Stephens, who had also been present throughout the morning, drove me to Chris Collison's house at Newton Flotman and then we visited Yew Tree Cottage Residential Home for the Elderly where I managed to have a chat with each one of the thirty or so residents. Next we visited Duffield's Mill, an old family firm which produces animal feed. Like the other two examples today, this is a well-run company and the hundred or so workers are committed and loyal, many of them having served for many years with the firm. After an interesting tour around the mill, I had a short chat with Tony Duffield, the Chairman, in his office. As a former churchwarden of Buxton, his main concern was to talk about the choice of a new incumbent. We had photographs taken in the boardroom, departing with gifts of golfing umbrellas advertising the mill.

We called in at a tea party for St Mary's Seekers, the Sunday school, in the church hall and then went to the church to meet the churchwardens and readers for a good talk about the parish. After a difficult period I sense there are new hopes and expectations with Chris Collison as their vicar. Because he is also Evangelism Officer he will only be part-time but there is potential here for effective lay involvement.

By now thick fog was descending and I went to the home of Roy and Christine Reason (Roy is a churchwarden) for supper and then back to the primary school at Newton Flotman for a Bible study. Chris Collison had not arranged for anyone to lead it. I said that it was not my custom to do this myself, so he led it and very well too, so that there was some valuable discussion in groups. Interestingly, the evening may perhaps have been the livelier for not having been prepared too carefully.

It is a relief that the temperature is rising but the associated fog may give us problems tomorrow morning. This has been another interesting day, but with only about twenty minutes free time on my own which I don't find enough.

Friday 23 February

The hundredth day of the pilgrimage began with a tour of the new Tesco Superstore on the Ipswich Road, just outside the city. It is a vast new supermarket employing 450 people; an impressive place, but one is conscious of the negative impact of these great stores on village shops. All the twenty or thirty employees I talked to were excited by the new venture and had been made to feel very much part of it. So for the time being at least morale is very high. As the General Manager outlined, various matters concerning the conditions of work, particularly styles of leadership and the giving of decision-

Barns at Swardeston

making even to check-out girls, have shown that his confidence was justified. Because of the effectiveness of computerised ordering, the storage space occupies only ten per cent of the total area whereas not long ago it would have occupied thirty or forty per cent. The variety of goods was astonishing and it was encouraging to see free-range and RSPCA endorsed products taking up proportionately more and more shelf space. When inspecting the bakery I dropped heavy hints about my love of doughnuts, but to no avail, though the Manager did offer me a Polo mint from his pocket as we toured his store.

Because we had spent so much time in the store, Michael Jones, the Vicar of Swardeston, and I arrived late for a Communion service at the East Carleton Cheshire Home. A reader was present and had sensibly started the service, so I took over and then chatted to the residents. As with all Cheshire Homes, they suffer from physical not mental disability, some of them in the advanced stages of multiple sclerosis. Many are unable to communicate but, as the Warden later pointed out, one has constantly to remember that these people are not mentally ill – indeed, most of them have all their mental faculties very much intact.

After lunch with the Jones's and a short walk, Peter Stephens took me to Little Melton where we had great fun on the Little Melton Railway run by Bob Brett in the grounds of his house which used to be a timber yard. He has two miniature trains running, a model railway exhibition, various skittle alleys and games for children. He opens it once or twice a month for charity and even on a rather bleak afternoon it was crowded with families with young children. I rode on the train and gave badges to all the children present, then judged a limerick competition and had a hot dog and cup of coffee which were most welcome since I was freezing after half an hour riding round in open carriages.

Bob Brett then drove me away in his own 1927 Austin 7 for a ride through country lanes to Little Melton where we stopped at the house of Ronnie and June Roberts. Ronnie used to be a churchwarden and worker on the Melton estate. They are a very hospitable couple, their house much used by friends who drop in at all times of the day for refreshment. June pays the rent by raising thousands of cuttings of geraniums which she sells at the roadside.

At a sheltered housing complex in the new part of the village Dan Shakespeare, a retired priest who looks after the home, introduced me to the residents and I chatted with them all. They included one lady who used to run an off-licence in Harpenden and remembered me when I was a curate – not, though, because I was a frequent customer but I had prepared her son for confirmation.

After a break at the home of Di Lammas, the new Vicar of Hethersett, the churchwardens and a few parishioners adjourned to the Little Chef on the Hethersett roundabout. Here we ate a hearty 'all day breakfast' filling ourselves with cholesterol, before a question and answer session back in the church hall, which was stimulating and entirely positive. Di seems happily settled and the leading churchgoers I met were certainly very appreciative of

Swardeston (pencil)

Swardeston

her ministry. Even her recent illness had a positive rather than a negative effect because it gave the parishioners an opportunity to minister to her. Once again Peter Stephens was with us for the whole afternoon and evening. He has been one of the most attentive rural deans during the pilgrimage, and it has been a pleasure to get to know him better on our journeys to and fro across his deanery.

Saturday 24 February

Pancake races were held on Swardeston Common in steady drizzle but with a good turnout of families and family dogs who consumed the often-dropped pancakes when the races were over. I took part in one race and came last, spending most of the time retrieving my pancake from the mud. We were all grateful to return to the Cavell Room, a wooden hall next to the church, where we had welcome hot soup and ploughman's lunch together.

After a damp walk, Peter Stephens came to drive me to Hingham where I spent the afternoon in this benefice of three parishes. John Bourne had arranged a whistle-stop tour which included two old people's homes, the offices of the Rural Community Council and then two little country churches. The first was Woodrising, a pretty church whose tower, which had fallen down in the eighteenth century, no-one had bothered to rebuild. It has interesting memorials of the Bedell family, with scallop shells in their coats-of-arms. I think this may have meant that in the Middle Ages a member of

Morley

the family went on pilgrimage to Santiago de Compostela or possibly Jerusalem, which made a nice link. The shell was also used by families who took part in the Crusades. They have a fine barrel-organ here which still works.

Following this, we drove to Scoulton, another interesting church where a group of a dozen parishioners had gathered, as everywhere in Norfolk villages, proud of their church and delighted that I should take such pleasure in it. Here again there are Bedell memorials with the scallop shells. None of the parishioners had noticed this before and they were interested in the link with pilgrimage. After chatting and praying the Pilgrimage Prayer together, we returned to Hingham. I travelled in a livestock trailer which normally carries pigs. The farmer assured me he had cleaned it up and indeed it only smelled slightly of its former occupants.

At the great church in Hingham more than a hundred people had gathered, which was pretty good for a wet afternoon, and we had choral evensong followed by tea and cakes at the back of the church. This benefice, on John Bourne's retirement, is to be taken over by Peter Stephens. It says much for the effective leadership of these two priests that the change seems to be going ahead without difficulty. In the two benefices, High Oak and Hingham, there are two LNSMs in training and another possibly on the way, so there are the makings of a good ministry team here.

Sunday 25 February

A Group Communion at Wicklewood was enhanced by a choir which sang like angels, and included an anthem from Verdi's *Aïda*. Peter Stephens, with me again for the whole day, then drove me across the deanery to Mulbarton where the Rector, Jess Stubenbord, at first did not notice me because he was so busy kissing members of his congregation! We made our way past wired-up guitars, two screens and overhead projectors, to the vestry in the medieval chancel. It was a family Communion service, better described as 'choruses with Communion'. There were several breaks in the liturgy which would have had Michael Perham tearing his hair, including a farewell and prayer for a family moving to Ireland, several chorus breaks and an extended Peace with much hugging. As at Wicklewood, this was a Group Communion with parishioners from the other, more traditional, villages attending who must have felt a little bemused. But Jess made them welcome and he has such a gentle, disarming manner that no-one could possibly take offence.

After lunch with the Stephens at Morley, I stood in the shelter of a children's slide in the local recreation ground and made a sketch of the church. We then drove to Wymondham Abbey for a fine choral evensong for the deanery with about 300 attending. I preached for the third time, as always on this pilgrimage unprepared.

We retired to the church hall for tea and yet another question and answer session for an hour, where the questions were intelligent and interesting, ranging from Church and state issues through the authority of the Bible to questions concerning death and life after death.

This has been another excellent week, well organised by Peter Stephens who has attended me every day for long periods. He has been like a faithful sheepdog – but I was not always sure if I was the shepherd or the sheep.

20

Redenhall

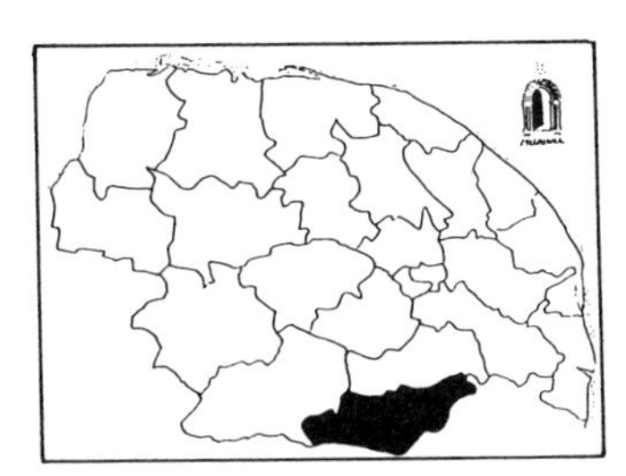

(The southernmost deanery lies along the valley of the river Waveney, which forms the boundary with Suffolk.)

Tuesday 5 March

I hoped in vain for some better weather on this pilgrimage week, but a steady drizzle whipped up by an easterly wind made the day exceedingly unpleasant from a meteorological point of view. However, it was brightened by a series of meetings with interesting people and visits to beautiful churches.

We began with a Bible study at Bressingham rectory where David Hunter gave the clergy chapter a well-prepared and profound introduction to the Passion narrative, which we have now reached in our study of St Luke. David has cystic fibrosis and is the oldest surviving person in England with this disease. He is a saintly man who bears his illness patiently and with good humour. His time in these parishes has been far from easy for he has had to cope with bitterly warring factions, but I sense the situation is now easier and certainly the atmosphere in all the parishes I visited today was happy, positive and forward looking.

We drove from the rectory to South Lopham Church, with its famous Norman tower. John Betjeman once said, 'This is a church worth going a long way to see,' and how right he was. It is quite beautiful, with parts of the Saxon church still visible, and the magnificent central tower, contemporary with the cathedral. A peculiar feature of South Lopham is the keyhole in the church door which is precisely the same height as the top of the spire of Norwich cathedral. Difficult to believe but true, the parishioners assured me, because this is almost the highest point in Norfolk. After prayers together, I was reluctant to leave the church, which has a truly prayerful atmosphere, but it was time to drive to the house of Jennifer and Richard Vere for a brief lunch, after which we travelled to Pulham Market where I joined the Rural Dean, Monty Ellson, his wife Marjorie, and a group of mothers and toddlers for their 'Tiny Tots' service. There was singing, stories, finger painting (very messy), tea and biscuits. After chatting to them all, I returned to the rectory for a good break. I went for a long walk in the icy drizzle and attempted once or twice to sketch but my fingers were freezing and the rain kept wetting my sketchbook so not much was achieved.

After a cup of tea, Monty drove me back across the deanery again to Bressingham, where we had high tea with the churchwardens and lay readers and interesting conversations with all the people there. They included Hilary Hammond, a churchwarden and also the County Librarian, who was most interesting on the subject of the new 'Technopolis' which is causing controversy in the city but about which he spoke persuasively and enthusiastically. I also met a potential LNSM who with his wife runs a youth club for North and South Lopham with about thirty-five young people attending.

At Bressingham Church the bells were ringing, having recently been restored and re-hung, and I met the band of ringers and parishioners. This is another fine church, much loved by its parishioners, and like South Lopham well on the way to full restoration.

Fersfield Church is another gem in this Group and contains a number of treasures, notably the fourteenth-century effigy of Sir Robert Dubois, carved from a single piece of oak, larger than life-size and still with its original paint visible. It is one of the finest examples of its kind and was a showpiece at the National Age of Chivalry Exhibition in 1987. A group of eight or ten parishioners sat in a circle and we read the Bible – literally. The four parishes are reading aloud in their churches the entire Bible from start to finish. This evening in the space of three quarters of an hour we read the whole of Ecclesiastes, each person reading ten verses. It was a remarkable experience. I have never taken part in such a Bible reading before. It is a simple exercise but one which has great benefit because even without any commentary the book somehow takes on new meaning. We spent a short time afterwards reflecting on some of the things we noticed. Interestingly, they all read from the Authorised Version. I asked if this had been deliberate and they said that when they first started people had read from different versions, but gradually, without saying anything, one by one they had all brought Authorised Versions, believing quite rightly that it was important to read from one edition – it doesn't matter which perhaps.

I was disappointed that the programme this week seems to have little involvement with the local community, industry and agriculture, but if it consists of spending time in conversation with lay people and visiting the beautiful churches that are a feature of this part of Norfolk, then I shan't complain too much.

Wednesday 6 March

Morning prayer at Rushall Church was a work of supererogation as I had already done this before I left Norwich but it was a delight to see another beautiful small church in good condition and talk to the parishioners for a while. I was to have travelled to Dickleburgh in the same benefice by horse-drawn caravan but the horses had not yet been shod, so instead I boarded a French farm cart which seated six of us and was probably used originally for shooting parties. Today the temperature had dropped but mercifully it was not raining and the journey, though cold, was most enjoyable. Elevated above the hedgerows and moving at a gentle pace one can really appreciate the countryside by this means of transport. The three miles took half an hour or so and I was told that the horse-drawn caravan went at such a slow pace it would have taken two hours, so perhaps it was just as well the arrangements were changed.

At Dickleburgh I talked, prayed and had coffee with a large group of parishioners. This has been a rather sad benefice; its priest having been ill for three years had then retired early. It is now looked after by a splendid NSM, Ben Sasada, and I found their morale high. The difficulties have clearly brought out the best in them and they are rightly proud of the way in which they have maintained the life of the church. Ben is well known already in this benefice and much loved and appreciated.

We drove to Thelveton Church, another delightful medieval building, on the estate owned by the Mann family. Sir Rupert Mann, who is very supportive of the church, was there, in his forties but sadly having had a stroke. He and his wife have abandoned the Elizabethan manor house and moved to Billingford Hall not far away. After looking around the church we drove along the one mile drive, lined with snowdrops, past the old Hall and on to Scole where I joined parishioners for the weekly Lent lunch.

I went for a good walk afterwards and then returned to the church where they had arranged a large upper room, furnished and heated, where I was able to thaw out and feel warm for the first time today. Monty Ellson collected me and we went to the house of Winnie Reeve, an old lady on an estate not far from the church, where she was joined by four friends for home Communion. Winnie was the daughter of the blacksmith, who was also the publican, local councillor and benefactor. All the ladies there remembered the burning of the church in 1963, set alight by a young man still serving a sentence in Broadmoor. It happened in January in intense cold and the water froze as it left the hosepipes. Much medieval work was destroyed but they have made a good job of rebuilding and used the opportunity to build an annex with kitchen, meeting rooms and lavatory, so the disaster was turned to good effect.

I joined William Bestelink for evening prayer in Roydon Church and thirty parishioners came too. William says morning and evening prayer each day and tolls the bell. This was a good move for him from his group of country parishes in mid-Norfolk; he seems happy and clearly his parishioners are very fond of him. A bachelor, now without a close living relative, he said to me later, 'The parish are my family,' which is touching and for him clearly true.

Roydon Church contains a memorial which I found particularly poignant and full of faith because, unlike the commemoration of young men killed in war, this happened to a family out of the blue. It is dedicated to the two sons of one of the rectors, called Frere, a famous local family. The memorial poem was written by a relative.

TEMPLE FRERE
was born March 2nd 1818.
He was drowned when saving
the life of a fellow student at
Trinity College Cambridge
on 4th April 1840, aged 22 years,
and is buried in the Vault beneath.

GRIFFITH TEMPLE FRERE
was born July 4th 1827.
He died in the fire which consumed
The Vicarage-House at Warfield, Berks,
in the night of the 14th March 1839
aged 11 years. His remains are
deposited in the Churchyard of
Little Marlow, Bucks.

A manly tender heart, a form and frame
Heroical, the pride of all his race,
Their pride and hope; in early youth he came
The unexpected inmate of the place
Ordained for all that breathe on earth below,
Exempted from the common ills of life,
Nor wearisome disease, painful and slow,
Nor wild excess, nor youthful hasty strife,
Consigned him to the Tomb; the prompt endeavour
Of a kind heart to succour and to save,
Darkened our dawn of hope, and closed for ever
His rising worth in an untimely grave.
Deem them not unprepared nor overtaken
At unawares, where daily life is pure,
God's chosen children never are forsaken,
His mercies and his promises are sure.

John Hookham Frere

In memory of these their eldest and youngest Sons, thus suddenly
and early taken from them by an Allwise God, their parents
Temple and Janet Frere have built this Vault and Porch.

Redenhall (pencil)

The churchwardens gathered at the rectory for supper cooked by Judith, a churchwarden's wife, delicious chicken, home-grown vegetables and apple pie produced from William's trees. There were two clergy widows there: Eunice Glass, whose husband was Vicar of Dersingham, among other places, and a great support to William; the other, the mother-in-law of Delia Smith, told me she was used for Delia's experiments in cooking which she clearly much enjoyed. A large group of parishioners turned up for the Bible study and there was a lively discussion followed by compline and coffee.

This has been a more leisurely day than many I have experienced but I was heartened by the parishioners, both in the Dickleburgh and Scole Groups, who have been cheerfully managing, on the one hand, a virtual interregnum with a priest who is sick, and on the other, a long interregnum since last June. Equally, it was encouraging to see, in William's case, how refreshing and life enhancing a good move can be for a priest.

Thursday 7 March

We returned to bitter weather again, with a strong easterly wind which blew all day with a flesh-numbing chill. This was a curious, unbalanced day, with a mad rush in the morning and nothing at all arranged for the afternoon.

I was met at Earsham by Sam Read and John Meade, the local squire and an imaginative and radical thinker about rural ministry. We dived straight into the primary school at Earsham for an assembly. Then on to the first of two old people's homes, one with twenty-five and the other with thirty-five residents, all of whom I spoke to individually, even though only half an hour was allowed for each visit. A highlight was meeting Cyril Piper who wore an Airborne badge and had fought with the Airborne Regiment throughout the war. His father had been a gardener at Hatfield House, where he was born in the Lodge, and now late in life he has had a stroke. He is a very competent artist and gave me a lovely bird picture and a book of local photographs he has produced. In his youth he was a fine sportsman and until recently was an expert amateur dahlia grower, producing a number of varieties which he himself cultivated and which are still grown. One of them was named after his encounter with a beautiful woman at a flower show. He walked up to her, a total stranger, and said, 'Excuse me, Madam, do you mind telling me the name of your lipstick? It's similar in colour to my unnamed dahlia.'

'"Venus" by Goya,' was the reply.

'That's it,' Cyril said.

So now 'Goya's Venus' is one of his dahlias.

Another highlight was a lovely old lady who the Matron told me had spent many years in Paris. The odd French word kept coming out as she talked, so I conversed a bit in French, and her eyes lit up as I told her about Lucy and Peter's year in Paris. I don't suppose people speak much French to her these days.

After these intensive visits we went to another primary school, a tiny one at Denton, with only twenty-one pupils.

'I'm afraid we haven't arranged for you to have a drink this morning,' Sam Read said, rather irritatingly, because by now my throat was very dry.

But I was rushed to Archbishop Sancroft High School in Harleston where I celebrated Communion and gave what I felt to be a rather unsatisfactory talk in the middle of it. We then went straight into a buffet lunch with the staff and by 2 o'clock I was feeling quite worn out after four hours' non-stop talking. I must have spoken individually to very nearly a hundred people.

Peter Morris took me back to the rectory and I was now free until 7 pm, which seemed to me daft, but I went for a long walk through the countryside around Harleston which is quite hilly and it was very enjoyable though cold. I returned to the rectory two hours later and chatted to Peter, a parishioner who turned up and his daughter Fiona who arrived home from school in Norwich. Then they left me and I fell asleep for an hour before being roused for supper cooked by Peter (Sue was away in York). A nice meal of baked potato with cheese and stir-fried vegetables.

The evening was spent with the local Mothers' Union who had a speaker, Pam Flowerdew, talking about 'Waste not want not'. It was good sanctified common sense but made most of us feel quite guilty. Afterwards we had a question and answer session which was lively and I had a chat with another interesting old lady, the widow of a Yugoslavian who had been a member of the Serbian Orthodox Church. I found myself suddenly listening to oral evidence of a major historical event. The father of this old lady's husband had planned the assassination of the Archduke Francis Ferdinand in Sarajevo, which began the First World War (though it was another young man who pulled the trigger). He was a priest and was imprisoned by the Austrians throughout the war but afterwards, on his release by the Serbs, was immediately made a bishop. One of his sons married an English teacher of classics, now long retired, who was the old lady sitting at a Mothers' Union meeting in the Methodist hall at Harleston.

Friday 8 March

We made our way through the crowded streets of Diss to the parish church for morning prayer taken by the Rector, Jimmy James, and afterwards spent an hour at the mini-market in the church hall – a popular event every Friday to which people come from as far afield as Ipswich. We then attended an ecumenical lunch which happens during Lent in a different church hall each week and this time it was at St Mary's. A crowd of about fifty or sixty people were there from all the local churches. There was a very real sense of fellowship among the lay people which once again reinforced my strong impression that ecumenical activity at local level is widespread and far in advance of the official negotiations that take place between Churches at national and international level. As I said to them during my talk, I think that in the long run it is local lay people who will drag the hierarchy screaming into unity – a sentiment which they loudly applauded.

Brockdish (pencil)

I had a short break in the garden of the rectory. It is a fine Georgian house with a beautiful garden created by Jimmy James' wife, Erica, which must be one of the loveliest small gardens in Norfolk.

On the way to Brockdish, the PCC treasurer of Diss told me that giving had been increasing in the parish and although as a treasurer he was hyper-cautious he had felt it right to give praise to the parishioners. There may be signs that financially, even if we are not over the hump, we are at least approaching the crest of the hill. We took tough decisions five years ago about manpower, and these are now beginning to bear fruit as we make our long-term forecasts. I believe some other dioceses are still experiencing major difficulties.

At Brockdish Primary School there are normally forty-two pupils but only twenty-eight were present, the rest being absent with a tummy bug which I hope I avoid. After tea with parents and governors, Ann Smart, one of the churchwardens, drove me to her home which I used as a base and I had a good walk around Brockdish Church. The day has been sunny but still very cold. However, I managed to find a warm place in a hedgerow where I sat and sketched the church for half an hour.

Evening prayer was at the delightful small church at Billingford, followed by tea at Thorpe Abbots village hall with a large number of parishioners from Scole, Billingford and Thorpe Abbots. Thorpe Abbots has another beautiful small church; all of them in this Group well-maintained gems. At Billingford their regular congregation amounts to more than ten per cent of the population, as I have found so often in rural parishes. As in so many other places, they were surprised but encouraged when I told them how favourably this compared with proportions in urban and suburban areas.

At Pulham Market rectory I celebrated a house Communion for the ministry teams of the two parishes, which included two LNSM ordinands. Afterwards we had a long meal together and interesting conversation. These are quietly impressive teams and they are handling the relationship with PCCs wisely. When Monty leaves he will certainly bequeath something valuable to his successor. The two LNSM ordinands are both high quality people who will be among the first batch to be ordained in September. Another twelve are following a year behind this first group of eight, and more are in the pipeline. This development in the life of the diocese is altogether encouraging and will surely lead to growth in the long run.

Saturday 9 March

A buffet lunch with parishioners at the home of a churchwarden in Winfarthing was followed by a fascinating afternoon visiting the churches of this Group. In each church a short service led by a lay person included a meditation on some feature of the church, each superbly done.

At Winfarthing a churchwarden talked about the parish chest, an ancient box provided at the time of Henry VIII in response to a royal command to keep records. This proved eventually too small and was replaced 200 years later by another chest, both of which are still in the church and in use. The latter interestingly has three padlocks, with originally three separate keys – one for each churchwarden and one for the incumbent – a symbol of team-work in one sense, or perhaps a precursor of the modern security methods applied to the launching of nuclear weapons.

At Shelfhanger we focused on the medieval wall painting discovered accidentally by a builder in 1965 as he was chipping away plaster in preparation for redecoration. The painting came to light for the first time in 750 years – an extremely well-preserved fresco of the nativity dating from the thirteenth century at a time when Giotto was painting frescoes in Italy. It is certainly worthy of anything done by the great masters of that time. The short service was led by Brian Paice, Headmaster of Archbishop Sancroft High School in Harleston. He is the lay reader here, a stocky, bearded man who reminded me of Simon Callow, with the same beautiful, deep, mellifluous voice. It was a treat to hear him speak and sing.

At Gissing, where there is an outstanding double hammer-beam roof with well-preserved angels, we once again had a good meditation led by a churchwarden.

At Tivetshall St Margaret there is an extraordinary screen which replaced the rood screen at the time of Elizabeth I. Again a churchwarden provided a meditation which was both scholarly and moving. Among the interesting features was a prayer saying, 'O God, save our Queen, Elizabeth' – an unusual and heartfelt form of 'God Save the Queen', with its emphasis on 'O' and 'our'. It was written in the year before the Spanish Armada, when the security of the realm was in some doubt. Also in this delightful church there is an organ which has to be pumped because there is no electricity here, and a lady pumped while the organist played a hymn.

In the same parish are the ruins of St Mary, Tivetshall, whose tower fell down in 1949 because of the vibration of a low flying aircraft. It was a blessing in disguise because the parish does not need two churches and they had been debating which one should be retained. They used some of the material from St Mary's to repair St Margaret's, and the ruin is now open to the sky but very carefully preserved and was the subject of a painting by John Piper. After a short service here we returned to Burston, driving in a Land Rover across the old Roman road which is now a farm track.

Burston is famous because of its Strike School when there was war between the Vicar and the local schoolteacher and her husband. For generations following there were bad relationships between the school and the church and it became a focus for the Trade Union movement. In recent years much healing has taken place and the present Rector, Des Whale, has really completed the process of reconciliation. I came to Burston two years ago to dedicate their new kitchens. The church is square with a single aisle, pews having been removed, and it is used now as a completely dual purpose building, hosting various activities during the week including old people's lunches, playgroups and other community activities.

The theme for the afternoon was the future and the meaning of the reordering of a church. We ended with tea and home-made biscuits and more talk with parishioners, many of whom had joined in the pilgrimage to all the churches. This is a very good Group where they have adopted my plea for a service in every parish every Sunday. They do this with a team of eight people in every parish who devise the worship when what they call the 'home team' operates on a Sunday. It works extremely well and I found a strong community spirit here and a real unity in the benefice.

Des Whale is leading this Group unobtrusively but very effectively. He represents a new style of team leadership, which is the antithesis of the individual parson, or 'strong leader' or 'great character'. I have now seen this style in action in a number of places, and there is no doubt that the best rural teams are always led by clergy with these qualities – a certain modesty, a determination to work closely in the context of the ministry team, generosity in listening and genuinely shared decision-making. They are qualities we need to analyse, because they can be taught, and I feel they have much to say about how leadership in the Church should develop in the years ahead. Lying behind this unobtrusive style must be a firm faith, because only those most secure in themselves are able to have the confidence to let go. It is also symptomatic that people like Des would be very surprised to read these words.

After a break at Diss rectory, we walked down to the Church Room, where about eighty people had gathered for an evening entitled 'Quiz and Fish & Chips'. Each of the ten tables formed a separate team and we were then given a series of quizzes on a variety of topics. It was all most entertaining and friendly with wine flowing and eventually fish & chips in plastic cartons. There is a great feeling of fellowship in this parish. A husband and wife at our table who had recently arrived said they had been overwhelmed by the friendliness of their welcome, and by how easy it had been to integrate into the community through the church. I left before the end but if only I did not have such an early morning in prospect I would have been quite happy to stay for another hour.

Sunday 10 March

After a very early start we arrived at Ranworth where the BBC 2 programme *Good Morning Sunday* was taking place. The visitors' centre was full of people enjoying coffee and croissants. The word had gone out on local radio

Diss Rectory

and about sixty or seventy people had turned up. I had two short interviews with Don McLean the presenter and then gave a talk. I had been asked to prepare it in advance but was unprepared for the fact that the talk was interspersed with laughter and comments when appropriate, but I think it went all right.

After breakfast back at Bishop's House, John drove me to Pulham St Mary where they were celebrating the restoration of the church, a magnificent large building with a parvis porch (where the priests used to stay overnight) still intact, the room in use as a storeroom. It is a large and magnificent church and yet again the parishioners have worked wonders restoring it to a high standard.

After coffee we had lunch at Starston in the small village hall. It was a small but friendly gathering, though apparently one or two parishioners stayed away, still not having forgiven me for uniting them with the Pulhams. They had pushed very hard some years ago to be independent with a retired priest looking after them. But for the common sense of most parishioners and the strong support of Richard Lombe Taylor, the local squire, and his son who farms the estate, it could have been very difficult. One of the parishioners said to me at lunch, 'You know you are still not universally popular here.' I said I knew and added that one could not exercise leadership and win a popularity contest at the same time, with which he good-humouredly agreed.

After a short break back at the rectory in Pulham, we went to Diss for the final service of the pilgrimage in the parish church, which was packed. At

Pulham Market

evensong I talked about the week and its encouragement. I had been asked, during the lunch at Diss, by the local Pastor of the Free Evangelical Community Church if I had, during my pilgrimage, noticed signs of growth and I replied, 'Yes,' before passing on to talk to someone else. But I thought hard about the question and answer and meditated on it in my address. We may not be witnessing growth in terms of dramatically larger numbers, though certainly congregations are increasing in many places. But there is certainly growth spiritually in terms of lay leadership, ministry teams, vocations to the ministry, ecumenism and excellent team work which I have seen everywhere in this deanery, not to mention once again the outstanding commitment to the church buildings, which itself, as people witnessed at Pulham St Mary this morning, has drawn Church and community together.

This has been a strange, uneven week, spent almost entirely with church people, but none-the-less very satisfying.

Interlude

Thursday 14 March
Kenneth Williams, the Chief Constable, noticed that I had not yet made an official visit to the police during my pilgrimage. So I spent half a day with them today, beginning with a long conversation with senior officers at the headquarters of the Norfolk Constabulary at County Hall. We talked about a range of matters and of course there is an enormous amount of common ground between us, symbolised in the motto of the Norfolk Constabulary, Serving the Community.

The terrible tragedy yesterday in Dunblane, where sixteen primary school children and their teacher were murdered by a gunman, has dominated not just the media but every conversation, and so it was with the police. They asked me if I had read the accounts and I said that I honestly found it difficult to read it all because it was just too upsetting. Significantly, they themselves felt the same way, although they were well used to dealing with violence and tragedy. But Dunblane was beyond 'normal' violence – it was overwhelming and deeply shocking to the whole community.

After lunch I went with Roger Sandall to the headquarters of the Norwich City Police and visited the cells where prisoners are kept immediately after arrest. This is an old police station and the cells are below ground level – rather grim, though I was assured that they had been modernised at great expense in recent years. The prisoners are in and out fairly quickly but the warders have a difficult time in an atmosphere which is without natural light and, of course, volatile.

They are reorganising the departments, particularly co-ordinating intelligence gathering, and have set up a new department dealing with domestic violence. The officers and civilians in the station are all highly motivated and professional but I was surprised at the lack of modern equipment. The person in charge of domestic violence, for example, works with card indexes and there are box files and old-fashioned filing cabinets in a place where one would have expected the best of modern computer equipment. There are one or two computers but far fewer than the task warrants. They are far less well equipped than my own secretary's office, and bear no comparison to the level of facilities available at the diocesan office, which gives pause for thought.

After a brief walk with a constable on the beat, mainly in order to allow the Press to take photographs, I spent two hours towards the end of the day in a police car – an 'Instant Response' vehicle – with Matthew and Malcolm, the driver and co-driver. Their task was to patrol the city and respond to requests for assistance. They explained that they only switched on flashing lights and sirens when it was a genuine emergency. For normal requests they would simply drive faster without scaring people with lights and noise. They wore earpieces so I could not hear anything over the radio from the back seat. When a message came through, they pressed the earpiece, the car accelerated and they passed the message to me. The first one concerned some boys smashing car windows and we drove fast but safely through the city until we were told to stand down because a Panda car had been able to deal with it alone.

We drove back into the city and a little later there was a call from Costessey, where neighbours had reported two young boys breaking into a house. Again, they did not feel flashing lights were justified and so we drove swiftly to Costessey. A Panda car with its one policeman was outside the house; Matthew and Malcolm joined him, surrounded the house and caught the two boys. In fact they lived there and having arrived home from school and forgotten their keys, were trying to get into their own house.

This all seemed a little tame but we had some interesting conversations, particularly about counselling which is an important subject in a profession faced regularly with great stress and traumatic incidents. We were driving slowly through Magdalen Street when Matthew, who was driving, pressed his earpiece and his hand immediately flew to the buttons on the roof activating the blue flashing signal and the siren. We surged forward with cars immediately pulling in to the sides, through a red light, and off at a great rate. I was curious to know what was happening but they were concentrating hard on driving.

Malcolm in the passenger seat was giving a running commentary: 'Three cars on left, now pulled over, clear to go; two cars coming on right, now they've pulled over, clear to go; car coming out of side street on right, it's stopped, clear to go; turn first left, van blocking, now clear, go.' And so forth. It was very like the kind of commentary co-drivers give on rallies and there was a perfect partnership between the two.

On a clear bit of road one of them managed to lean over and say, 'This could be serious, and actually we may need you because there's been a house fire and a child's clothing has caught fire.'

My stomach turned over but there was no time for thinking as we raced through the traffic and out towards Bawburgh. When we arrived at the cottage the ambulance had already got there and the child was in the ambulance being looked after by a paramedic. He was not too seriously burnt – it could have been a lot worse. I went inside and had a word with the mother and then sat with the child, who must have been four or five years old.

We then cruised slowly back to the city centre and it was almost time for me to be taken home when once again Matthew hit the roof buttons, yelled what sounded like 'gunshot' over his shoulder and we were off again – this time in rush hour traffic, roaring through red lights, over pavements, weaving in and out with great skill. My seatbelt was tightly fastened but even so I needed to hang on to the handle in the roof of the car as we raced around corners. Eventually we arrived in St Giles and went to the gun shop. ('Gun shop' had obviously been the message – but that was serious enough.)

We were the first to arrive. Matthew and Malcolm ran into the shop, telling me to stay where I was. They were, of course, unarmed but there was a man inside who had been demanding guns and ammunition. Naturally a shop like this is protected with hidden alarms and the police are very quickly called. It turned out that the man was mentally ill. They arrested him, took him into the car, and we all went back to the police station where he was put in the cell to await psychiatric examination.

Matthew then drove me home and I thanked him for an extraordinary and exciting afternoon which will live in my memory for a long time.

Sunday 17 March

Today I returned to Beaconsfield to celebrate the twentieth anniversary of the formation of the team ministry, which happened while I was Rector. The family Communion was even larger than in my day, with about 500 present. We were very happy in this parish and I have always found the one or two occasions I have returned moving, as I did today. There were still many people whom I remembered – the young, now middle-aged, and the middle-aged, elderly – but recognisable and making one poignantly aware how much one loses when one moves from parish life to senior responsibility. Never since 1977 have I been involved in a community which one knows intimately, which is supportive, and in which one feels, as a family, totally integrated.

I arrived at the church as the bells were ringing and at 9.30 they stopped and kept a minute's silence for Dunblane before resuming in preparation for the service at 10 o'clock. It was Mothering Sunday, and at the end of the service children came in with posies to give to their mothers and to all the women in the congregation; no-one was left out. Then, as the children stood silently, one little girl walked from the back of the church with sixteen white carnations and placed them on the altar.

The new Rector, John Wynburne, told the congregation what was happening and said, 'There is, of course, no need to say why we are doing this.'

I stood in the sanctuary, opposite Tenniel Evans, an old friend from Beaconsfield days – an actor who is now ordained as an NSM. Tears were streaming down our faces, as they were, I think, among most of the congregation. It was a deeply touching moment.

Afterwards in the fine new Fitzwilliams Centre, named after my successor, we had coffee and I talked to old friends. We then went to Hall Place for drinks. This in our day had been the rectory, a beautiful Queen Anne house in which the children grew up. It had a very special atmosphere and a lovely garden of four and a half acres. It had been a paradise for little children, but naturally could not have continued indefinitely as the parsonage house. It was bought from the Church by a wealthy couple and then sold to the present owners, who are very keen on its history and are restoring some of its original features. They knew we loved the house and were generous in letting us poke around everywhere, in the cellar, in cupboards and into every room. Betty had so loved this place that on previous occasions she had found it difficult to come back, but after a distance of twenty years she enjoyed the experience and it was good to know that it is loved as we loved it. Joanna and her husband Simon came for the service and to look round the house. The present family have generously given an open invitation to the others to come when they wish, which I know they will want to do.

After lunch with Joan and Bernard Frost with whom we stayed (he was a churchwarden when we were in the parish and both of them have been close friends ever since), we drove back to Norfolk, leaving brilliant sunshine in the Chilterns to enter fog once we reached the Suffolk border.

21

Heacham and Rising

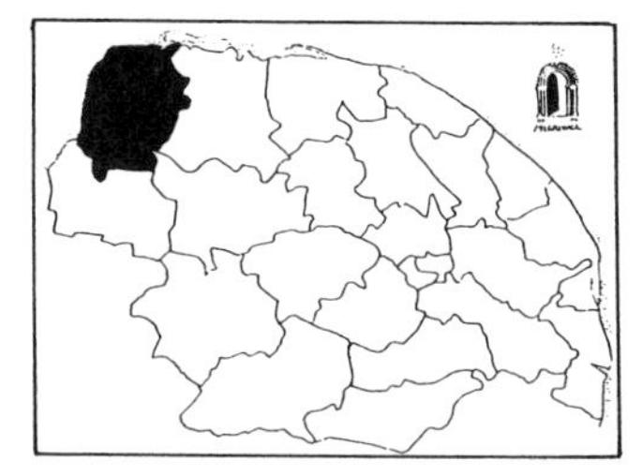

(The far north-west of the diocese, dominated by the holiday industry around Hunstanton and agriculture inland. The Sandringham estate is part of one of the original Norfolk Groups pioneered by Bishop Launcelot Fleming.)

Tuesday 19 March

This deanery is geographically the furthest from Norwich, so it means longer journeys than normal and we made an early start in order to arrive at Brancaster Staithe village hall for a session with a group of elderly tap dancers. A group of a dozen or so enthusiastically demonstrated their skills after which we had a chat over coffee. Tap dancing is enjoying something of a revival, not least among the elderly, for whom it is good exercise in co-ordinating body and mind. There has also recently been a wonderful musical called *Riverdance* which is very popular and has awakened people's interest in what has always, I suspect, been a minority pastime except among the Irish.

We drove along the coast to the tiny school at Brancaster which has only twenty-five pupils. They are celebrating because, having been threatened with closure, their campaign to remain open has been successful. It is an excellent small school with bright pupils which deserves to continue and I hope grow in the long run. Michael Sellors, the Vicar of Hunstanton, took me next to the community centre at Hunstanton where I had lunch with sixty old people – one of the liveliest such gatherings I have attended, with people full of fun. Clearly the sea air is good for them. One told me she had been advised by her doctor to get out of London or her husband would have less than a couple of years to live. The therapy of Hunstanton gave him another twenty years.

I went for a walk along the cliffs and climbed down to the beach. It was chilly but the sun had come out briefly in contrast to the dull, misty weather in Norwich. Back at the vicarage, and after a short interview with Radio Norfolk, David Grundy, the new Rector of Snettisham, took me to a Sue Ryder Home where we had a short service, tea and then a session visiting a number of patients in their rooms. Like all Sue Ryder and Cheshire Homes, this is well run, though I gather at the moment they are making a substantial loss each year, which must cause them concern. John collected me at 5 o'clock and we drove home, back into overcast weather. It was good to have an easy schedule for the first day of this pilgrimage week.

Wednesday 20 March

Smithdon School at Hunstanton, built in the sixties, is considered by aficionados to be an architectural gem and is apparently listed in magazines for architectural tourists visiting Britain from abroad. It seemed to me just another example of the kind of flat-roofed box typical of that period, but perhaps I am a Philistine. The visit to the sixth form was a sadly wasted opportunity. About a dozen sixth formers had obviously been told to meet me but there had been no preparation; they had not a clue who I was, and nobody had thought of asking them to prepare questions for discussion. They were not very forthcoming and it was extremely hard work for half an hour. They were obviously bright young people and we could have had a fruitful time together if only someone had given a little thought in advance to our meeting. I was then taken to the Headmaster who is to retire this term, and found him wrapped toga-like in an MA gown! We had coffee in his study while I listened to him extolling the architecture. I was therefore relieved when Michael Sellors arrived to take me off on a visit to the Wednesday market in the town centre. He was furious about the lack of preparation because in fact there are some very good RE teachers in the school, who had clearly not been asked to help.

The Wednesday market was rather desultory in freezing weather with only a few stalls operating and after chatting for a while we moved to the Princess Theatre, which was an altogether more pleasant experience. The head of leisure services for the area, John Barratt, was in fact an undergraduate at Fitzwilliam when I was chaplain. He had been accident prone in those days – a promising schoolboy cricketer who wrecked his chances in his first year with a torn ligament and at the beginning of the cricket season in his second year fell off his bicycle and broke his shoulder. But he played for Norfolk and indeed still plays cricket at club level. The theatre is owned by the local authority and is very lively, open all year round with both live shows and cinema, and is clearly a great asset, not just for holidaymakers, but for the local community. I had a most interesting hour with the senior staff until I was collected by David Sturdy, who took me to a hospice called Tapping House at Snettisham.

Brancaster

This is a day care centre founded by Hugh Ford, a local GP, where people come for one, two or three days a week. There were a dozen or so women there, mostly elderly but one in her forties. They give each other tremendous mutual support and there is a wonderful atmosphere of happiness and contentment. They had recently watched a programme about St Christopher's Hospice (the first hospice founded by Dr Cicely Saunders), which they thought was appalling because it emphasised the negative aspects of hospice care and featured mostly people who were at the point of death.

'Here,' they said, 'we are concerned with living day by day and enjoying life to the full.'

We had an excellent lunch together, with much laughter and mutual teasing. This is a real community where genuine friendships have been formed, fostered by Judith Clarke, the sister-in-charge. There is need for some residential care and Michael Sellors has a plan to launch an appeal for an extension to the hospice as a project for the Millennium.

I left Tapping House on yet another original form of transport, this time a tandem owned by David and Judith Grundy. Photographers were there in the hope of seeing me fall off but David safely guided me the mile or two to Snettisham vicarage, from where I set off for a walk across the fields. On my return, two ladies were waiting to take me to Docking where the Mothers' Union from the whole deanery had gathered for an enormous tea. I had a happy hour chatting to them before David Roper took me back to Brancaster rectory for a break.

From there we went to St Edmund's, Hunstanton, for a deanery Eucharist and the church was full for a good celebration of Rite B. I preached, had coffee with parishioners afterwards, and departed to spend the night at Burnham Thorpe just half an hour away.

Thursday 21 March

At Dersingham church hall, PHOBBIES (Physically Handicapped Hobbies) meets on Thursday mornings. Here people with a range of disabilities from blindness, through brain damage in accidents, to multiple sclerosis, engage in a number of crafts. It is a happy and fulfilled group of people to whom no doubt the acquiring of skills has given a new sense of self-confidence and worth. Certainly the standard of the work that I saw was in some cases very high. It was particularly interesting to see one man painting skilfully with his left hand – a natural right-hander who had lost the use of his right arm after a stroke.

Martin Adams, the Vicar, then took me to Monks Close at Bircham. This is a small rural housing estate, locally notorious, consisting of houses which formerly belonged to the airforce base which has long since disappeared. The housing was built in the 1940s, and is unmodernised. After a time with the playgroup in the tiny community centre which used to be one of the administration buildings on the aerodrome, we visited two families in their homes. In one, a young couple with their small children have worked hard on the house, redecorating it, though it is still damp and causes frequent illnesses within the family. However, they are full of fighting spirit and determined to make improvements and raise the image of the estate. It used to be a place where problem families were dumped, and although that is true no longer, its reputation still survives, as in all such places.

We next visited a mother and her children in a house where the wallpaper is peeling off the walls because of the damp and the conditions are pretty awful. The local authority is due in the autumn to begin installing solid fuel central heating, which will improve the living conditions considerably. This young mother is struggling mostly on her own with her three children. Her husband, who had been unemployed, eventually found work in Diss, where he has to stay in a flat and can only get home once a fortnight. They have been trying without success to find accommodation in Diss and so far have had little help from local authorities. The mother suffers, rather naturally, from bouts of depression and life is obviously pretty grim. She has no transport and this housing estate is three miles from the nearest shop. Yet here again there is a determination to survive, to hold the marriage together and to do the best for the children. There is real courage in this place.

The whole atmosphere is reminiscent of the North Lynn estate, the first young family typical of those who are determined to change things, and the other typical of courageous fighting against the odds. There are other families like these on this estate and they are well supported by Martin Adams, who gives this place priority, quite rightly, even though he is criticised for not spending more time visiting homes in Docking. This is a prime example of rural deprivation. The estate is set in beautiful countryside and from the road you cannot imagine there would be problems. The local authority apparently painted the sides of the houses facing the roads, but not the hidden backs.

Lunch was at the church hall in Docking where a group of twenty or so met for a well-cooked lunch and I chatted, taking my food from table to table. After a walk in drizzling rain, we visited the Docking Rural Workshops, one of the new enterprises that are springing up in many places in Norfolk. We visited an engineering workshop, art gallery and, most curious of all, a workshop where coffins for pets are being made. This is the enterprise of a solicitor who left the law, and his wife, an undertaker by profession. They proudly showed me their product – cardboard coffins of varying sizes, ranging from those which would be suitable for a gerbil to others which would accommodate an alsatian. They strongly believe there is a market for this product and they may well be right.

I was collected by a retired NSM – Herbert Karrach, a former doctor – who took me to Dersingham where I had sandwiches, cakes and sausage rolls with Nancy, the Lay Chairman of the deanery synod, the secretary and treasurer and we had some interesting conversation about the pilgrimage and the deanery. They are proud of the fact that they always manage to pay their parish share, and rightly so. There is good mutual support here, thanks, not least, to a good rural dean and these excellent ladies, one of whom is the sister of Linda Taylor, wife of Bishop John Taylor, formerly of St Albans.

George Hall collected me and took me to the fire station. The fire-fighters here are all volunteers and like all such encounters during this pilgrimage, I was impressed with their qualities of professionalism and team work. As well as talking about the fire service, they were full of questions about the pilgrimage, and we had an interesting hour together. I mentioned my time with the lifeboatmen and said how appalled I had been at the problem some lifeboatmen faced whose employers would not give them time off, or docked their pay during the hours spent on lifeboat work. I said, 'I don't imagine the same problem applies to fire-fighters like you.' To my astonishment, they said that it did.

Another retired priest, Victor Challen, then took me across the road to the old TA Drill Hall where the Sandringham detachment of the Army Cadet Force was meeting. This was an impressive group of young people, commanded by a woman, whose second-in-command is a staff sergeant and one of the churchwardens at Castle Rising. I toured the activities: a young corporal lecturing recruits in field-craft; another group having an examination; a third planning an exercise and a fourth being drilled, fearsomely, by a pretty, female staff sergeant. Her sister had been in this cadet detachment and is now in the Military Police and she, too, is headed for a military career. It was all very interesting and full of purposeful activity. Of course a number of these young people will have at the back of their minds the possibility of a career in the army, and so there is a strong sense of motivation around. They have good facilities here including an indoor range, and they regularly produce cadets who are good enough to shoot at Bisley each year. After handing out Certificates of Proficiency and a Duke of Edinburgh's Award, I told them that I had been a cadet in my youth and then in the regular army.

'But you can never tell where that will lead,' I said. 'Look at me now – so be prepared for anything.'

Friday 22 March

Norfolk Lavender is a growing enterprise near Heacham where most of the profits now come from a large mail order business selling almost 200 products from lavender. It seemed to occupy quite a small site at a crossroads, but is a little like the *Tardis* – the further into the complex you go, the larger it becomes, and I visited huge processing sheds and a drying plant. One of the major hazards for workers is the bees who are still harvesting nectar when the flowers are cut. Since at one stage of the process the dried flowers have to be put in great vats and then trodden down, I imagine this can be very uncomfortable, but the workers spoke lightly of the hazard and actually rather sympathised with the bees who found their habitat so rudely disturbed.

Lawrence Campbell took me to Brancaster Staithe where there is still an active fishery with about six boats and twelve fishermen earning a living from shellfish and oysters. I met some lovely old characters and much enjoyed the walk around the Staithe, still with its original oyster shed used for cleaning shellfish. It was a misty morning with only working boats and a few dinghies on the mud. These little north coast staithes and harbours are among the most attractive parts of Norfolk and are much loved both by yachtsmen and artists.

We returned to the hall where I had met the tap dancers on Tuesday morning for a Lent lunch with parishioners, and I learned that our next door neighbour in the cottage at Burnham Thorpe had died suddenly. He was a retired doctor, Sir William Shakespeare, a delightful man and a direct descendant of the playwright. I had seen his wife, Sue, that morning and simply waved at her, not knowing what had happened, and felt an idiot, but I hope to be able to visit her later in the day.

I returned to the rectory at Old Hunstanton and went for a walk in the park of the Old Hall, nearby. We have still not seen the sun, though it is somewhat milder today, but at times very foggy.

Bob Whitehead, a retired gunner major and former Headmaster of Glebe House School, took me to the Sandcastle Holiday Home where they have holidays for the handicapped. The main purpose is respite care for families, but occasionally, as today, a grandmother, mother and two boys were staying. There are about twelve residents and a large number of friends of the Home, who are active and very supportive. Once again I was impressed by the quality of the staff and the general atmosphere which was relaxed and caring.

On the way home I visited Sue Shakespeare in Burnham Thorpe, with her two sons, Tom and James.

Saturday 23 March

A leisurely day began with a meeting at Dersingham with all the churchwardens of the deanery. After coffee we had a question and answer session with some worthwhile talk ranging from homosexuality to the Church Commissioners. George Hall and I then walked to the local barber's shop where Albert cut my hair. He is an old-fashioned barber, the centre of village gossip and a delightful man. He has less hair than I have, so is not a good advertisement for the trade, but he cuts hair well. After chatting to two small boys sitting on the wall outside, waiting their turn, and giving them badges, we walked to a coffee shop being run by the church, where we had a simple lunch. This is an initiative led by a lay woman who must be in her sixties. They have converted an old carpet shop into a delightful small café and they open every day from 10.00 until 4.00. It is staffed by volunteers from the church and is much used by local people. It is a Christian organisation, but not obtrusively so. However, it is known that the staff are all Christians and so a real ministry is based here. In a very natural way the lady in charge spoke of prayer for all their needs being constantly answered: the money to convert the shop, people to staff it, furnishings and maintenance. I was impressed.

After lunch we went back to Sandringham rectory and I walked through the park down to the lake in the grounds of Sandringham House. I was leaning over the fence watching the ducks when I was confronted by a policeman. Scores of them were scouring the grounds because the Prince of Wales is arriving soon for a stay and security is now very tight indeed. I explained who I was, but that was not good enough and he asked for identification. The only thing I had was an envelope in my satchel, addressed to me, which he seemed to think was okay. On my way back to the house another plain clothes policeman walked across the grass to see me and explained that I had been seen on camera and what was I doing here? I managed to give a satisfactory explanation, and was allowed to return to the rectory.

From there we went next door to Park House which used to be the home of the Princess of Wales' family many years ago, now owned by the Cheshire Foundation and is an hotel for the disabled – very much five star with superb facilities. I chatted to a dozen or so guests who had just arrived for a week with a gardening theme, and then looked round the hotel, which is certainly beautifully equipped. At 5.30 I left for home and worked in the car at the correspondence which has piled up during the week.

Sunday 24 March

This morning's service took place in a school on an estate at Heacham. This is a church plant from the parish church, a number of worshippers having established a church centre in the school to serve the needs of people on this new estate. About fifty or sixty of them were there and the service was led by two lay readers, one an LNSM candidate due to be ordained in September. Given the churchmanship of the parish church, I rather expected a charismatic rave-up but it was, in fact, restrained with most of the liturgy taken from the *ASB* morning prayer. It was well conducted by Dee with a weighty address from Penny, the other lay reader. At the end of the service Roy and Janet Barrow, two parishioners, were wished God speed as they set off as missionaries to the Philippines. This is an adventurous step for a middle-aged couple who have taken a full part both in the life of the parish and the diocese in recent years.

Back at Sandringham, George took me to the West Newton Social Club for a pint of beer before lunch. There are a series of such social clubs in the Sandringham Group, all established by King Edward VII. When his mother Queen Victoria bought the Sandringham estate she disapproved of the pubs and they were all closed down and social clubs established instead. They are really rather good institutions which families attend, with normal evening opening times during the week but on Sundays are only open at lunchtime between midday and 1 o'clock. This dates from King Edward's time when he insisted that drinking should stop in time for families to have lunch together. I talked to a good number, many of them workers on the estate, including one of the fire-fighters from Dersingham and some former crew members of the royal yacht. George Hall said to me afterwards that they were very appreciative of the fact that I drank a pint of beer rather than a gin and tonic. After a delicious lunch back in the rectory, I went for a walk again on the estate, carefully avoiding the boundaries of Sandringham House. A much chillier afternoon but at least it was dry.

We were due at Heacham Church at 4 o'clock to attend a rehearsal of Fauré's Requiem which they were performing this evening under the direction of Alan Warren, the retired Provost of Leicester who lives at Old

Shernborne

Hunstanton. George had been rather irritated with Alan because he had had to rearrange the deanery programme to accommodate this rehearsal, which Alan insisted I should attend. So he was less than pleased when we arrived at Heacham Church to find the rehearsal had just finished and they were all having tea. But I chatted for a while and listened to the soloist rehearsing the 'Pie Jesu' which was very well sung, and after looking round the church and seeing the memorial to Pocahontas (who married a member of the Rolfe family of Heacham) we went home a little earlier than planned.

Although the programme this week has not been as heavy as some, I have felt very tired each day. Betty mentioned this to David Conner, who suggested that it may be the 'marathon' syndrome – that is, I am now in the last stages of a long race and beginning to flag. The programme for the final pilgrimage week looks very heavy indeed, with exceedingly long hours, but perhaps I shall be like the marathon runner entering the stadium with the end in sight and will find a fresh burst of energy. It has been very good to spend time with George Hall, who is an old friend from Westcott days and who has proved to be an outstanding rector of Sandringham, much loved and respected both by the parishioners in his Group and by the royal family, for whom his ministry during these difficult years has, I believe, been very important.

22

Sparham and Ingworth

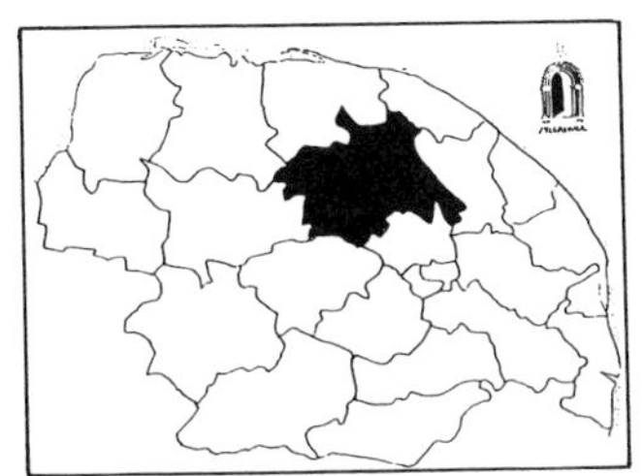

(Apart from the market town of Aylsham and the attractive small town of Reepham, these two small deaneries are entirely rural and set in beautiful landscapes. As in every deanery, there is a large number of outstanding medieval churches.)

Monday 1 April

The last week of the pilgrimage. A brilliantly sunny day gave the first promise of spring and a most welcome change from the dreary weather of the last few months.

All Saints, Bawdeswell, is an interesting architectural curiosity since it was built in the 1950s to a Georgian design by James Fletcher-Watson, now a well-known watercolour painter. As an architect, his last work was the building of Bishop's House. The interior furnishings are all in the Georgian style, including a three-decker pulpit. After prayers with the parishioners, we visited the Bawdeswell stores and post office – a large shop which serves a number of surrounding villages and is clearly prospering. The owner drove me in his delivery van to visit Aaron, an old man living in a cottage, who used to work on the estate at Horsey. We delivered a bundle of kindling and after a chat visited an old lady in Folland Court, which is sheltered housing nearby.

Floranova is a specialist seed propagation nursery and this was a fascinating visit. They produce new varieties of flowers and export the seed all round the world. I visited acres of greenhouses where they raise young plants and test new varieties, and at the end was presented with some boxes of pansies. They also promised to let us have plants for the garden this summer if we wished to have them.

The visit lasted longer than anticipated and for the rest of the day we were half an hour late everywhere. Grahame Humphries drove me to Itteringham at the far side of the deanery, where there was lunch in the village hall for parishioners from the whole Group. A large number had gathered and a choir of children and adults sang as I entered and then we had a sumptuous buffet lunch while I gave away badges and prayer cards. There was only time for a fifteen-minute break before beginning a tour of the churches.

We began at Itteringham where I planted a tree in the churchyard to replace a beech that had blown down, visited the church and talked to parishioners. We then drove to Mannington Hall in a marvellous old Armstrong Siddeley Sapphire driven by David Green, the owner, who comes from Exmoor. He told us his father was a well-known poacher on the river Exe and had taught him how to catch salmon with a stick and a bit of wire. At Mannington Hall, in the grounds of the ruined old chapel, I planted another tree. Robin and Laurel Walpole were there with two of their children and we looked inside the ruined church where there is a font in which one of the children, Henry, was baptised and he showed me photographs of his baptism, thirteen years ago. We then followed their Land Rover to Wolterton Hall where Robin's father and mother had lived. Here we planted yet another tree and after saying farewell to the Walpoles, we continued on our tour.

We visited Wickmere, Little Barningham, Edgefield, Saxthorpe, Oulton and Blickling. There was a good gathering of parishioners in each church who showed me round and we prayed together before moving on to the next church. They were all in their way delightful and memorable – all so different. At Little Barningham a large wooden carved skeleton which sat on the end of a pew had been stolen a few weeks ago. They showed me a photograph of it, and I think the church looks better without it. The church at Edgefield is remarkable because one hundred years ago it was rebuilt with stone from the old medieval church, which was falling down, so Edgefield Church is in a good state of repair. The famous Marcon family were rectors here for generations and there is a delightful modern window with a picture of Canon Marcon, incumbent for sixty-five years, wearing a broad-brimmed black hat and riding on a bicycle. As President of the Norfolk Show this year, I have to wear a hat during the day according to custom. Most presidents wear bowlers, but I cannot possibly wear that with purple shirt and dog collar. I rather fancied Canon Marcon's hat and asked the parishioners what their advice was. They suggested that gaiters and frock coat would be most suitable with a black top hat (which is what I wore in the end).

As the afternoon wore on, the temperature dropped, and although it was still sunny the churches became colder. We were glad to arrive at Blickling Hall for a cup of tea in an elegant dining room overlooking the park, before setting off for home.

Itteringham

Tuesday 2 April

Spring lasted one day. Today there was a bitter east wind and drizzle with overcast skies, so it was back to long johns and two pullovers. Because of the Royal Maundy, to be held in Norwich Cathedral this year, the annual service for the blessing of oils and renewal of ordination vows was held in Aylsham this morning, and a good crowd turned up for a service masterminded by the cathedral staff and including the delightful new cathedral girls' choir who sang beautifully. Immediately afterwards I was taken to the Methodist church hall where there was an old people's lunch and from there we drove to the railway station, the headquarters of the Bure Valley Railway. This is a splendid narrow gauge line, running between Aylsham and Buxton. It is quite extensive with engine sheds, three steam engines and a mobile crane; the train I was on was pulled by a half-size diesel engine. I sat with the driver and much enjoyed the journey through lovely countryside.

We arrived at Buxton in pouring rain, but a large group of parishioners had gathered and I was given a ride in an old farm cart pulled by two heavy horses, owned by Arthur and Olive Clouting, celebrating today their thirty-sixth wedding anniversary, who were dressed in traditional costume. Half a dozen parishioners also sat on the hay bales in the back and the rain mercifully stopped for a most enjoyable ride to the village hall.

Here I judged a painting competition over tea with parishioners from Buxton, Brampton, Hautbois and Lammas. They expressed anxiety about a new vicar, having rejected the one candidate who has been sent to them so far. They are still going through bereavement following Graham Drake's departure, and I think a reasonable interregnum would be a good idea. Nevertheless, we must try to get on with the appointment and see if we can get a married man (they are not ready for a woman yet). There is no doubt about the potential for ministry among young people here. There is an excellent Adventurers' group and numbers of young families in the villages.

I mounted the cart again and was allowed to drive the heavy horses – very tricky, because you have to watch them all the time, especially as one of the horses was stronger than the other and tended to pull to one side. We drove towards Stratton Strawless where I was due to meet the village social club, but the journey would have taken an hour at the rate we were going and so half-way there I was picked up in a huge limousine and driven the rest of the way in sumptuous comfort.

At the village hall I talked for twenty minutes or so about the pilgrimage, telling funny stories of my encounters and journeys. I had a microphone which I held in my hand and the club members were sitting round at tables. They were very responsive with their laughter, and I felt for all the world like a northern club comedian. After a jolly half hour, Patrick Foreman took me to Mill House nursing home, where I visited a member of the club who was ill, and then at 4.30 we arrived at Horstead House, the youth centre.

I was met by Neville and Val Khambatta, the Wardens, who completely understood that I was now ready for a break and I had an hour and a half on my own. I walked by the river and up through woods and sketched for a while. Though by now the temperature had dropped considerably, it was no longer raining. A group of eighteen young people from Rotherham was staying in the house and we had a barbecue supper together in the garden. There was a choice of beefburgers or Bernard Matthews turkeyburgers. I tried the turkeyburger, which was tasteless, but the beefburger was quite delicious. They buy them from the local butcher who uses ninety per cent good meat in each, so despite the beef scare we all enjoyed them enormously.

After supper, Heinz Toller, the Vicar of Coltishall, took me to the Salvation Army Hall where about thirty people had gathered for a Bible study and we had a good evening together – particularly good, I think, because once again a number of those present had been studying St Luke throughout the pilgrimage.

Wednesday 3 April

Spring returned this morning as we drove out to Salle Church, a spectacularly beautiful perpendicular church in this tiny village. A group of about twenty parishioners had gathered and we prayed together. I marvelled at this lovely building and then in bright sunshine set off with the son of Sir John White, the local landowner and descendant of Timothy White the chemist, and Ben Stimpson, churchwarden and one of a large farming family, who drove us in a kind of buggy used for small loads and shooting. We made a stop in the village at the home of an old man who had recently lost his wife, another stalwart of the church and a dear old boy who was touchingly grateful for my visit. Then we set off across country, literally, driving across ploughed fields to Reepham, where Ben dropped me in the market place.

Reepham is an almost perfect little town with its Georgian houses lining the small square, interesting side-streets and the curiosity of two parish churches built next door to each other by rival benefactors. We visited the W.I. market in the Bircham Centre, an old house given to the community and used as a library, meeting room and location for this weekly market. Next Michael Paddison took me to the Old Brewery House Hotel, revived by the new owners, and then we drove to a compact industrial area. Here small businesses are established and we visited first the Reepham Brewery, which used to be famous in times past and has been revived by a son and his parents. After what I sensed were years of struggle, they seem to be doing well and are winning prizes at beer festivals. We sampled their brew and then went next door to 'Slogans', a T-shirt printing unit, where I was shown the processes and at the end presented with a sweatshirt with the pilgrimage and 900 logos printed on them.

We drove back into the town centre where I attended an old people's lunch in one of the old parish churches, now redundant and converted to a church hall, enjoying an excellent lunch and chatting to all the people there.

Michael Paddison dropped me at Bernard Matthews' factory at Great Witchingham where I was met by Paul Illingworth, the Rural Dean and local Rector, together with the Manager of the factory, whose son is to be baptised on Easter Day. We were dressed in suitably hygienic white wellington boots, hairnets and white coats, then taken round to see the processes from turkey meat via the adding of ingredients to cooked turkey slices, packaged ready for the supermarket shelves. Before entering every room we had to wash our hands and clean our boots. The standards of hygiene are very high, as I suppose one would expect, and the workers I talked to enjoy their job, many having worked there for years. We talked about the methods of raising and killing birds and although the Manager was not evasive, I did not find it entirely reassuring. On the other hand, one has to remember that this very successful firm employs 2,000 people locally, mostly from the villages, and if they were not there it would be an employment disaster for a large chunk of countryside.

We met Michael Sayer, local landowner and churchwarden of Sparham, at a gravel works and had an interesting tour of the workings of this complex where they extract gravel for road building. I was shown the way in which they restore the land after they have finished their extraction, which is impressive.

Next stop was the Lakeside Leisure Centre at Lyng – a new sports complex with a vast indoor bowling green where I had fun playing bowls extremely badly with a group of local people. They included William Brigham, whom I have known for many years, a dairy farmer and local representative of the NFU, now much affected by the crisis over beef. The bowlers all wore white pullovers so I stripped off my cassock and proudly put on my new white sweatshirt, so I felt more part of the bowling scene. I may have looked the part but my bowling soon revealed me as a crass amateur.

After tea in the leisure centre I was taken to the White House at Lenwade, the home of David and Sally Acloque. Sally is the sister of David Gurney, and I have known the family for years. They knew I wanted to be free of conversation and I walked by the lake behind their garden and sketched for a while in the cool early evening sunlight. I returned to the house for supper with them and their two children, Peter and Sarah Jane, with Paul Illingworth there, too. The children had very kindly made me trout flies based on the 'Bishop of Norwich' salmon fly, with which I caught my first salmon years ago. It was a fly invented by Colin Reid, a gillie on the Spey who, when he knew I was coming, created a fly with a purple hackle, white collar, yellow and green body (for Norwich City Football Club), and a dark blue tail. Today's was the first trout fly that had been made to this pattern and I shall look forward to trying it out sometime.

After a delicious and friendly meal we drove to Swannington Church where thirty people had gathered for a Bible study, rather freezing round a table at the back of the church. However, it was a good evening and attended by a churchwarden from Castle Acre and her husband, which was a lovely gesture. They said they had shared the first week with me and wanted to share something in my last week. At the end of the Bible study we held the ancient service of Tenebrae, saying psalms, singing hymns and reading scriptures as candles were extinguished one by one until the church was in darkness and we walked out into the moonlight.

Thursday 4 April Maundy Thursday

It was a perfect spring day for the Royal Maundy. The family and I arrived in the cathedral an hour before the service was due to begin and already it was almost full. There were 140 recipients of the Maundy Money – seventy men and seventy women, one for each year of the Queen's age. They were placed in various parts of the cathedral, each with a companion, and there were representatives of the diocese, the cathedral, city and county. Colourful figures from the Queen's Bodyguard were getting ready in the aisles and John Taylor, the Lord High Almoner and formerly Bishop of St Albans, was there with his wife, Linda, who the day before had taken the Queen's part in a rehearsal. She chuckled when I told her that local Press the day before had

Cawston (pencil)

headed an article about her part in the rehearsal 'Queen for a Day'. There were no less than three choirs – our own cathedral choir, the choir of the Chapel Royal and the girls' choir.

A group of us waited at the Erpingham Gate for the Queen to arrive, with crowds lining the grass around the west entrance. After meeting the Lord Mayor, High Sheriff and Chief Executive of the city, I took the Queen to meet the Suffragan Bishops and Dean. She was thankful for the weather because she said that Prince Charles had told her that the week before in Norfolk he had experienced snow and bitter cold, which I knew all about. She remembered the pilgrimage and asked me if it was nearly over. After introducing the Dean, I then took the Duke of Edinburgh to meet the canons and we formed up for the procession to begin this marvellous service, hardly changed, I understand, for many centuries. It was beautifully simple with the passage from John 13 about the feet washing read with great feeling by Prince Philip, and everything went very well, thanks to extremely careful preparation and many rehearsals.

I spent the entire service sitting on the ancient throne behind the High Altar. It is said to be the only bishop's throne in this traditional position north of the Alps. In medieval times bishops always sat here but when cathedrals adopted patron saints, they usually removed the throne and replaced it with a window commemorating the saint. I always find it a strange experience. From the congregation's point of view it looks very grand, but it does not feel like that, for two reasons. First, from the throne you can see the entire length of the roof of the nave, and one is conscious of the height and length of the cathedral and its grandeur, hence one's own littleness. Secondly, looking down at the congregation, particularly a full one like today, one is conscious of the responsibility one bears. So the experience is curiously humbling. One also realises that thrones are lonely places.

It was strange and very moving to see the Queen from the height of the throne – a small figure moving among the congregation, giving the Maundy Money. The singing was glorious and at the end we emerged from the west end to a barrage of photographers. After five minutes or so, we walked through the cloisters to the deanery for drinks, where Stephen Platten looked after the Queen and I introduced people to the Duke of Edinburgh for half an hour or so. The royal party then left for a walk-about in the centre of Norwich and we followed on foot. Because of heavy security we were not allowed, as we had hoped, to have a car, so John Taylor, Stephen, Willy Booth the Sub-Almoner and I, with our wives, walked through the streets to the crowded market place and thence to the City Hall, where a splendid lunch had been laid on, courtesy of the Mayor and City College catering department.

After lunch we walked back again through the city and arrived home where the children were preparing for William Nott's second birthday party – just tea and a birthday cake in the kitchen. John and Linda Taylor called briefly to give Lucy his nosegay, because she had missed the service, being unwell. It was a kind thought and much appreciated. The nosegays are beautiful bunches of fresh flowers, held by the Queen and the royal party when distributing the Maundy Money. In ages past, when distributing gifts to the poor who smelled rather, the nosegays held close to the face kept the odours at bay.

In the early evening I set off on the pilgrimage again, this time to Marsham for a Maundy Thursday Eucharist. It was attended by students on their traditional pilgrimage to Walsingham. Parties of students from many parts of the country converge on Walsingham at Easter and the Oxford leg usually calls here en route. Sadly, half the party had gone to the Roman Catholic Mass, which struck me as unusual because young people these days break ecumenical barriers more easily than most. Their leader, the chaplain of Kent University, preached a sermon berating us all for our lack of unity. I thought it was rather unnecessary since my ecumenical encounters on this pilgrimage have given me great hope and encouragement, and indeed I think many of our villagers have progressed much further in the ecumenical pilgrimage than these young students.

I attended the first part of the service as a pilgrim with the young people, and had my feet washed. They had all been in the vicarage beforehand, having baths. Had I known it, I would have washed my own feet, so it cannot have been a pleasant experience for Robin Hewetson, the Vicar. I then took over and presided for the rest of the Eucharist, which was a well attended and prayerful service.

Afterwards Grahame Humphries told me he had been sitting high up near the roof of the cathedral that morning, overlooking the sanctuary, while he recorded the Maundy service for Radio Norfolk. He jokingly asked a senior security man what would happen if he fell over – because he would land just in front of the Queen's chair.

With a straight face the policeman answered, 'Don't worry, sir, my marksmen are so good you'd be dead before you hit the floor, so you wouldn't even have to apologise.' I don't think he'll try to make jokes with security men again.

So, home for a meal with the family – the first this week – at the end of a truly memorable day.

Friday 5 April Good Friday

Erpingham Church was full with parishioners from the seven-church benefice for a well-devised liturgy in which I was able to be a member of the congregation, which was a treat. The theme of personal suffering was strangely and quietly present in the church. I greeted Angela Parkes before the service, who was playing the organ. She is the widow of a courageous former vicar of Aylsham, whose dying of cancer was a period of great grace and blessing to his parishioners. She had been in Aylsham for the Chrism Eucharist on Tuesday and reminded me that the last time I celebrated Communion there had been at David's funeral. Pensively I sat with Helen and Nicholas Corbin (one of the churchwardens) in their pew. I noticed on the wall a memorial to Phyllis Corbin, aged thirty-seven and their oldest daughter, aged ten, who both died at sea in 1961. I had not realised that Helen was Nicholas' second wife and that such a terrible tragedy was part of his life.

The church at Erpingham is delightful, with a fine east window. The original is in Blickling Hall, discovered by Nicholas Corbin himself who used to be Director of the National Trust in Norfolk. He found the original medieval window, which had been dismantled from the staircase, and had it put up in the east window of the church. Then eventually Blickling Hall wanted it back, so a replica was made for the east window. It is a most interesting series of scenes and a fine focal point for this church set on a hill.

From the church we all walked the half mile or so to the rectory and had coffee and hot cross buns. The rectory here is one of the old houses of manageable size and a truly charming house which the churchwardens, led by Nicholas Corbin, fought for some years ago in the face of the Board of Finance's wish to sell. I'm glad they succeeded.

After the parishioners left, I went for a short walk down a lane nearby. The landscapes of this rolling countryside are very beautiful. I passed a farm and in the field was a mare with a foal, born that morning. Back at the rectory I had a light lunch with Brian and Eleanor Faulkner who love the house and garden and have worked extremely hard on both, which the parishioners appreciate, as well as their hospitality.

Brian drove me to St Michael's in Aylsham, a local hospital, which, like so many others, is shrinking and has an uncertain future. Here we had an open-air service on a terrace. There was a cold wind but the sun was shining and luckily I managed to find a seat out of the wind and enjoyed the sun beating down on my face. Afterwards I went on a round of the wards, visiting a number of patients.

After a cup of tea in the canteen, Bob Branson, the Vicar of Aylsham, took me to visit three residential bungalows for the disabled. Two of them are used for respite care and one is a residential home. In the first there were five children with severe learning disabilities and I played with them for a while before moving on to another bungalow where there were older patients – again, here for respite care to give their carers a break. The patients in this house were quite severely handicapped and in one or two cases badly deformed, but the lady in charge had a good relationship with them and was skilful in helping me to communicate. In the third bungalow I met a group of permanent residents with varying degrees of handicap. As always, the company of handicapped people is rewarding and the response of a smile from a severely handicapped person is worth a thousand words of praise.

We had taken far longer on these hospital visits than the programme had anticipated. I had been due for a break at 4 o'clock, but it was already past 5. We drove to Cawston rectory where Jean King informed me that a visit to sheltered housing nearby had been arranged for me. My heart sank because I was desperate to have some space, but I girded up my mental loins and went across the village to the Community Room where a large crowd of about thirty residents had gathered for hot cross buns. I chatted to them about the pilgrimage and the meeting became quite animated.

When I mentioned my ride the other day in the farm cart which featured in the film *The Go-Between* one old man said, 'I was in that film,' and to everyone's astonishment (because no-one apparently knew about it), he explained that he had been the butler in that well-known film which was produced in Norfolk. He had himself been butler to the Ketton-Cremers at Felbrigg. Lady Billa Harrod knew the director, Joseph Losey, and told him that for the part of the butler he could do no better than hire a real one, which he did. John Ritchie, a Scotsman, obviously enjoyed having these memories revived and it clearly delighted his friends, too. I think perhaps he will now be something of a celebrity.

At last I got away for a walk on my own. By now the sun was going down

Erpingham Rectory

and it was very cold, but I strolled along a disused railway line for a while and then returned to the rectory to prepare for an evening at the Wesleyan Chapel. This was a traditional service of hymns, anthems, prayers and Bible reading in the small chapel, with a full choir. The singing was stupendous and we sang all the old favourites, including The Old Rugged Cross at full volume. I gave an impromptu exposition of the Bible reading for the day and then afterwards trays of refreshments were brought in and I chatted to the people for a while. Many of them were full of the Maundy visit of the Queen and one of the people there had actually been a recipient of the Maundy Money. It had been an interesting, but long Good Friday.

Saturday 6 April Easter Eve

At St Swithun's, Bintree, parishioners were preparing the church for Easter. The programme had mentioned the odd proposal that I was to help arrange flowers. I was greeted by the chief flower lady who said that she had heard that I was very keen on flower-arranging. Where on earth she got this story from, I cannot think, but I promised to put one flower in a vase. I actually made a mess of that, breaking the flower when I took it from the bunch, which made them realise that I was not being falsely modest.

After talking for a while, a Dutch farmer, Cuhl Van Beuningen, took me for a visit to his farm at Twyford. This is a very interesting mixed farm – part of it commercial crops, cereal and sugar beet, and also fields devoted to organic farming, on which he is very keen. None of this is yet making a profit, but he is determined to persevere. He is committed to conservation, and evidence of this, with the planting of hedgerows, is everywhere. He is also raising a small herd of wild boar in the hope that in the long run they might prove an edible and commercial delicacy. The boar are in a large area, including woodland, where they are able to roam free, but they were gathered at a fence when we arrived, no doubt hoping to be fed. Cuhl scattered some nuts which they scrabbled around for and proceeded to bite each other viciously – not the kind of animals you would want as pets.

Eric Barrett, local farmer and member of the Board of Finance, and father of Maggi Sprange, Bishop Hugo's secretary, drove me to Guist, where I met another group of parishioners with children and had a cup of coffee. Afterwards, Alan Coulson, the Manager of the farm on the Sennowe estate, took me on a tour of the farm and estate. We began by examining all the machinery available to see if there was anything that I had not yet ridden. To my delight, there was a 1928 Fordson Tractor which had been lovingly restored by one of the workers. As we drove around I remembered the noise and the smell from the short period I had spent selling these old workhorses when I left the army. We next travelled, by contrast, in a huge crop-sprayer which unfolded its wings like some gigantic insect and we then sprayed water on a field. It was quite easy to drive, very comfortable, like most modern tractors, heated in the winter and air-conditioned in the summer.

Alan then took me on a tour of the estate where we saw flocks of sheep and herds of cattle grazing right up to the house itself, a large Edwardian pile built by what must have been an eccentric millionaire, but soon bought by Sir Thomas Cook, the founder of the travel firm, inherited now by a descendant and namesake. There are also large lakes created by gravel workings, huge areas of water now much used by migrating birds, a feature of which Tom Cook is very proud, being a keen nature lover.

After thanking Alan, I drove with Tom Cook in a fourteen-year-old open Porsche to Stibbard village hall where a large crowd of villagers and children met and I had more coffee while the children showed me their exhibition. There seemed to be masses of youngsters who belonged to organisations such as Explorers, Adventurers and the curiously named Conkers. I then left on the school bus, accompanied by all the children, to Wood Norton village hall. The children stayed on the bus and rode back to Stibbard for their lunch, though a few rebelled and came with me. A smaller crowd this time was waiting at the hall and we had a ploughman's lunch together.

After lunch I made a brief visit to parishioners where both the husband and wife had been quite ill, then drove with Alan Greenhough to Foxley Wood, where Tony Foottit and a crowd of about twenty parishioners and the same number of children were waiting to go for a walk through the nature reserve. We had a fascinating afternoon with Tony enthralling us with his stories of flowers, plants, trees and their theological significance. The day was cold and overcast, but in the woods it was quite warm out of the wind and the children frolicked around, shooting at us from bushes with machine-guns made from twigs. Near the end we stopped for a prayer at a circle of tree stumps in a clearing, which Tony calls 'The Chapter House'. The children put down their weapons and devoutly joined us.

It was now time to go to Themelthorpe, a delightful tiny church where another good group of parishioners had gathered for Bible study and prayers. We then returned to the rectory at Guist where I had a walk before supper with Alan, June and their son, Hugh. The day in this benefice has been delightful. Alan is clearly a good, unostentatious, caring country parson who knows his sheep and is known by them. The parishioners of the seven parishes were very supportive of all the events throughout the day and children were everywhere. Alan made little of it, but there is obviously an outstanding ministry among children and young people in these parishes. Everywhere I went today I was tripping over children who were, without exception, friendly and very much at home in church buildings and among church people.

In the evening at Foulsham we had a Service of Light and the renewal of baptismal vows. Chris Engelsen, the new incumbent, had devised a good liturgy. There was not a large crowd, but the singing was good in this church which has a wonderful acoustic – one of the best I have encountered. After a cup of coffee I wished them happy Easter and left for home.

Sunday 7 April Easter Day

The whole family is staying in Bishop's House and they waved me goodbye as John drove me for the last time on this pilgrimage. He has been marvellously patient and uncomplaining about the hours he has had to drive which have frequently been unsocial, to say the least. He is not always very good at finding his way, but that is nothing compared to his constant good humour and easy companionship.

We arrived in cold drizzle at Weston Longville Church for the Easter morning Eucharist. The church was packed with 350 people and we had a splendid service with many children present, which has been a feature of this week. Again, I preached off the cuff, with little preparation, as I have done throughout this year, but it has been good for me and having had so many appreciative comments, I think perhaps in former years I have over-prepared.

After coffee and sandwiches in the village hall, I went for a short walk and did my last sketch in a nearby estate belonging to Lady Anne Prince-Smith, the queen of the flower arrangers in the cathedral.

I rode into Norwich on the back of a BMW motorbike, accompanied by ten outriders. It was an exciting, if rather chilly journey, and when we arrived at St Julian's Church we were met by a phalanx of photographers and Anglia Television. After interviews and the statutory photographs, I prayed for a while in the Cell and then with twenty or so local parishioners and clergy, walked to the Cathedral Close.

Here I was met by the children's marching band (The Falconers) from Sprowston, the same group who had met me when I arrived at Pulls Ferry last May. Crowds had gathered from deaneries throughout the diocese. My family were there and two of the grandchildren walked with me for a while until we were met by the choir, chapter and Bishops Hugo and David. We processed into the cathedral, as I did last time, while the men of the choir sang a plainchant psalm, and once again I knelt at the tomb of Herbert de Losinga, the first Bishop of Norwich. I prayed my Pilgrimage Prayer and then the choir sang, 'The Lord bless you and keep you; the Lord make his face to shine upon you and be gracious unto you; the Lord lift up the light of his countenance upon you and give you his peace' – the anthem by Rutter, sung for the first time in the cathedral at my enthronement. I moved into the sanctuary and there my stick and old satchel were taken from me and I was vested in cope and mitre before mounting the steps of the ancient throne for evensong. It was all beautiful and moving, with, for me, tears never far away.

Just before the blessing I thanked the diocese for sharing the pilgrimage and for allowing me to share the personal pilgrimage of so many groups and individuals. I reminded them that the most telling evidence for the truth of

Near Weston Longville

the resurrection of Christ was the life of the Church itself, and during this year I have had much evidence of that life which has strengthened and deepened my own faith.

I have made many friends during the year, but there is, of course, never enough time to spend with people so, as I told the congregation, I consoled myself with a phrase which I believe to be part of the resurrection hope – 'This is the life in which we make friends, the next is the one in which we enjoy them.'

So I pronounced the Easter blessing, and we processed out, through the great west door, and into the forecourt, where I greeted everyone. I walked home, very tired but very fulfilled, to be greeted by the family on the doorstep with party-poppers and champagne.

This has been the most memorable year of my whole ministry and it has been marvellous that I have not missed a single day through sickness or other cause. Throughout I have been daily conscious of the support of people's prayers and of the strengthening presence of the Holy Spirit without which the journey would have been impossible. Thanks be to God.

The Bishop's Pilgrimage Prayer

O LORD GOD,

FROM WHOM
WE COME,
IN WHOM
WE ARE
ENFOLDED,
TO WHOM
WE SHALL
RETURN:

BLESS US
IN OUR
PILGRIMAGE
THROUGH LIFE;
WITH THE POWER
OF THE FATHER
PROTECTING,
WITH THE LOVE
OF JESUS
IN DWELLING,
AND THE LIGHT
OF THE SPIRIT
GUIDING,
UNTIL WE COME
TO OUR ENDING,
IN
LIFE
AND LOVE
ETERNAL.

AMEN

SOME COMMENTS

'These diaries have always been regarded as social histories and of enormous value as histories of how people lived in the past . . . it is an account full of humour as well as care and compassion.'

John Timpson

'The reader's discovery is that the Bishop is an artist in water-colours which, with his sketches, make this a gem: those pleasing pictures and the wonderful gossip.' **Church Times**

'The Bishop of Norwich's Diary has been hailed as being in the finest tradition of Norfolk clerical diaries. It is written from the heart, showing in his own paintings and words the humour, compassion and faith of the author.' **Eastern Daily Press**

'I loved your frank comments and I also loved your optimism and encouragement about all that is going on. Of course I was thrilled by your enthusiastic comments about church buildings.

Lady Harrod

'I want to say how much I enjoyed it, was encouraged by it; and in a significant way, challenged by it.'

The Provost of Portsmouth

'Your book made a great impact on me. It was like finding something precious that had long been lost. "All sorts and conditions of men" you encountered, their problems of life and death, sickness and health, youth and age, freedom and imprisonment, which will have touched your readers at various levels. Your example in setting out and accomplishing this pilgrimage is just as greatly affecting. And your honesty in correcting without intending to wound was, at times, breathtaking. For your courage, grit, forbearance and insight, thank you.'

Martial Rose